THE BETRAYAL kNoWs MY NAME

HOTARU ODAGIRI

Translation: Melissa Tanaka † Lettering: Abigail Blackman

URAGIRI WA BOKU NO NAMAE WO SHITTEIRU Volume 11 © Hotaru ODAGIRI 2012. First published in Japan in 2012 by KADOKAWA SHOTEN Co., Ltd., Tokyo. English translation rights arranged with KADOKAWA SHOTEN Co., Ltd., Tokyo through TUTTLE-MORI AGENCY, INC., Tokyo.

Translation © 2013 by Hachette Book Group, Inc.

Yen Press
Hachette Book Group
237 Park Avenue, New York, NY 10017

www.HachetteBookGroup.com
www.YenPress.com

Yen Press is an imprint of Hachette Book Group, Inc. The Yen Press name and logo are trademarks of Hachette Book Group, Inc.

First Yen Press Edition: September 2013

ISBN: 978-0-316-24311-7

10 9 8 7 6 5 4 3 2 1

BVG

Printed in the
United States of America

HoTaru oDagiri

Today as I was walking along the street, I saw an old woman in an electric wheelchair coming toward me from the opposite direction, so I moved aside to make way. "Thank you," she said to me as she passed. It felt so nice to be thanked even though I'd only done it automatically because it was the proper thing to do. I hope that as I grow older, I can be grateful for the things people do for me rather than taking them for granted.

MESSAGE FROM VOLUME 11
(Japanese edition)

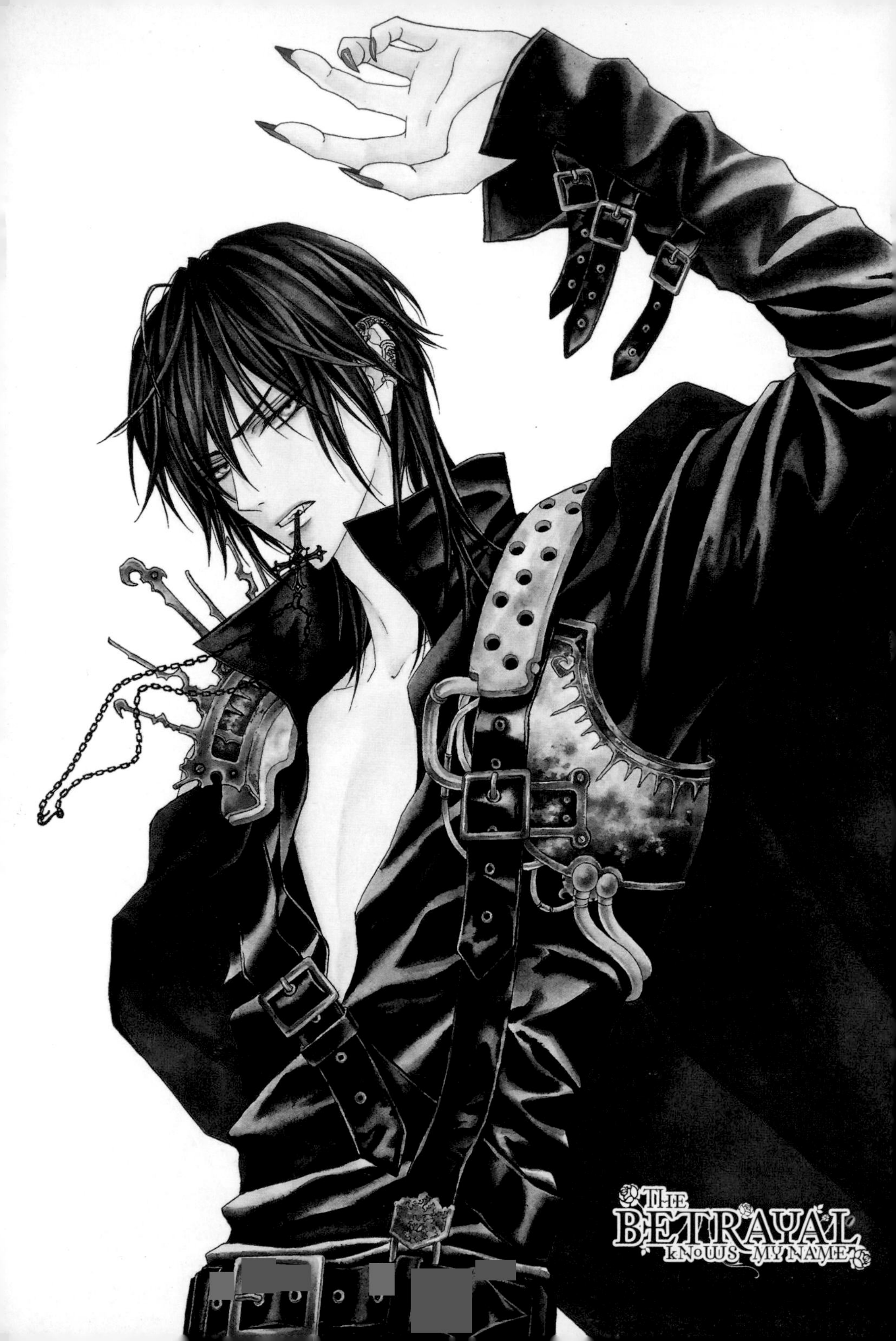
THE BETRAYAL KNOWS MY NAME

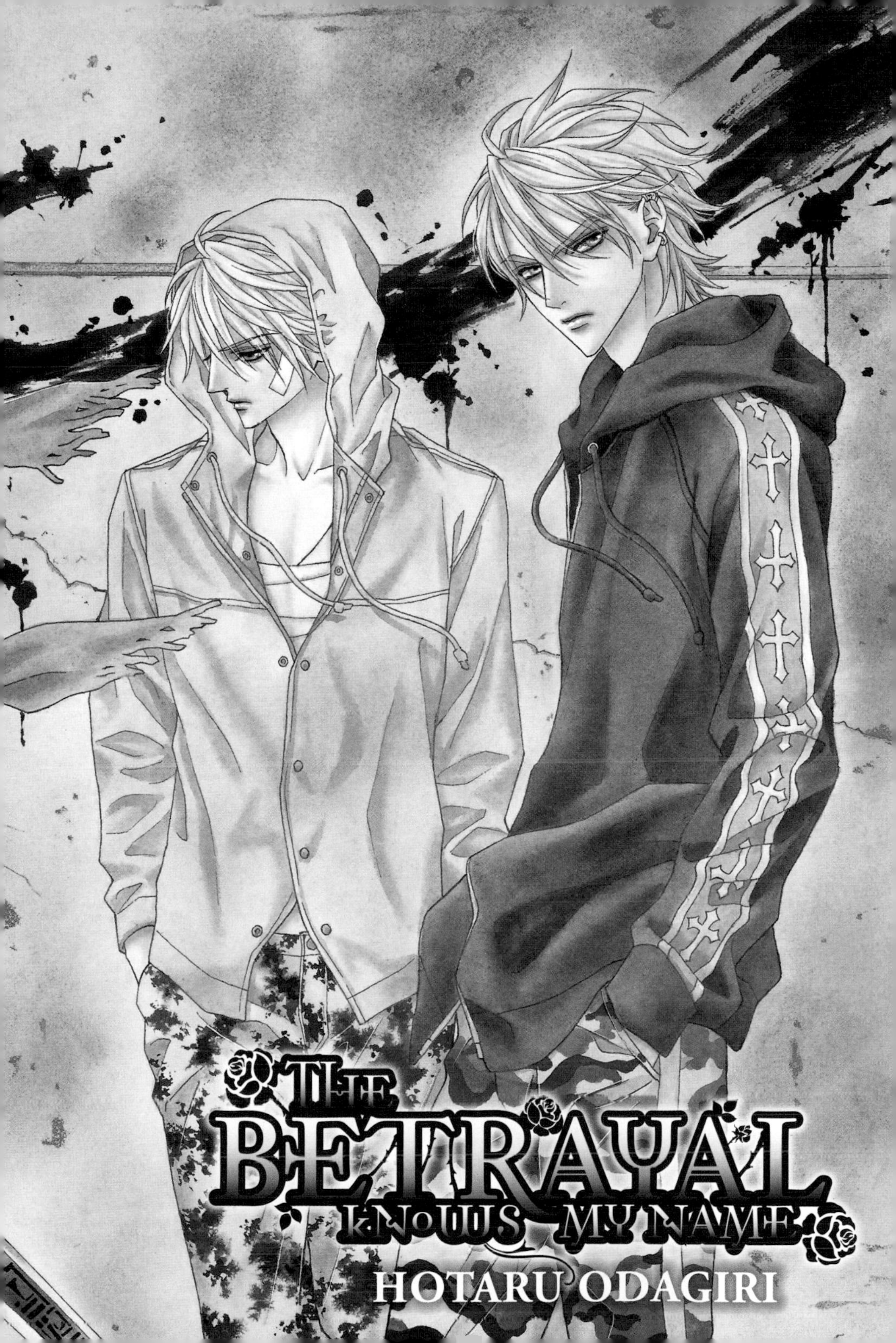

THE BETRAYAL KNOWS MY NAME
HOTARU ODAGIRI

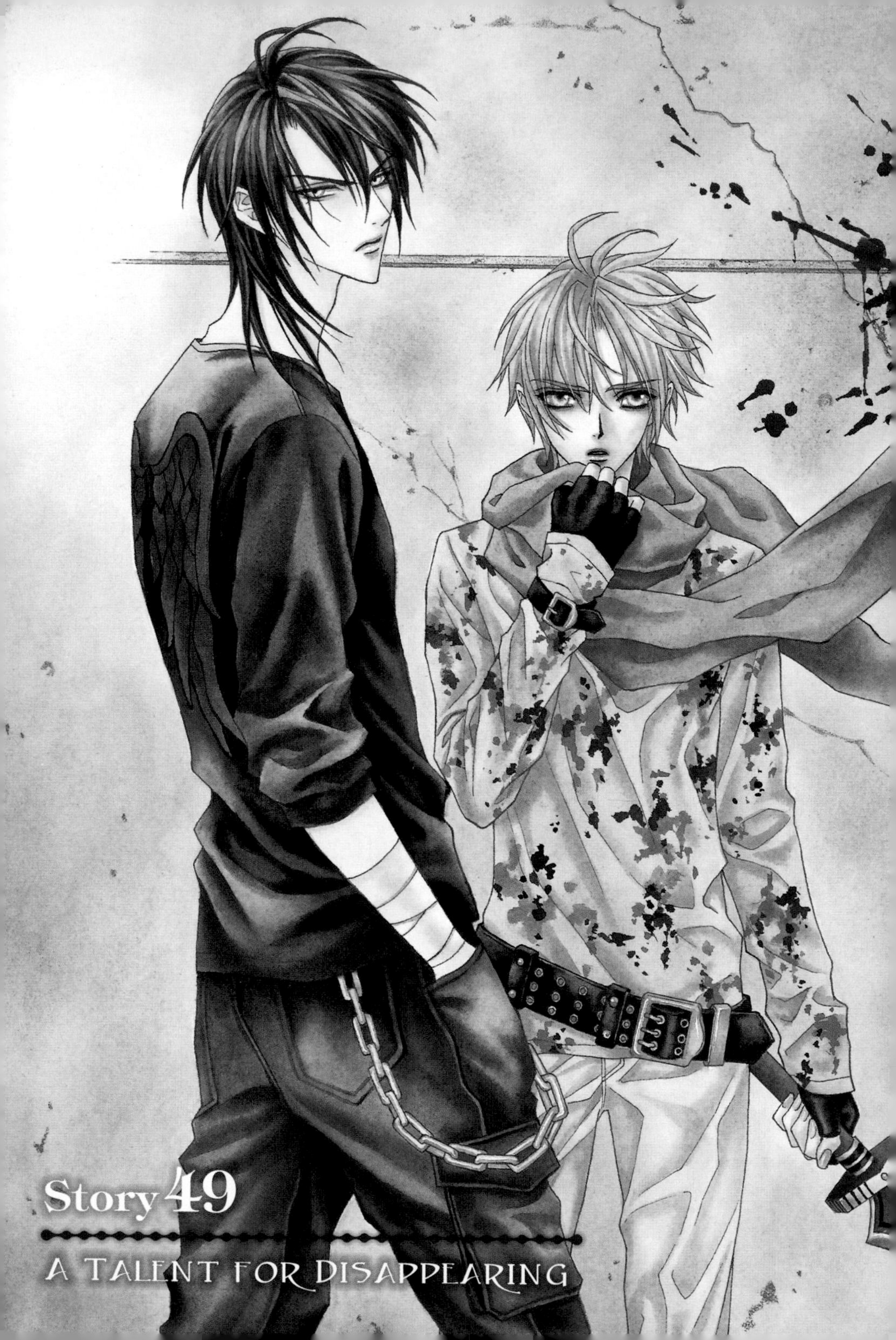
Story 49
A Talent for Disappearing

6
Contents

Story 49   A Talent for
           Disappearing 2

Story 50   Signal..39

Story 51   Trembling 73

Story 52   The Command of God 107

Extra   Afterword Manga:
           Behind the Scenes 140

THE
BETRAYAL
KNOWS MY NAME

6

Hotaru Odagiri

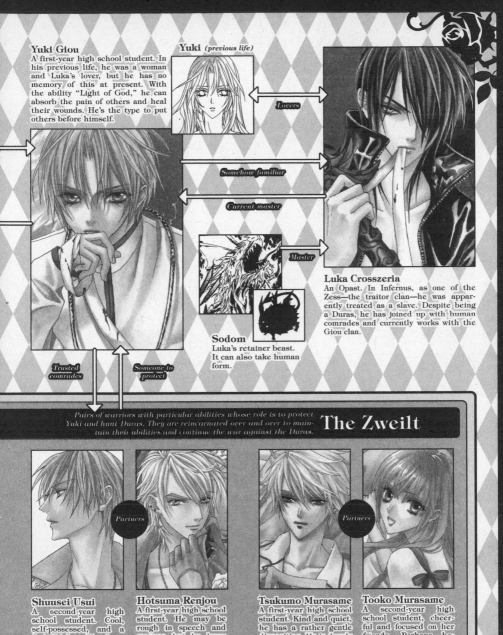

Yuki Giou
A first-year high school student. In his previous life, he was a woman and Luka's lover, but he has no memory of this at present. With the ability "Light of God," he can absorb the pain of others and heal their wounds. He's the type to put others before himself.

Yuki *(previous life)*

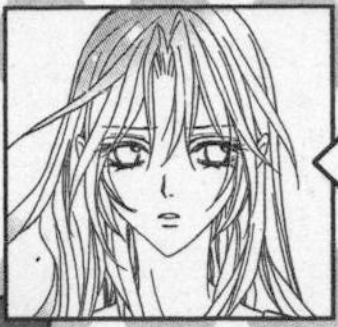

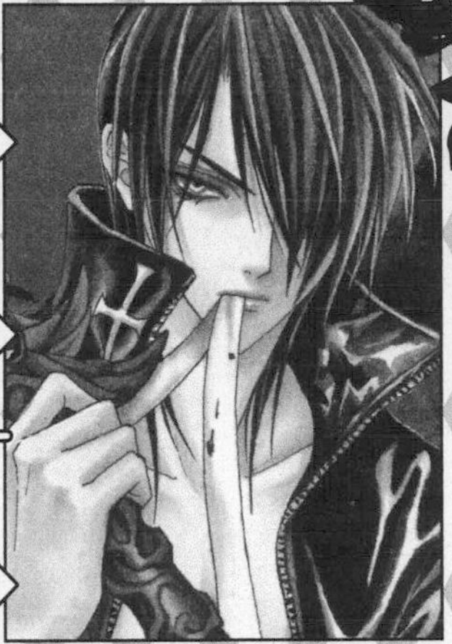

Lovers
Somehow familiar
Current master

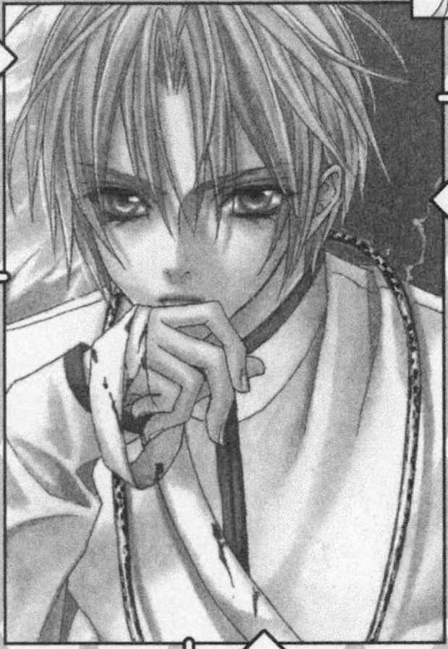

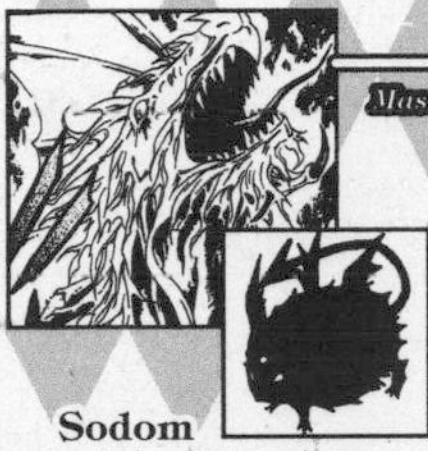

Master

Luka Crosszeria
An Opast. In Infernus, as one of the Zess—the traitor clan—he was apparently treated as a slave. Despite being a Duras, he has joined up with human comrades and currently works with the Giou clan.

Sodom
Luka's retainer beast. It can also take human form.

Trusted comrades

Someone to protect

The Zweilt

Pairs of warriors with particular abilities whose role is to protect Yuki and hunt Duras. They are reincarnated over and over to maintain their abilities and continue the war against the Duras.

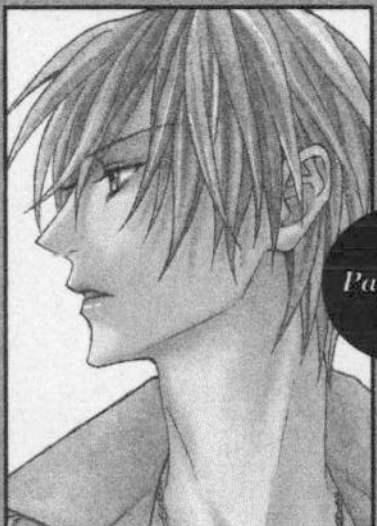

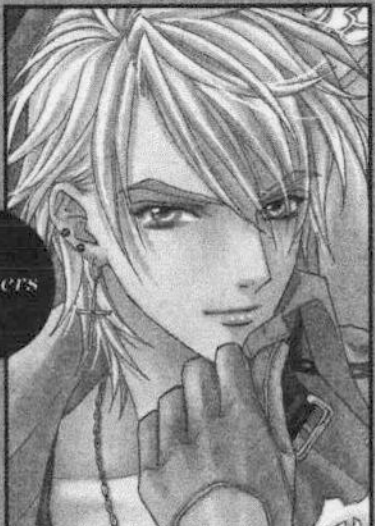

Partners

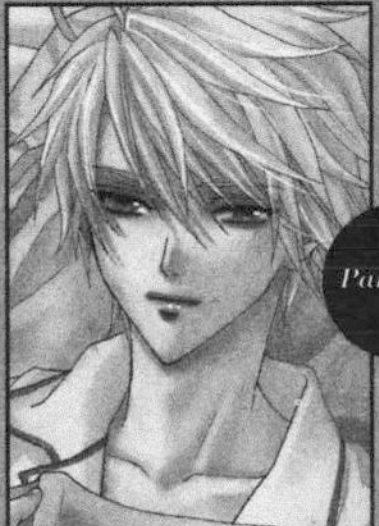

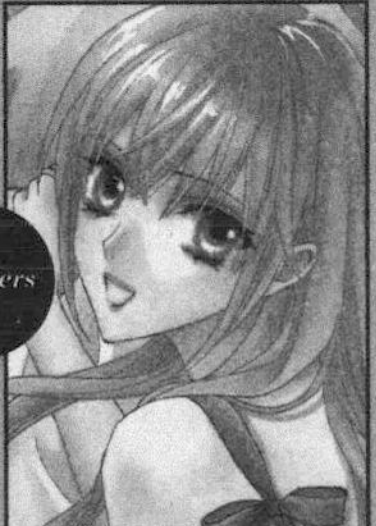

Partners

Shuusei Usui
A second-year high school student. Cool, self-possessed, and a fast thinker. Has burn scars on his chest that won't fade, caused by Hotsuma. Has the special ability "Eyes of God." Alias "The One Who Sees Through All."

Hotsuma Renjou
A first-year high school student. He may be rough in speech and manner, but he loves people deep down. He once tried to kill himself. Has the special ability "Voice of God." Alias "The One Who Burns to Cinders."

Tsukumo Murasame
A first-year high school student. Kind and quiet, he has a rather gentle disposition. He is deeply devoted to his sister, Tooko. Has the special ability "Ear of God." Alias "The One Who Inquires."

Tooko Murasame
A second-year high school student, cheerful and focused on her friends. Perhaps because he resembles someone she loved in a past life, she seems to have Luka on her mind. Has the special ability "Ear of God." Alias "The One Who Inquires."

character

The Giou Clan

Betrayed

Not his brother after all, but still important to him

Formerly close friends

Was like an older brother

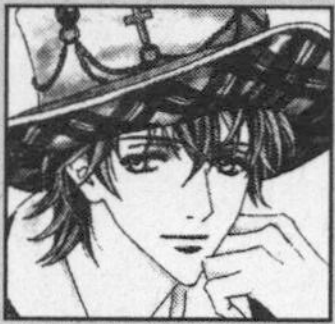

Tachibana Giou
Steward of Twilight Hall. Supervises the Zweilt.

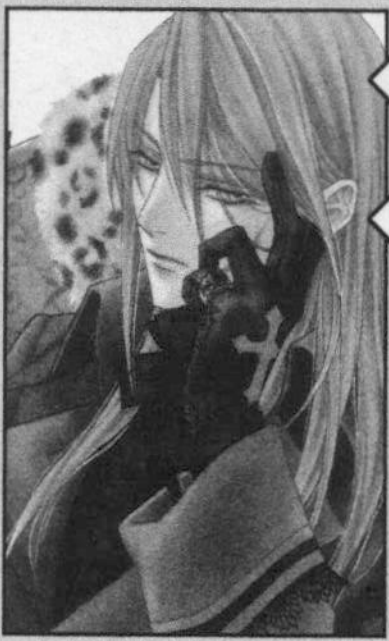

Takashiro Giou
Commander of the Giou clan. He introduced himself as Yuki's brother, but that was a lie, as he has been alive since the "Sunset of the Underworld" a millennium ago. The most powerful of the clan, he is both a wotes and a necromancer. But might he still be hiding things from Yuki...?

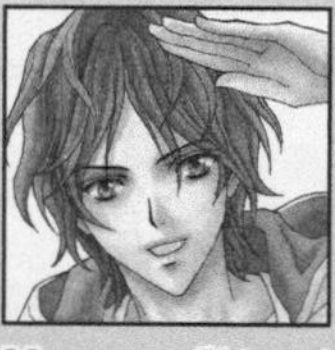

Masamune Shinmei
A second-year high school student and apprentice necromancer residing at the main residence in Kamakura.

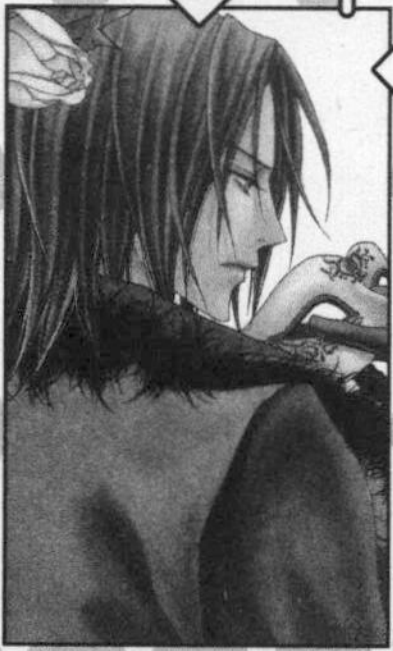

Reiga Giou
As Kanata Wakamiya, he grew up with Yuki at the Morning Sun House and made it to college, but awakened as "Reiga" and became Yuki's enemy. A child of mixed blood, born to an Opast father and a Giou mother. Also a peerless necromancer.

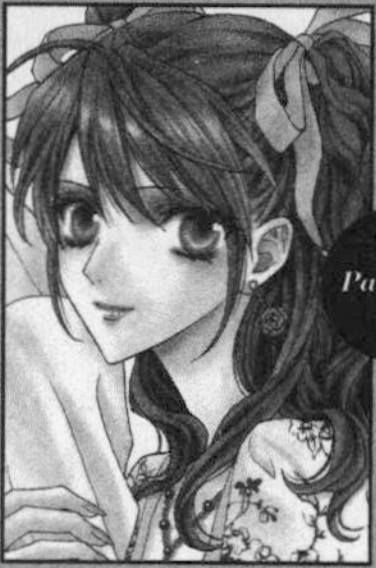

Lia Otona
A first-year high school student and an idol singer. The lively bohemian type. Having lost her partner in the previous war against the Duras, she is now paired with Sairi.

Partners

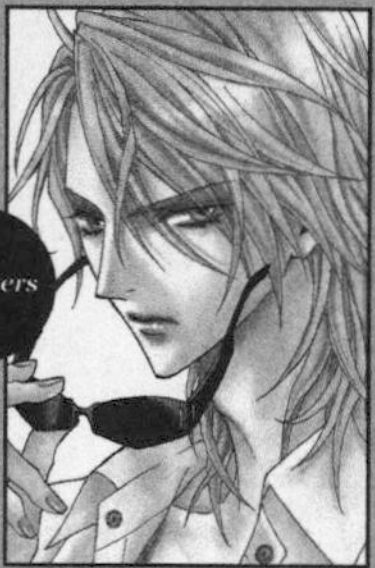

Sairi Shinmei
A university first-year. Active in show business as an actor of some renown. A gentleman... and a ladies' man. He was overseas retrieving a Grimoire, but has returned to join up with the others. Masamune's cousin.

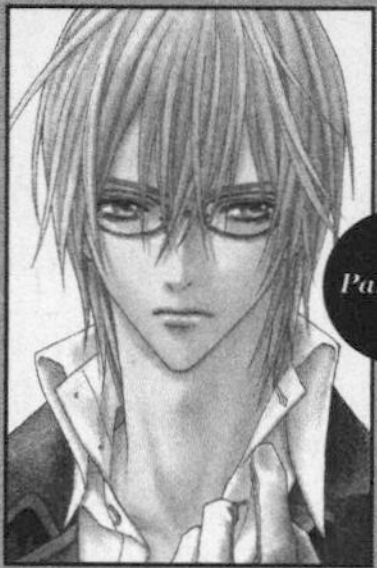

Senshirou Furuori
A first-year in art school. Likes cooking and taking care of people. Completely devoted to Kuroto. A "newbie" Zweilt, who has just joined for this round of the war. He has vowed to take revenge on the Opast Cadenza.

Partners

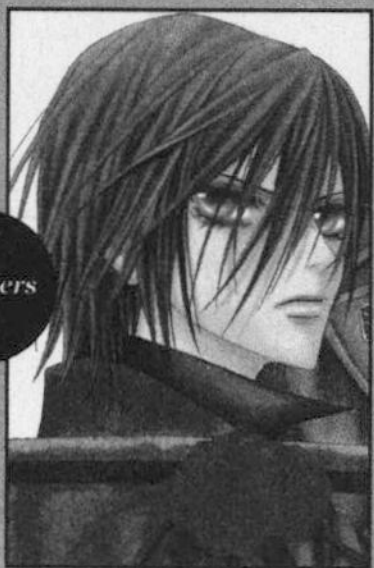

Kuroto Hourai
A first-year high school student. He grew up as a rich boy and has a self-important attitude. He was active as a professional shogi player, but quit to join the fight against the Duras. Has the special ability "Feet of God." Alias "The Swift One."

story

The Giou clan——known as the "descendants of the gods" for the special abilities possessed by many among them——has existed silently in the margins of history. Among those with such abilities, there are "necromancers," who summon and control beings known as Duras from the other world, or Infernus. It was said that these necromancers would bestow great blessings upon the people.

But a day came when the necromancer Reiga betrayed the clan. Using the Duras, he drove the Giou halfway to annihilation, then deserted them for Infernus. That was the beginning of the long war between the Giou clan, led by Takashiro, and the Duras, led by Reiga.

Time rushed onward——and now, over a thousand years later, a new battle is beginning for the Zweilt and for Yuki Giou, the boy who holds the key to a millennium-long struggle...

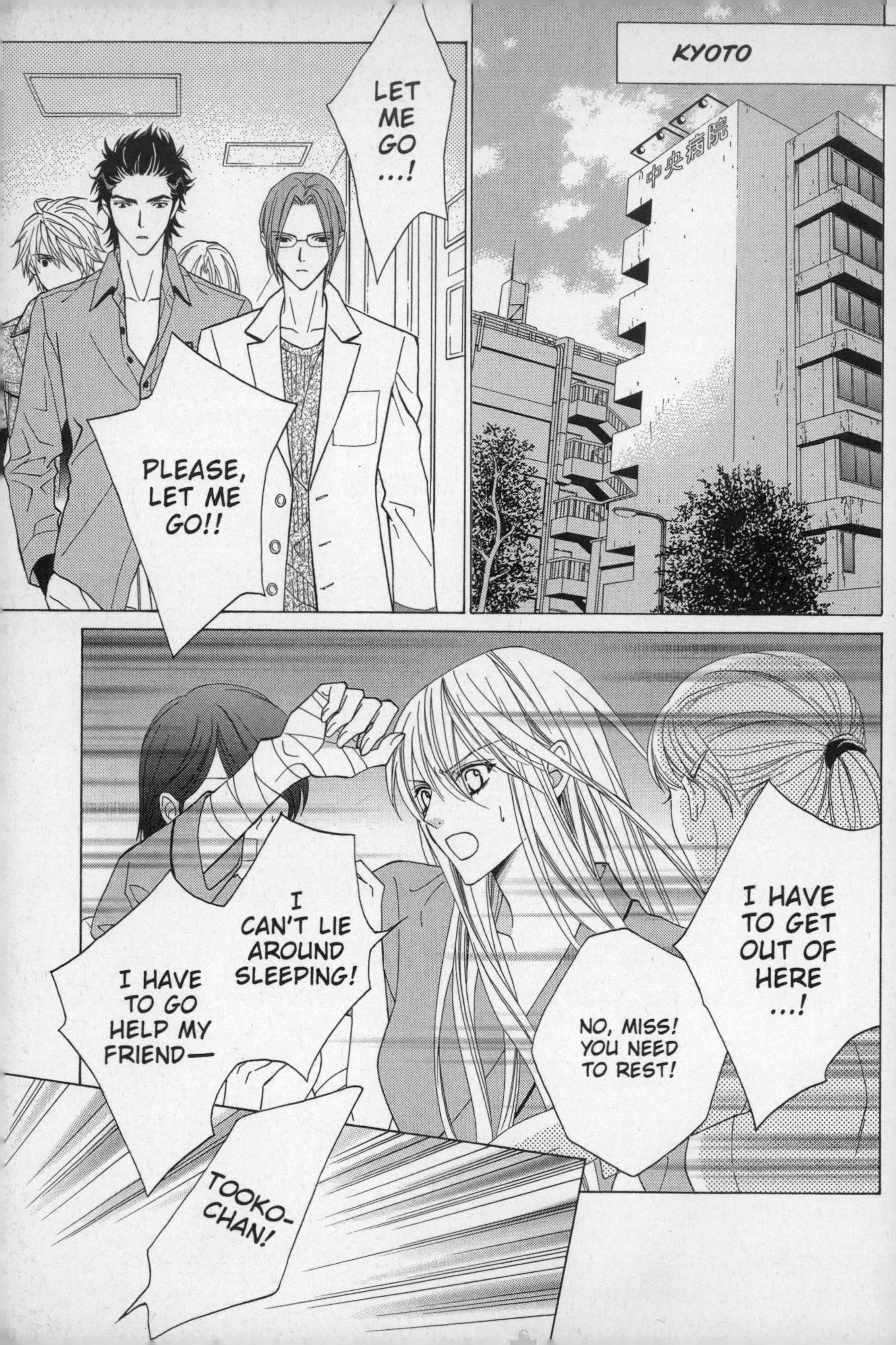
KYOTO
中央病院
LET ME GO ...!
PLEASE, LET ME GO!!
I HAVE TO GET OUT OF HERE ...!
NO, MISS! YOU NEED TO REST!
I CAN'T LIE AROUND SLEEPING!
I HAVE TO GO HELP MY FRIEND—
TOOKO-CHAN!

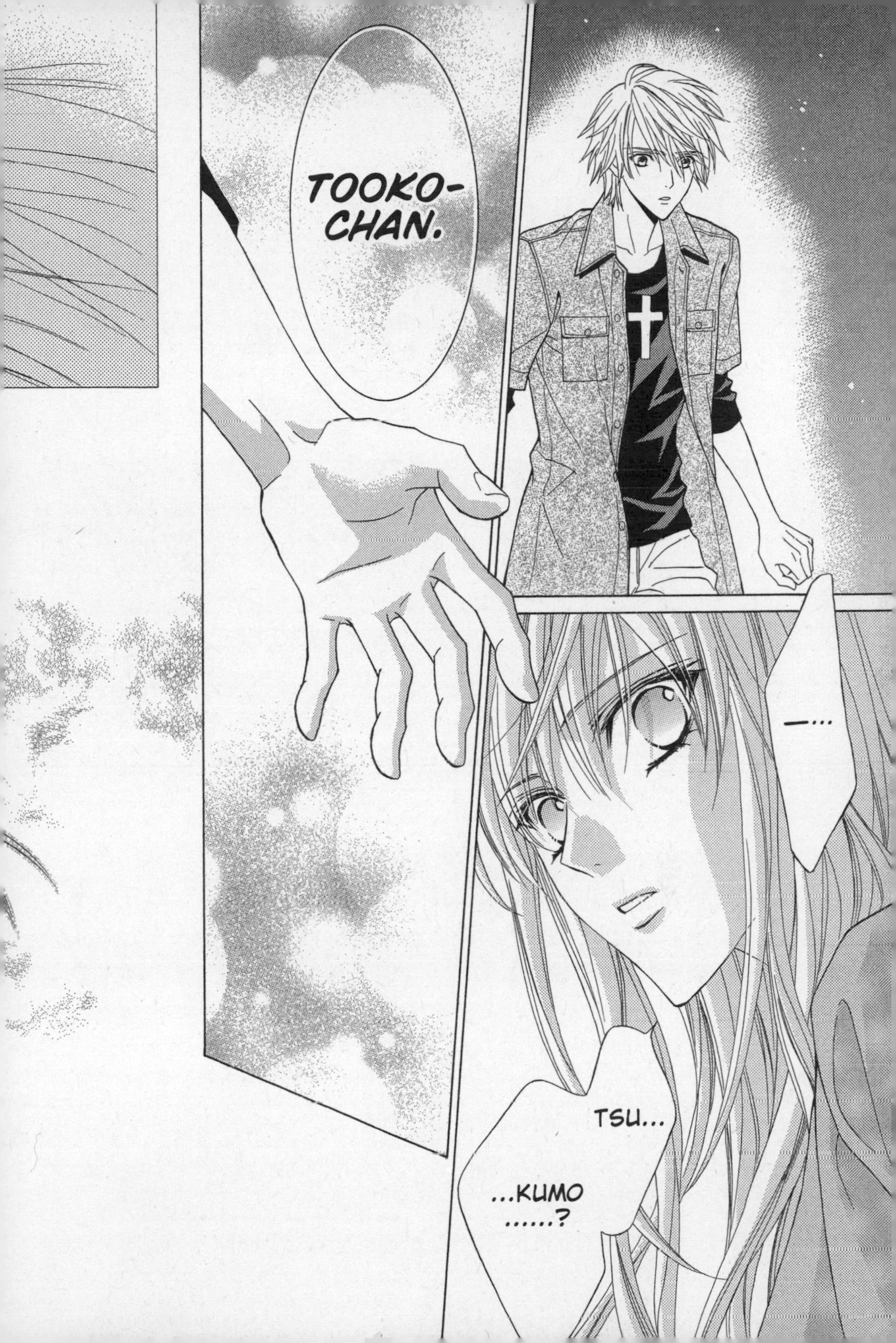
TOOKO-
CHAN.
—...
TSU...
...KUMO
......?

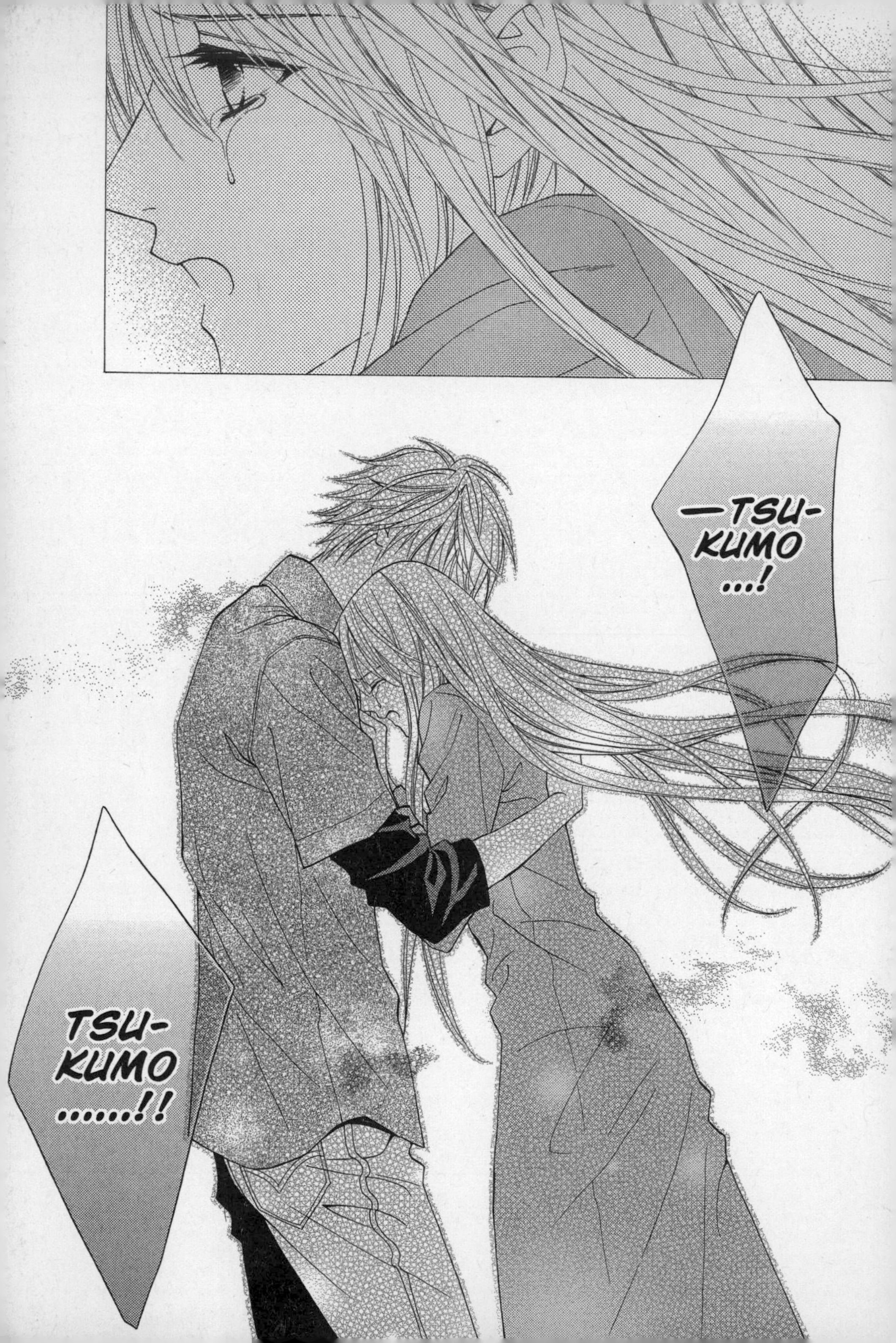
—TSU-KUMO ...!
TSU-KUMO ......!!

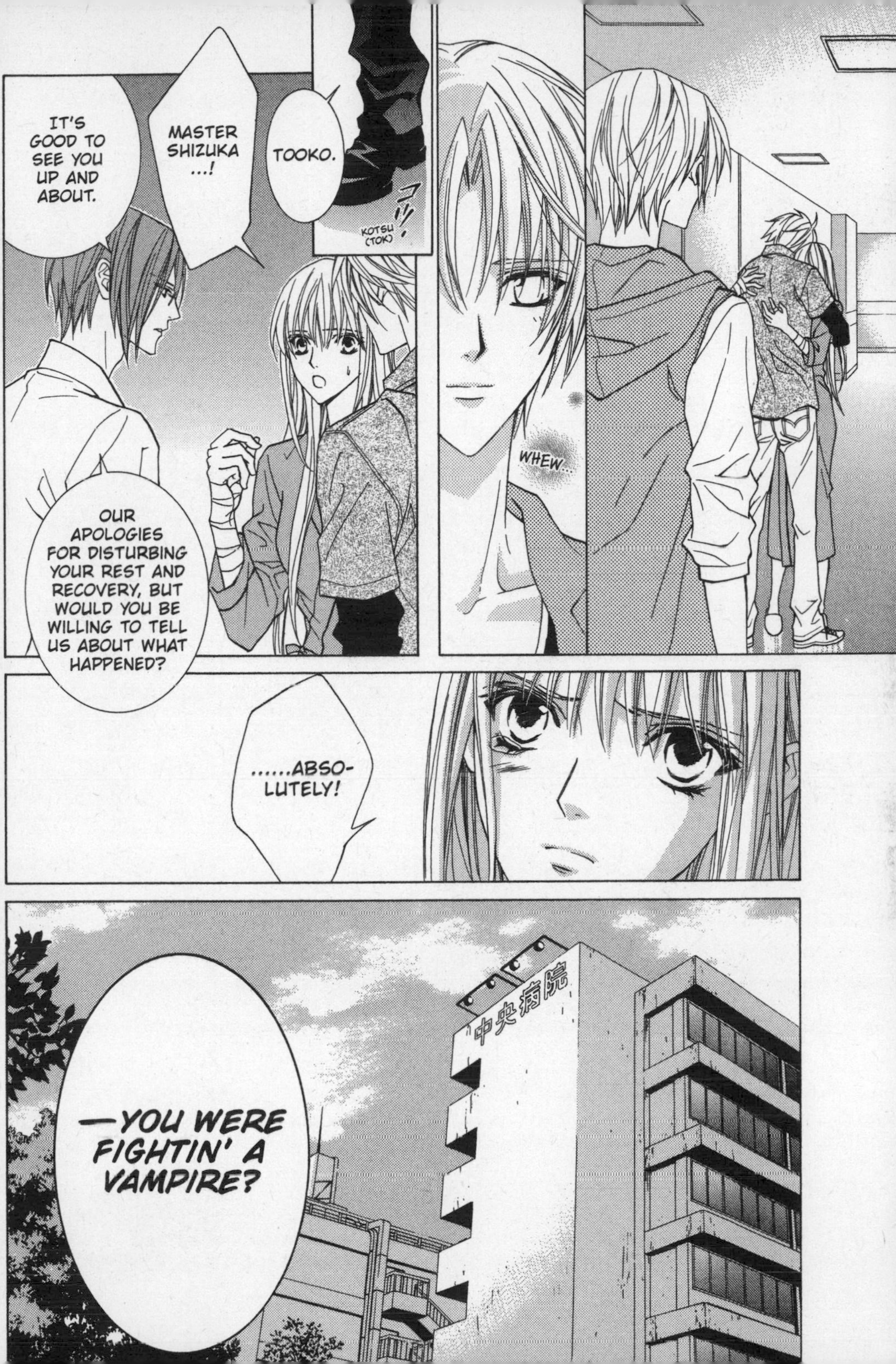
WHEW...
TOOKO.
KOTSU (TOK)
MASTER SHIZUKA ...!
IT'S GOOD TO SEE YOU UP AND ABOUT.
OUR APOLOGIES FOR DISTURBING YOUR REST AND RECOVERY, BUT WOULD YOU BE WILLING TO TELL US ABOUT WHAT HAPPENED?
......ABSO-LUTELY!
中央病院
—YOU WERE FIGHTIN' A VAMPIRE?

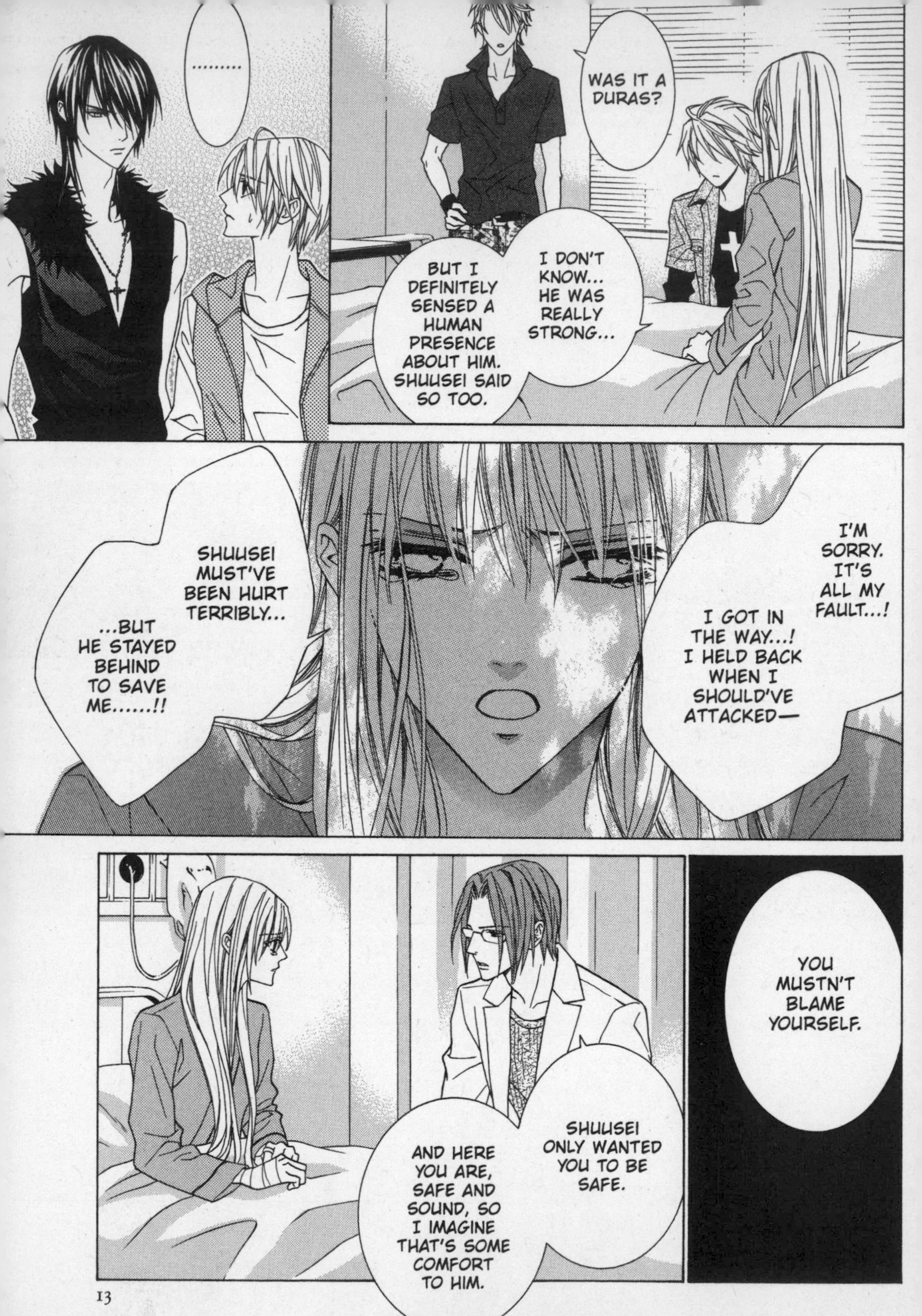
WAS IT A DURAS?
I DON'T KNOW... HE WAS REALLY STRONG...
BUT I DEFINITELY SENSED A HUMAN PRESENCE ABOUT HIM. SHUUSEI SAID SO TOO.
....
I'M SORRY. IT'S ALL MY FAULT...!
I GOT IN THE WAY...! I HELD BACK WHEN I SHOULD'VE ATTACKED—
SHUUSEI MUST'VE BEEN HURT TERRIBLY...
...BUT HE STAYED BEHIND TO SAVE ME......!!
YOU MUSTN'T BLAME YOURSELF.
SHUUSEI ONLY WANTED YOU TO BE SAFE.
AND HERE YOU ARE, SAFE AND SOUND, SO I IMAGINE THAT'S SOME COMFORT TO HIM.

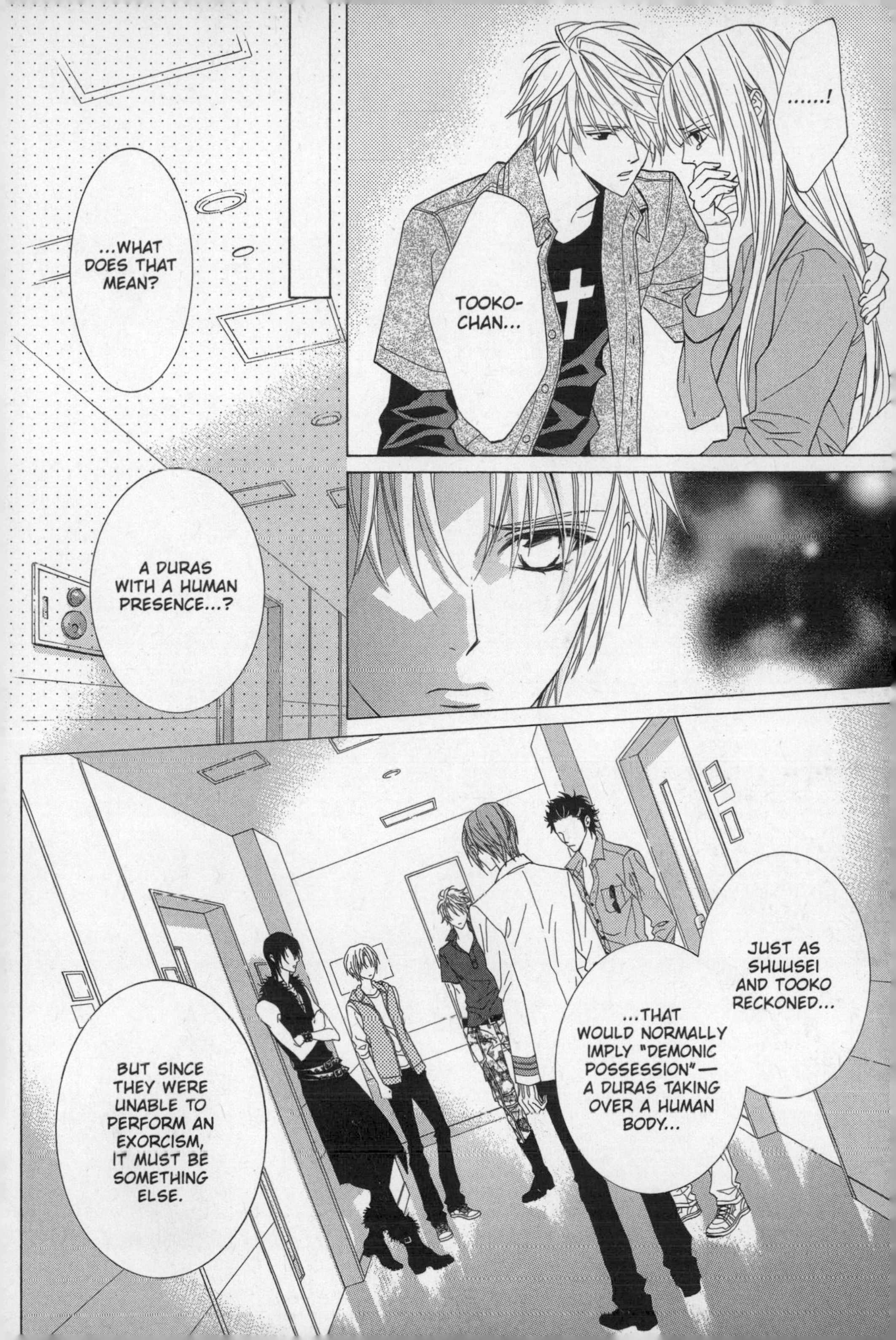
......!
TOOKO-CHAN...
...WHAT DOES THAT MEAN?
A DURAS WITH A HUMAN PRESENCE...?
JUST AS SHUUSEI AND TOOKO RECKONED...
...THAT WOULD NORMALLY IMPLY "DEMONIC POSSESSION"— A DURAS TAKING OVER A HUMAN BODY...
BUT SINCE THEY WERE UNABLE TO PERFORM AN EXORCISM, IT MUST BE SOMETHING ELSE.

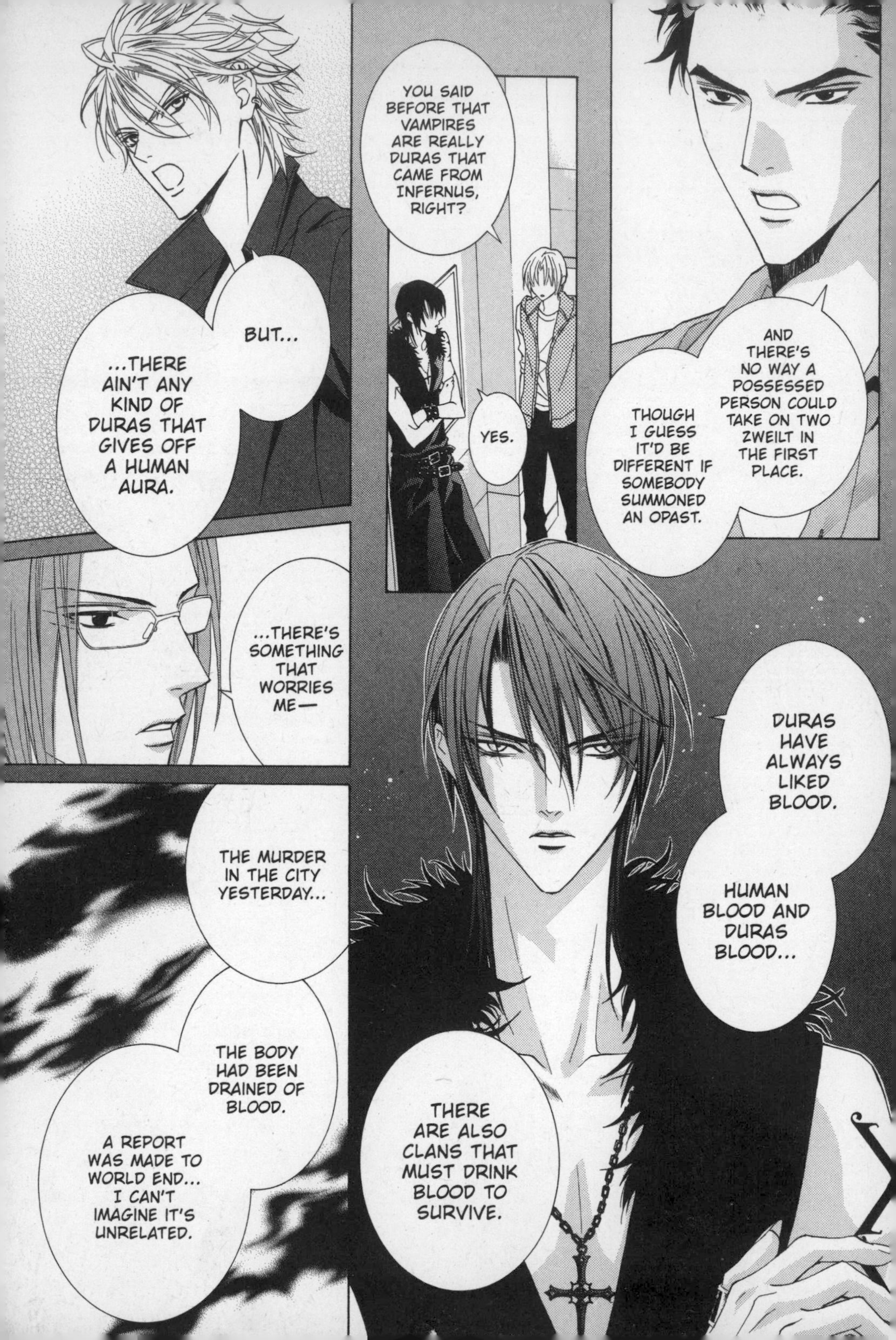

AND THERE'S NO WAY A POSSESSED PERSON COULD TAKE ON TWO ZWEILT IN THE FIRST PLACE.
THOUGH I GUESS IT'D BE DIFFERENT IF SOMEBODY SUMMONED AN OPAST.
YOU SAID BEFORE THAT VAMPIRES ARE REALLY DURAS THAT CAME FROM INFERNUS, RIGHT?
YES.
BUT...
...THERE AIN'T ANY KIND OF DURAS THAT GIVES OFF A HUMAN AURA.
DURAS HAVE ALWAYS LIKED BLOOD.
HUMAN BLOOD AND DURAS BLOOD...
THERE ARE ALSO CLANS THAT MUST DRINK BLOOD TO SURVIVE.
...THERE'S SOMETHING THAT WORRIES ME—
THE MURDER IN THE CITY YESTERDAY...
THE BODY HAD BEEN DRAINED OF BLOOD.
A REPORT WAS MADE TO WORLD END... I CAN'T IMAGINE IT'S UNRELATED.

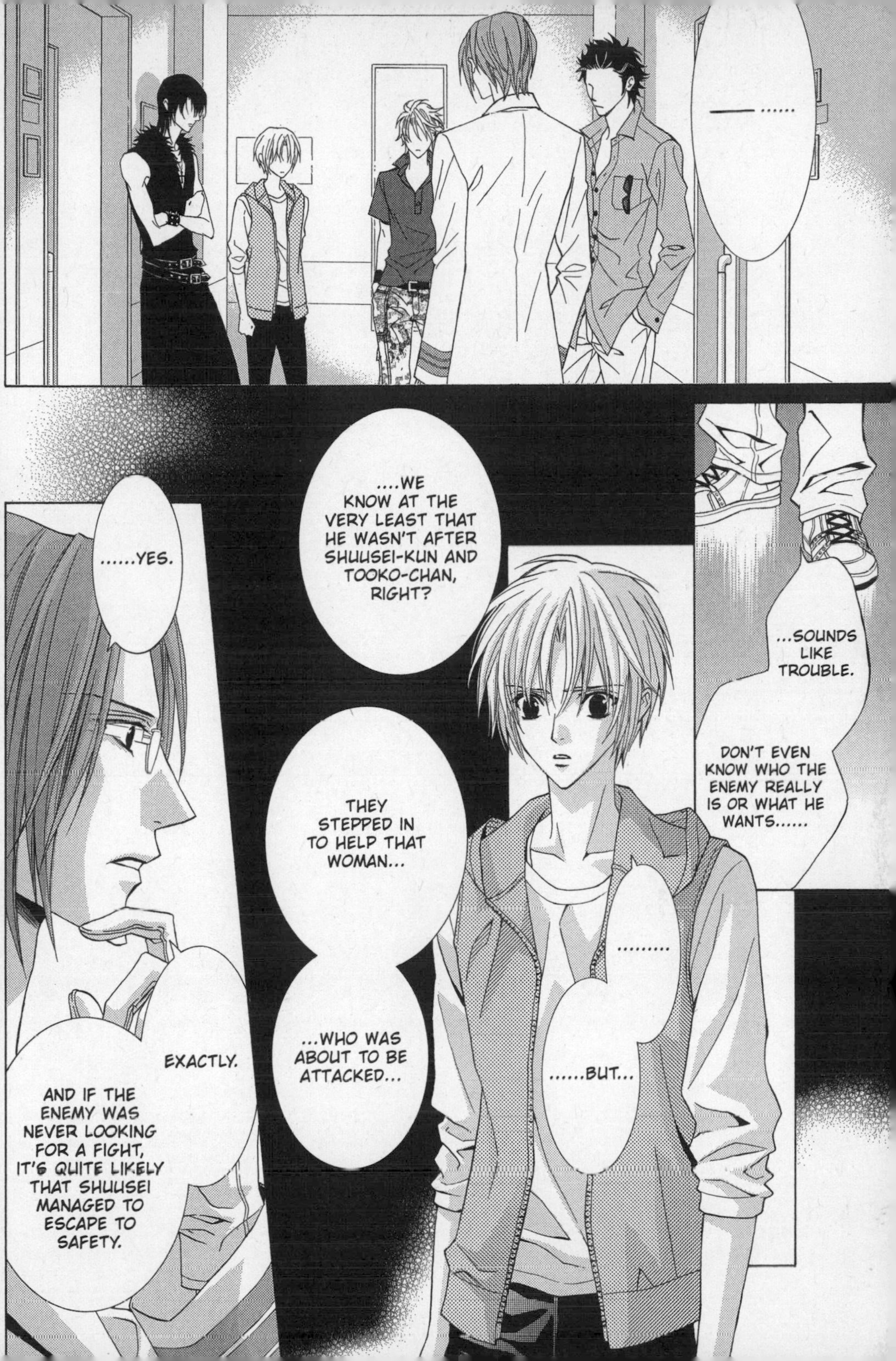
—— ......
...SOUNDS LIKE TROUBLE.
DON'T EVEN KNOW WHO THE ENEMY REALLY IS OR WHAT HE WANTS......
....
......BUT...
....WE KNOW AT THE VERY LEAST THAT HE WASN'T AFTER SHUUSEI-KUN AND TOOKO-CHAN, RIGHT?
THEY STEPPED IN TO HELP THAT WOMAN...
...WHO WAS ABOUT TO BE ATTACKED...
......YES.
EXACTLY.
AND IF THE ENEMY WAS NEVER LOOKING FOR A FIGHT, IT'S QUITE LIKELY THAT SHUUSEI MANAGED TO ESCAPE TO SAFETY.

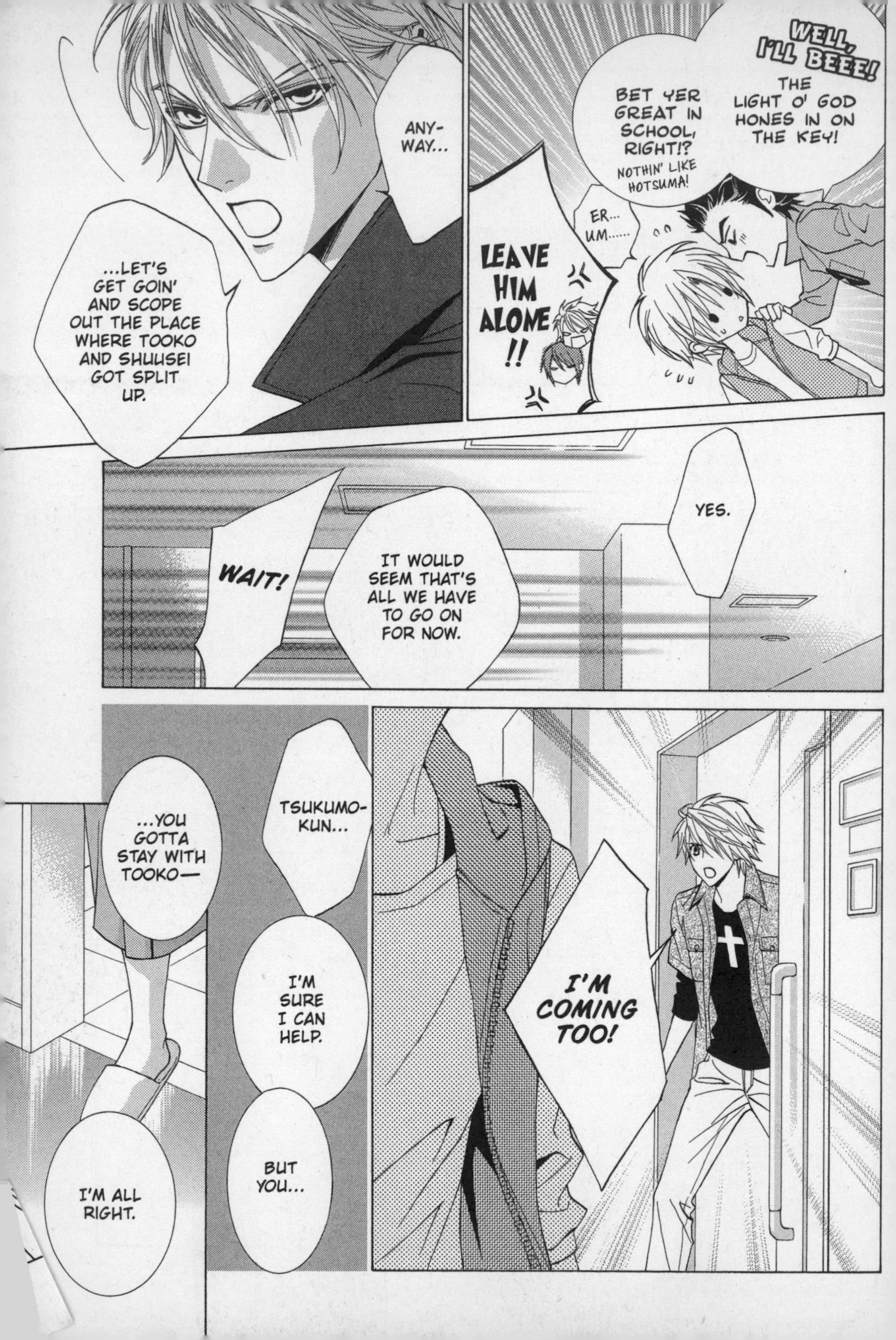
WELL, I'LL BEEE!
THE LIGHT O' GOD HONES IN ON THE KEY!
BET YER GREAT IN SCHOOL, RIGHT!?
NOTHIN' LIKE HOTSUMA!
ER... UM......
LEAVE HIM ALONE!!
ANY-WAY...
...LET'S GET GOIN' AND SCOPE OUT THE PLACE WHERE TOOKO AND SHUUSEI GOT SPLIT UP.
YES.
IT WOULD SEEM THAT'S ALL WE HAVE TO GO ON FOR NOW.
WAIT!
I'M COMING TOO!
TSUKUMO-KUN...
...YOU GOTTA STAY WITH TOOKO—
I'M SURE I CAN HELP.
BUT YOU...
I'M ALL RIGHT.

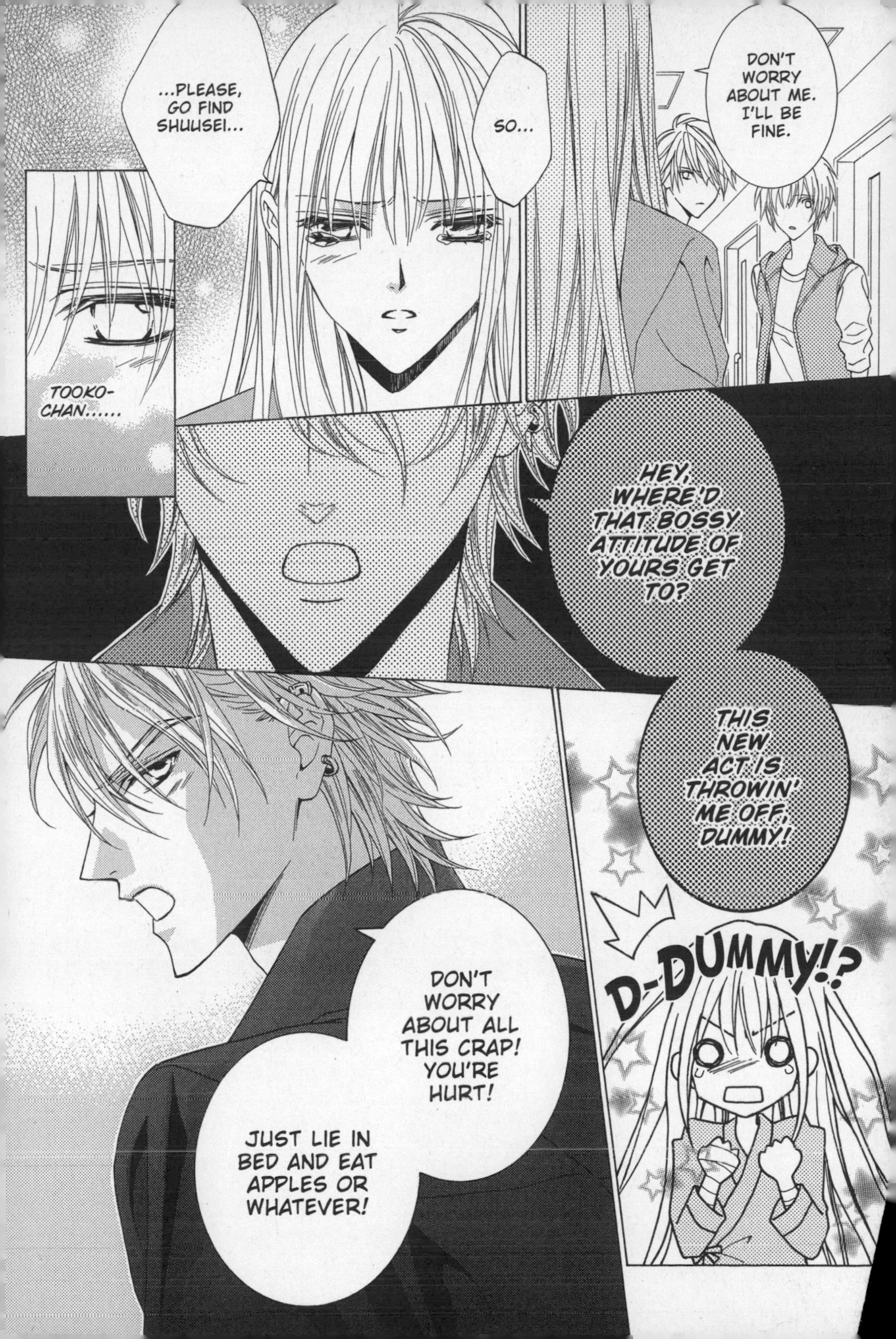
DON'T WORRY ABOUT ME. I'LL BE FINE.
SO...
...PLEASE, GO FIND SHUUSEI...
TOOKO-CHAN......
HEY, WHERE'D THAT BOSSY ATTITUDE OF YOURS GET TO?
THIS NEW ACT IS THROWIN' ME OFF, DUMMY!
D-DUMMY!?
DON'T WORRY ABOUT ALL THIS CRAP! YOU'RE HURT!
JUST LIE IN BED AND EAT APPLES OR WHATEVER!

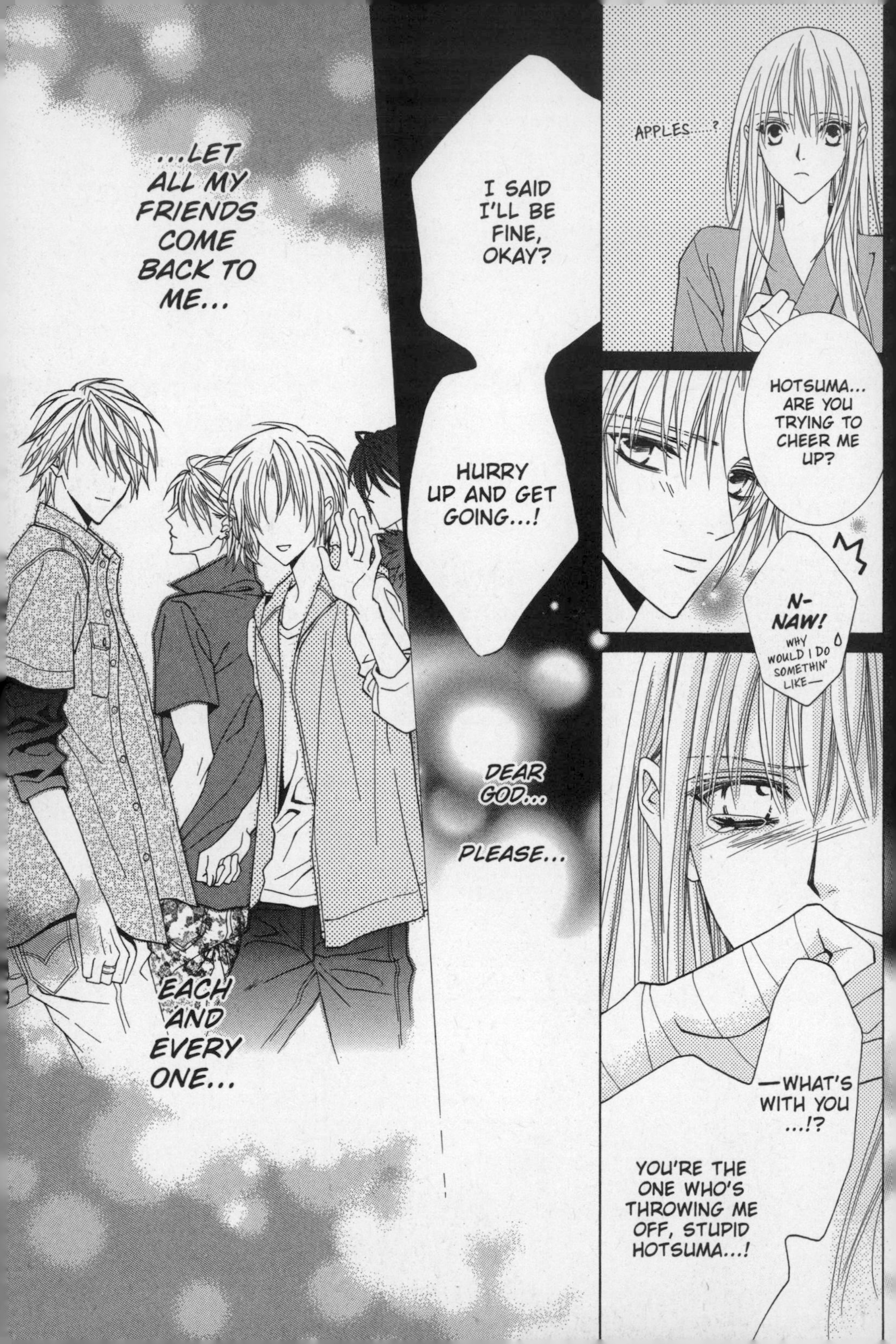
APPLES...?
HOTSUMA... ARE YOU TRYING TO CHEER ME UP?
N-NAW! WHY WOULD I DO SOMETHIN' LIKE—
—WHAT'S WITH YOU ...!?
YOU'RE THE ONE WHO'S THROWING ME OFF, STUPID HOTSUMA...!
I SAID I'LL BE FINE, OKAY?
HURRY UP AND GET GOING...!
DEAR GOD...
PLEASE...
...LET ALL MY FRIENDS COME BACK TO ME...
EACH AND EVERY ONE...

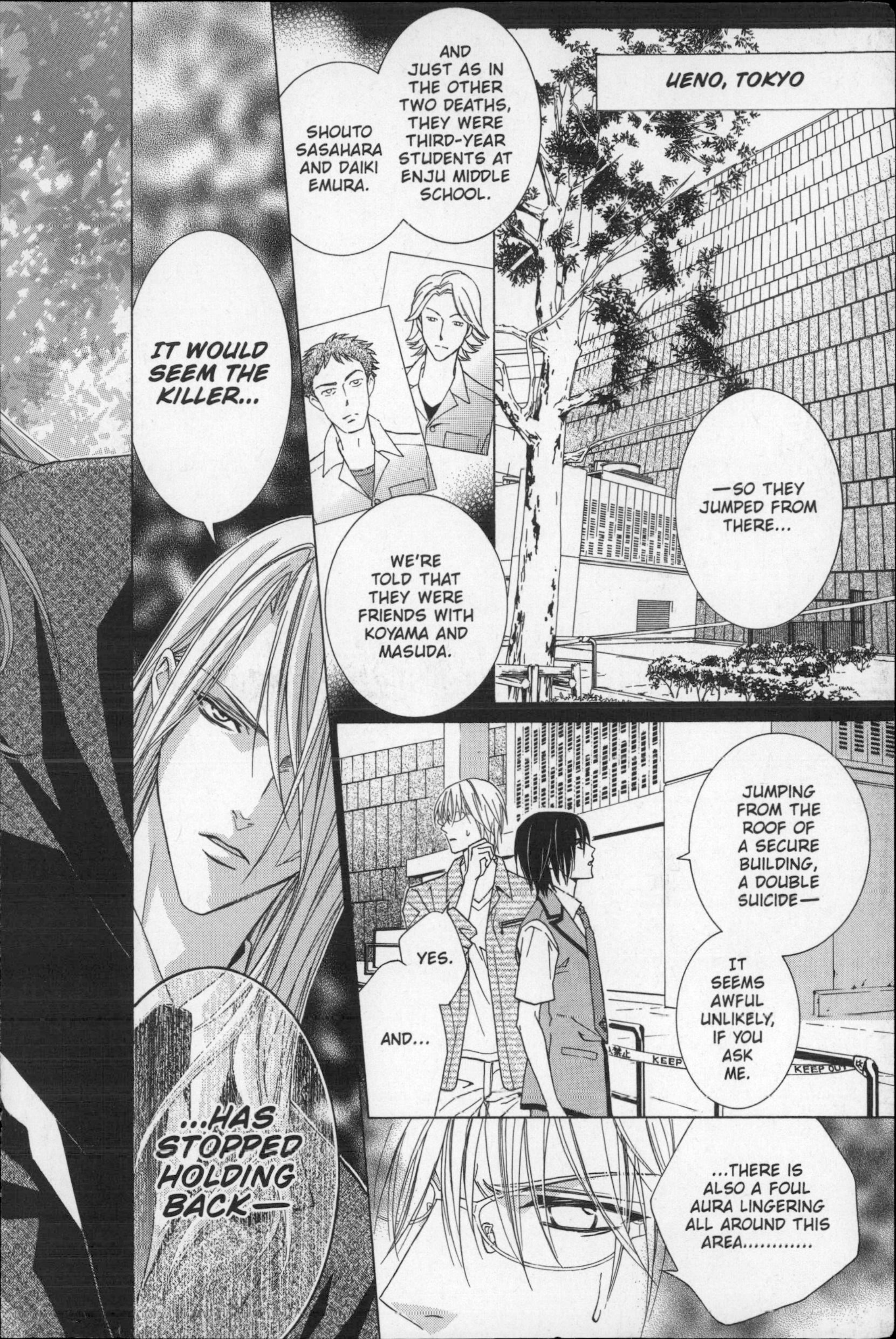
UENO, TOKYO
—SO THEY JUMPED FROM THERE...
AND JUST AS IN THE OTHER TWO DEATHS, THEY WERE THIRD-YEAR STUDENTS AT ENJU MIDDLE SCHOOL.
SHOUTO SASAHARA AND DAIKI EMURA.
WE'RE TOLD THAT THEY WERE FRIENDS WITH KOYAMA AND MASUDA.
JUMPING FROM THE ROOF OF A SECURE BUILDING, A DOUBLE SUICIDE—
IT SEEMS AWFUL UNLIKELY, IF YOU ASK ME.
YES.
AND...
KEEP
KEEP OUT
...THERE IS ALSO A FOUL AURA LINGERING ALL AROUND THIS AREA............
IT WOULD SEEM THE KILLER...
...HAS STOPPED HOLDING BACK—

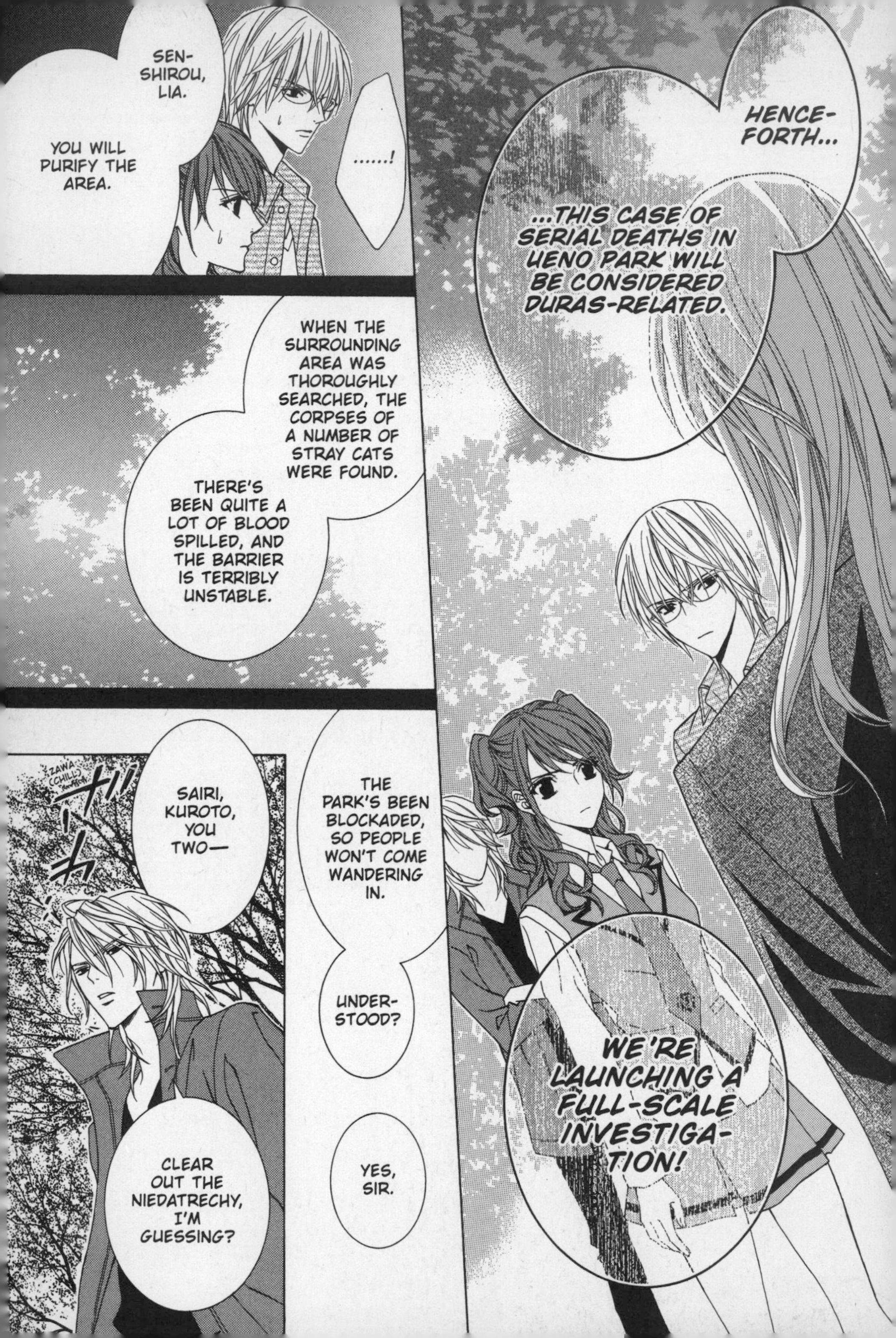
HENCE-FORTH...
...THIS CASE OF SERIAL DEATHS IN UENO PARK WILL BE CONSIDERED DURAS-RELATED.
WE'RE LAUNCHING A FULL-SCALE INVESTIGATION!
SEN-SHIROU, LIA.
YOU WILL PURIFY THE AREA.
......!
WHEN THE SURROUNDING AREA WAS THOROUGHLY SEARCHED, THE CORPSES OF A NUMBER OF STRAY CATS WERE FOUND.
THERE'S BEEN QUITE A LOT OF BLOOD SPILLED, AND THE BARRIER IS TERRIBLY UNSTABLE.
THE PARK'S BEEN BLOCKADED, SO PEOPLE WON'T COME WANDERING IN.
SAIRI, KUROTO, YOU TWO—
UNDER-STOOD?
ZAWA (CHILL)
CLEAR OUT THE NIEDATRECHY, I'M GUESSING?
YES, SIR.

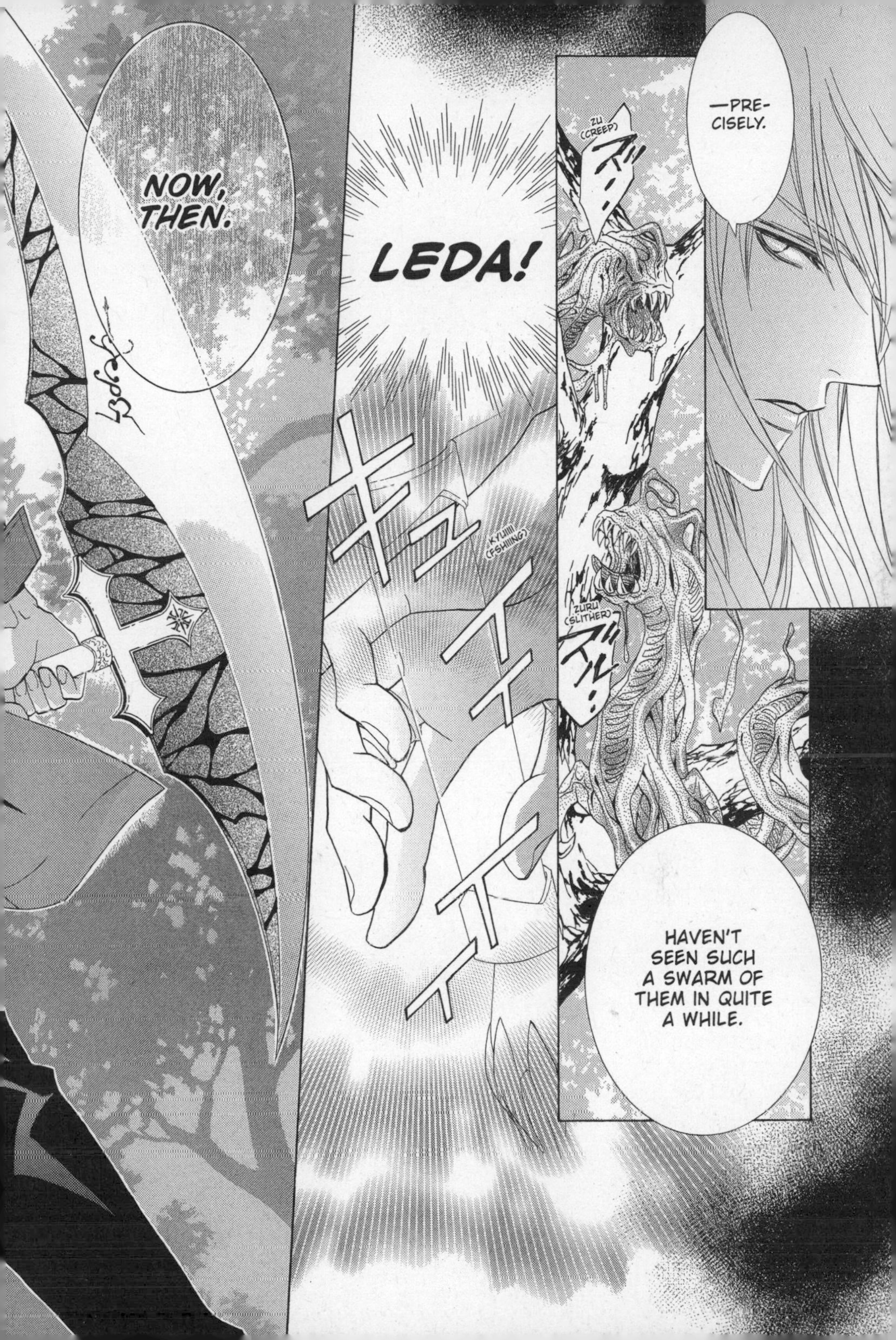
—PRE-
CISELY.
ZU
(CREEP)
ZURU
(SLITHER)
HAVEN'T SEEN SUCH A SWARM OF THEM IN QUITE A WHILE.
LEDA!
KYUIII
(FSHIIING)
NOW, THEN.

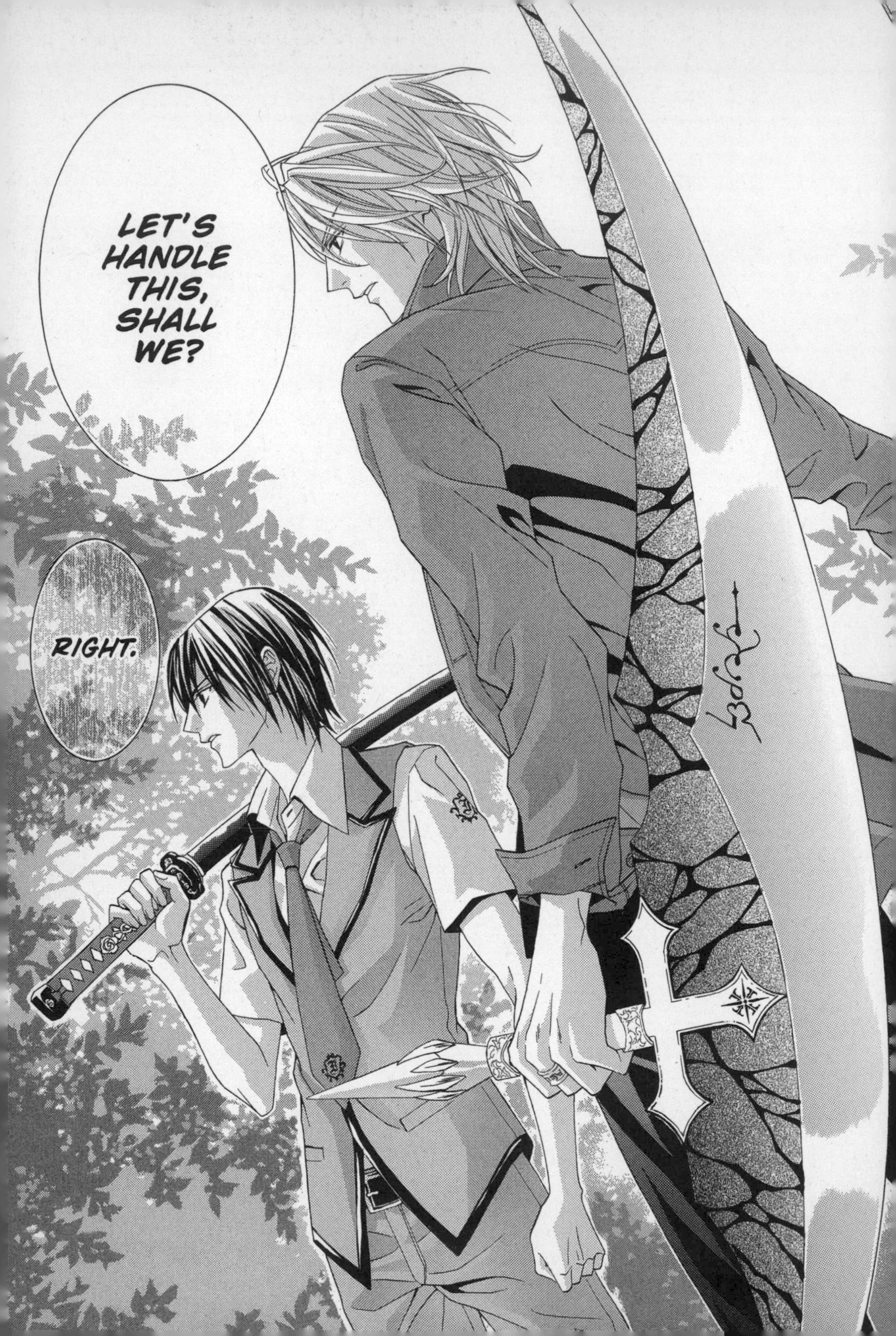
LET'S HANDLE THIS, SHALL WE?
RIGHT.

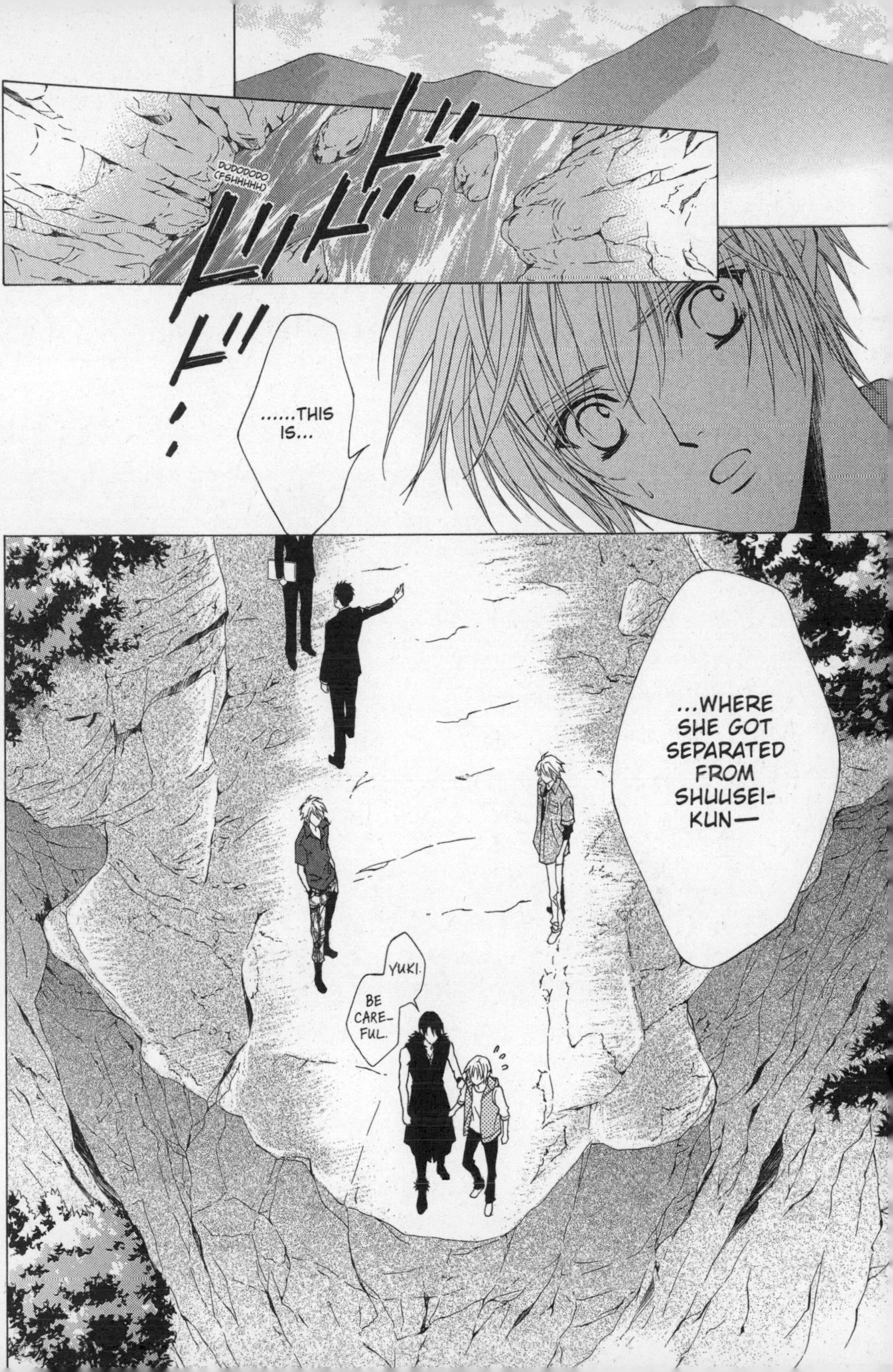
DODODODO (FSHHHHH)
......THIS IS...
...WHERE SHE GOT SEPARATED FROM SHUUSEI-KUN—
YUKI.
BE CAREFUL.

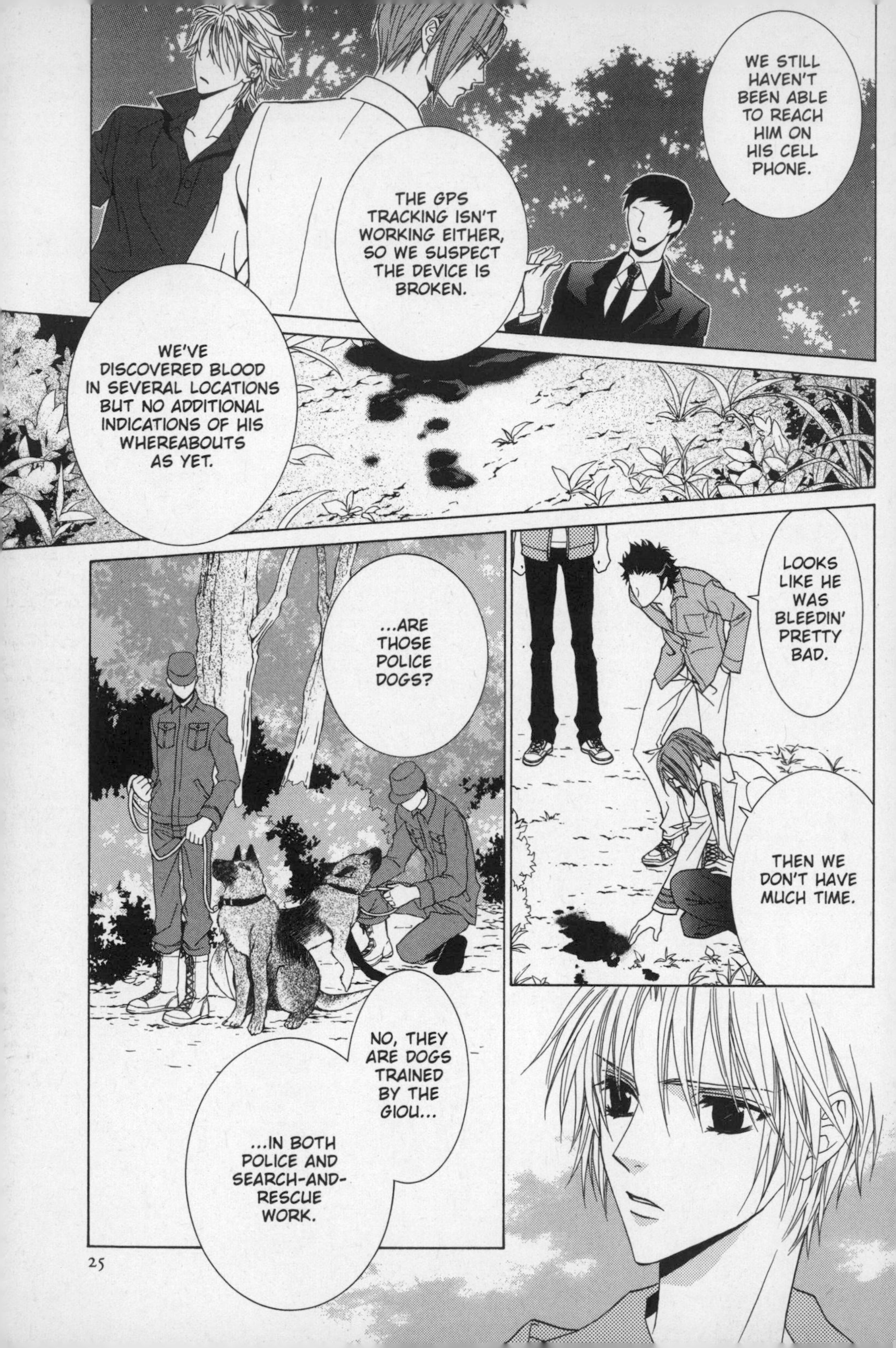
WE STILL HAVEN'T BEEN ABLE TO REACH HIM ON HIS CELL PHONE.
THE GPS TRACKING ISN'T WORKING EITHER, SO WE SUSPECT THE DEVICE IS BROKEN.
WE'VE DISCOVERED BLOOD IN SEVERAL LOCATIONS BUT NO ADDITIONAL INDICATIONS OF HIS WHEREABOUTS AS YET.
LOOKS LIKE HE WAS BLEEDIN' PRETTY BAD.
THEN WE DON'T HAVE MUCH TIME.
...ARE THOSE POLICE DOGS?
NO, THEY ARE DOGS TRAINED BY THE GIOU...
...IN BOTH POLICE AND SEARCH-AND-RESCUE WORK.

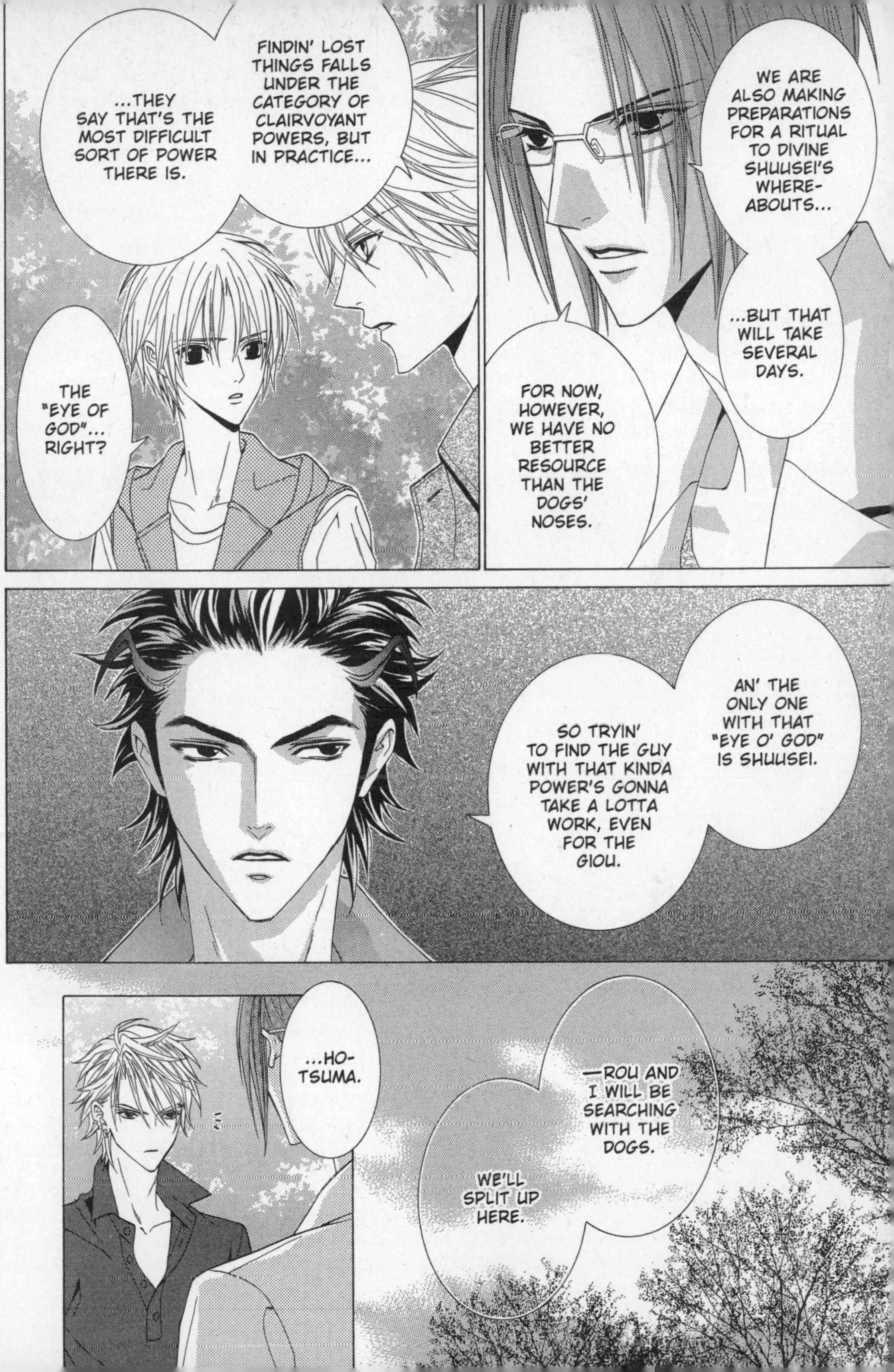
WE ARE ALSO MAKING PREPARATIONS FOR A RITUAL TO DIVINE SHUUSEI'S WHERE-ABOUTS...
...BUT THAT WILL TAKE SEVERAL DAYS.
FOR NOW, HOWEVER, WE HAVE NO BETTER RESOURCE THAN THE DOGS' NOSES.
FINDIN' LOST THINGS FALLS UNDER THE CATEGORY OF CLAIRVOYANT POWERS, BUT IN PRACTICE...
...THEY SAY THAT'S THE MOST DIFFICULT SORT OF POWER THERE IS.
THE "EYE OF GOD"... RIGHT?
AN' THE ONLY ONE WITH THAT "EYE O' GOD" IS SHUUSEI.
SO TRYIN' TO FIND THE GUY WITH THAT KINDA POWER'S GONNA TAKE A LOTTA WORK, EVEN FOR THE GIOU.
—ROU AND I WILL BE SEARCHING WITH THE DOGS.
WE'LL SPLIT UP HERE.
...HO-TSUMA.

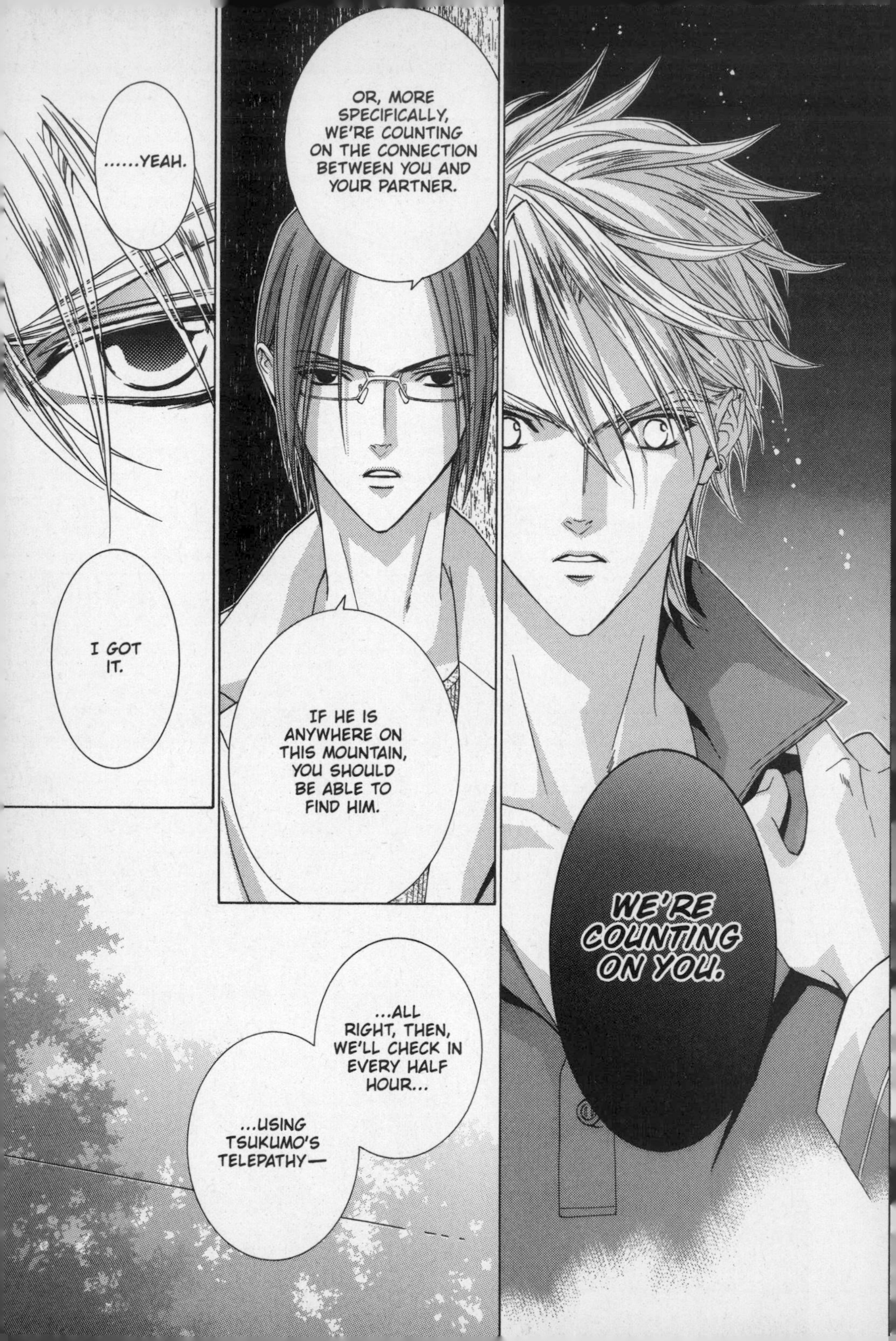
WE'RE COUNTING ON YOU.
OR, MORE SPECIFICALLY, WE'RE COUNTING ON THE CONNECTION BETWEEN YOU AND YOUR PARTNER.
IF HE IS ANYWHERE ON THIS MOUNTAIN, YOU SHOULD BE ABLE TO FIND HIM.
......YEAH.
I GOT IT.
...ALL RIGHT, THEN, WE'LL CHECK IN EVERY HALF HOUR...
...USING TSUKUMO'S TELEPATHY—

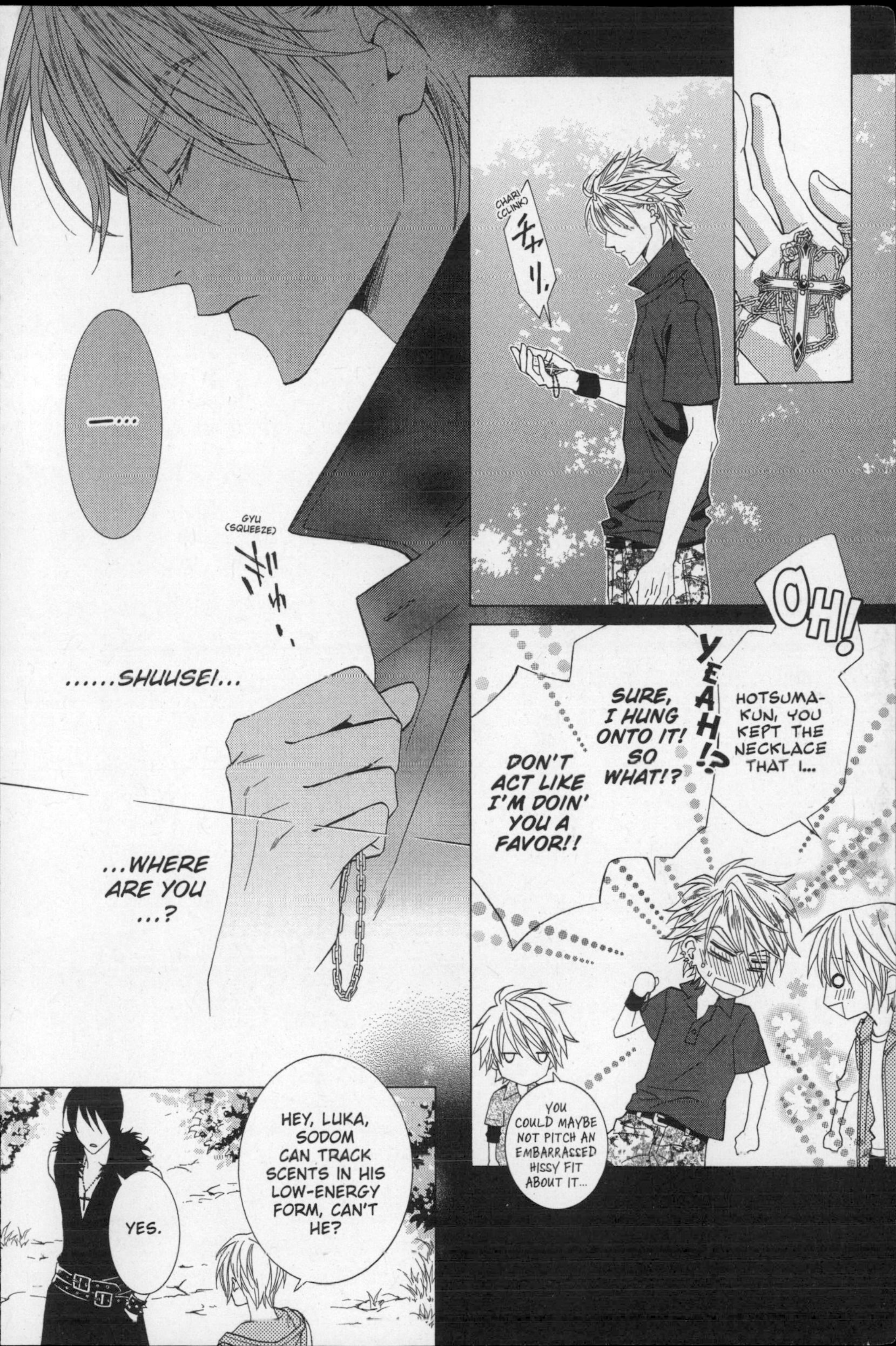
CHARI (CLINK)
チャリ
OH!
HOTSUMA-KUN, YOU KEPT THE NECKLACE THAT I...
YEAH!?
SURE, I HUNG ONTO IT! SO WHAT!?
DON'T ACT LIKE I'M DOIN' YOU A FAVOR!!
YOU COULD MAYBE NOT PITCH AN EMBARRASSED HISSY FIT ABOUT IT...
—...
GYU (SQUEEZE)
ギュ
......SHUUSEI...
...WHERE ARE YOU ...?
HEY, LUKA, SODOM CAN TRACK SCENTS IN HIS LOW-ENERGY FORM, CAN'T HE?
YES.

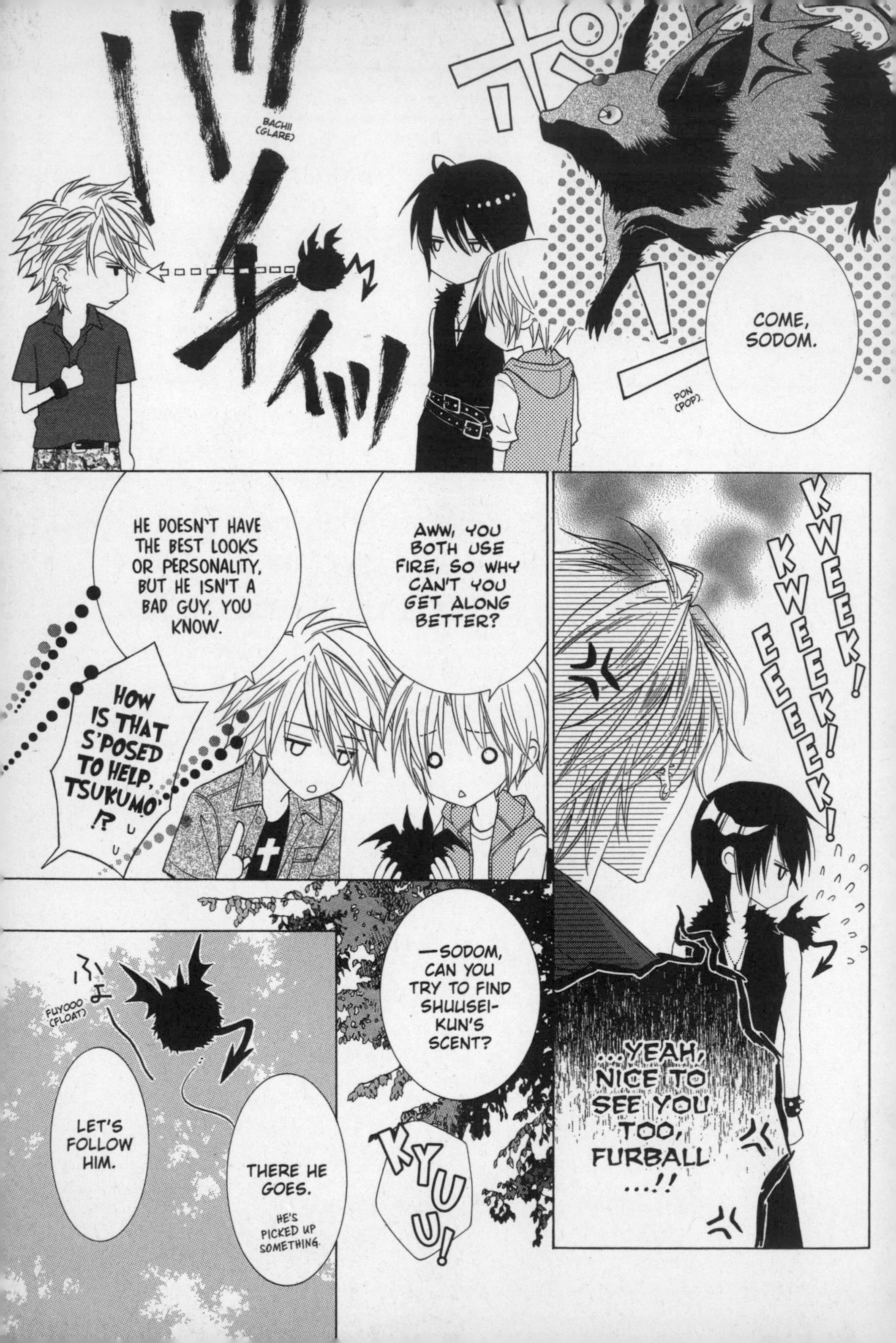
COME, SODOM.
PON (POP)
BACHII (GLARE)
KWEEK! KWEEK! EEEEK!
...YEAH, NICE TO SEE YOU TOO, FURBALL ...!!
AWW, YOU BOTH USE FIRE, SO WHY CAN'T YOU GET ALONG BETTER?
HE DOESN'T HAVE THE BEST LOOKS OR PERSONALITY, BUT HE ISN'T A BAD GUY, YOU KNOW.
HOW IS THAT S'POSED TO HELP, TSUKUMO !?
—SODOM, CAN YOU TRY TO FIND SHUUSEI-KUN'S SCENT?
KYUUU!
FUYOOO (FLOAT)
THERE HE GOES.
HE'S PICKED UP SOMETHING.
LET'S FOLLOW HIM.

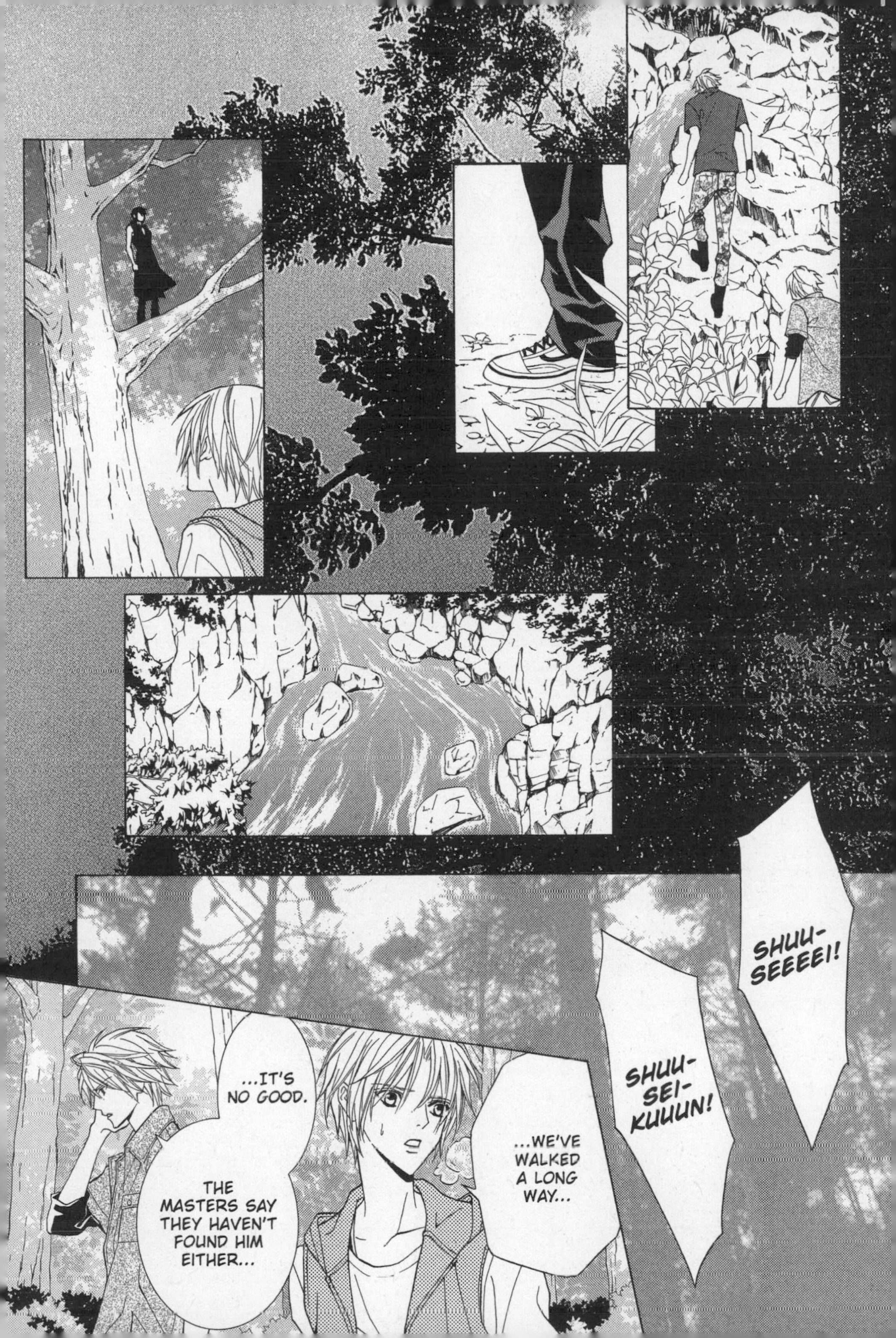
SHUU-SEEEEI!
SHUU-SEI-KUUUN!
...WE'VE WALKED A LONG WAY...
...IT'S NO GOOD.
THE MASTERS SAY THEY HAVEN'T FOUND HIM EITHER...

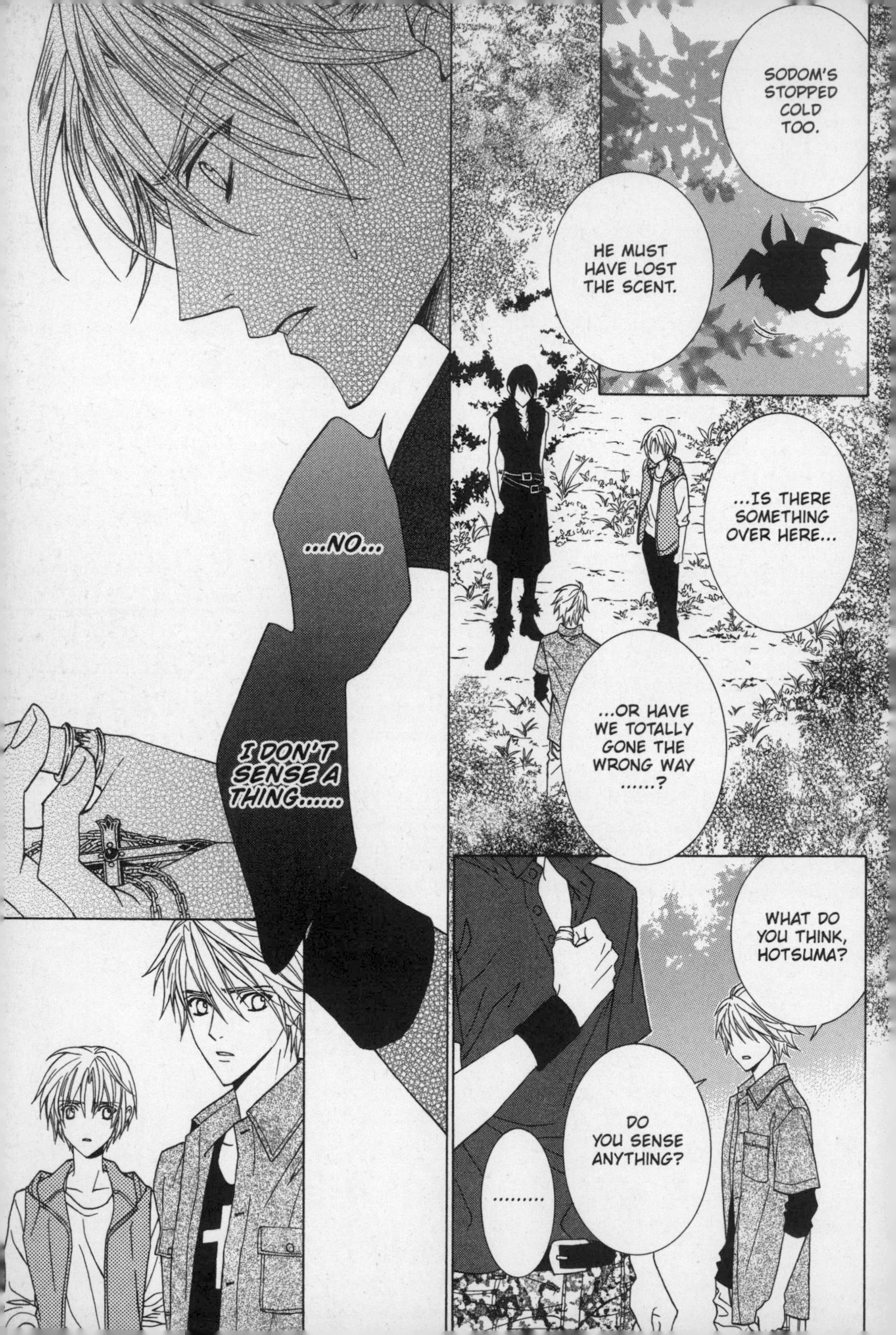
SODOM'S STOPPED COLD TOO.
HE MUST HAVE LOST THE SCENT.
...IS THERE SOMETHING OVER HERE...
...OR HAVE WE TOTALLY GONE THE WRONG WAY ......?
WHAT DO YOU THINK, HOTSUMA?
DO YOU SENSE ANYTHING?
....
...NO...
I DON'T SENSE A THING......

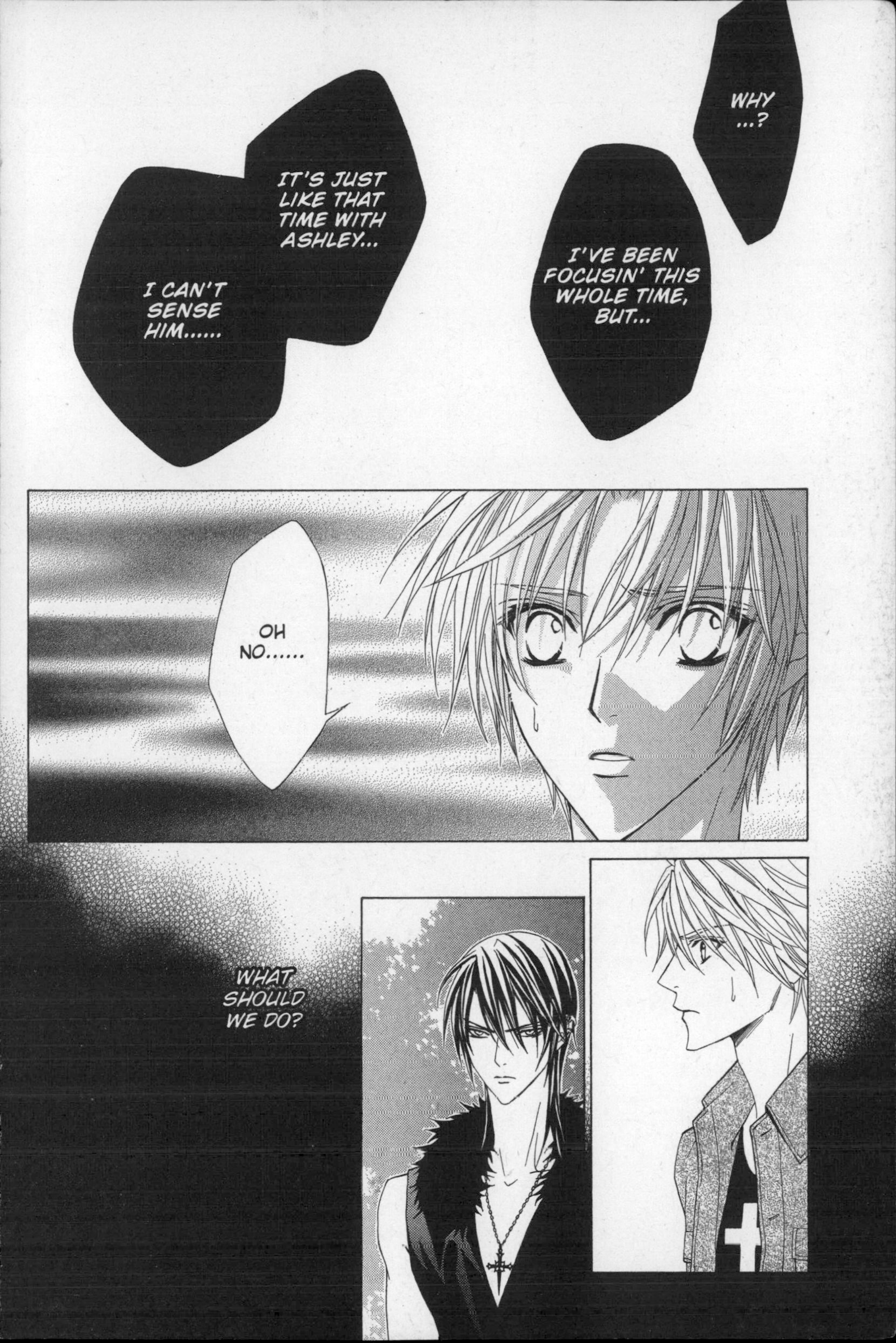
WHY ...?
I'VE BEEN FOCUSIN' THIS WHOLE TIME, BUT...
IT'S JUST LIKE THAT TIME WITH ASHLEY...
I CAN'T SENSE HIM......
OH NO......
WHAT SHOULD WE DO?

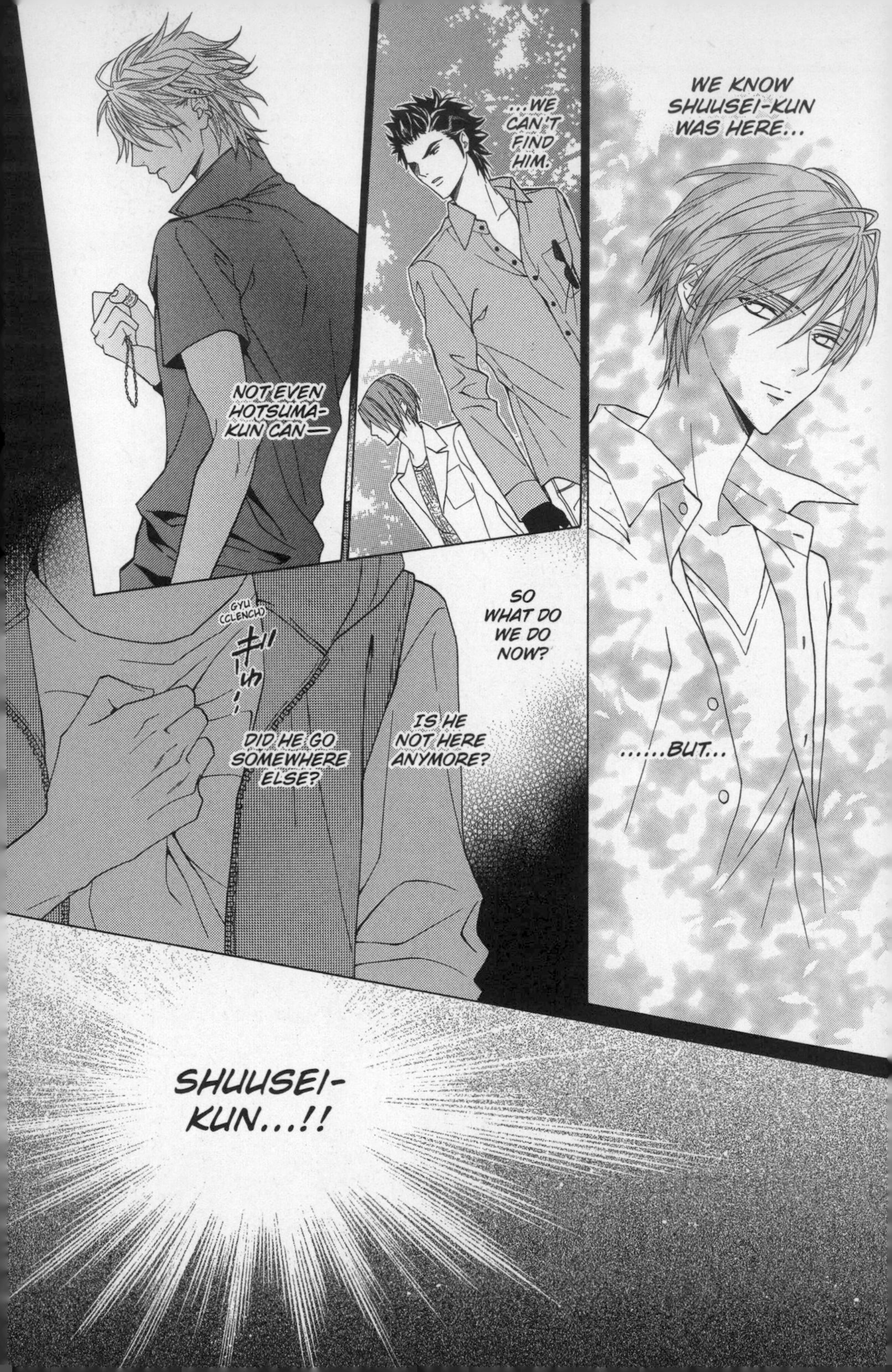

WE KNOW SHUUSEI-KUN WAS HERE...
......BUT...
...WE CAN'T FIND HIM.
NOT EVEN HOTSUMA-KUN CAN—
SO WHAT DO WE DO NOW?
IS HE NOT HERE ANYMORE?
GYU (CLENCH)
DID HE GO SOMEWHERE ELSE?
SHUUSEI-KUN...!!

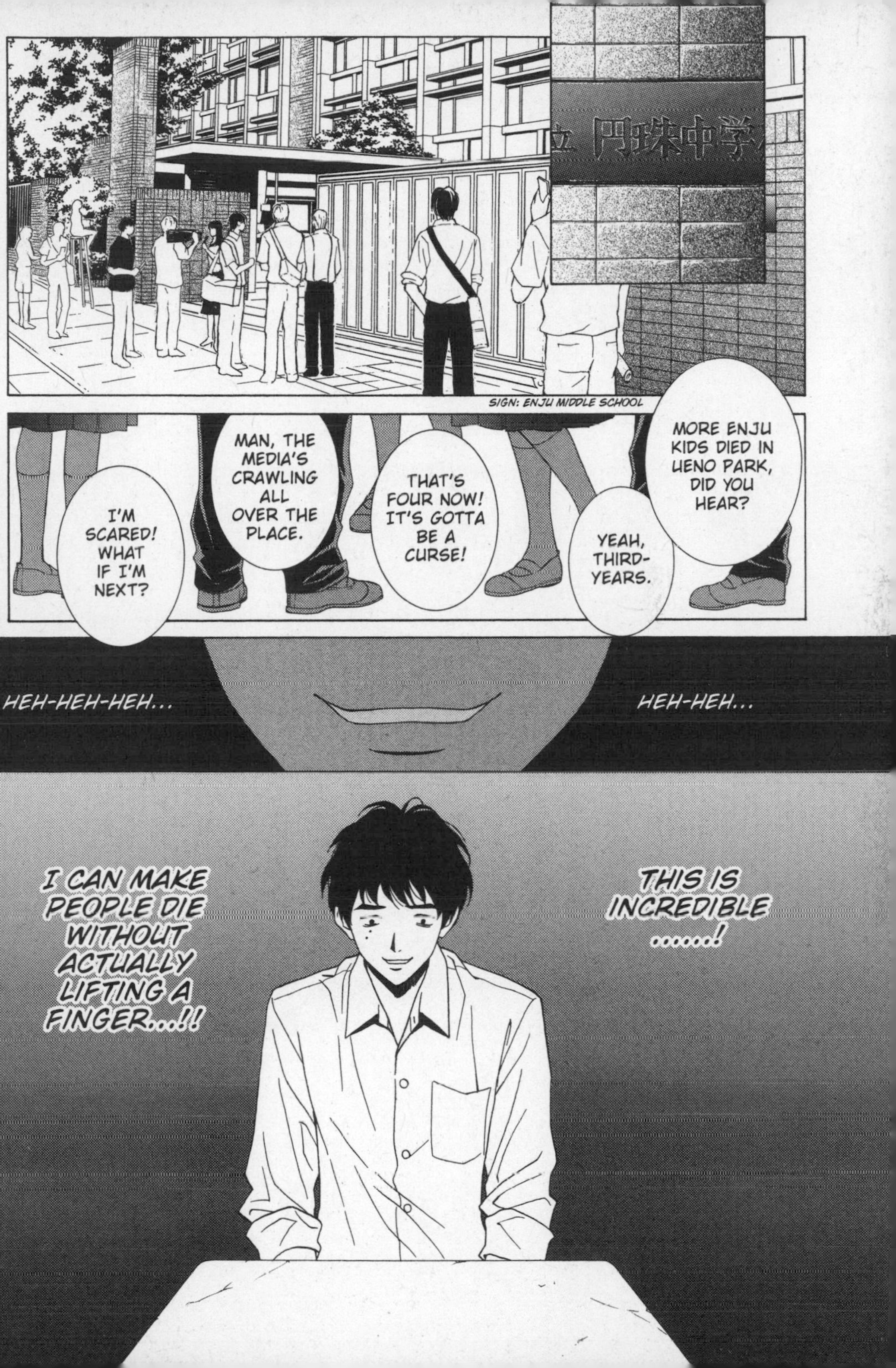
円珠中学
SIGN: ENJU MIDDLE SCHOOL
MORE ENJU KIDS DIED IN UENO PARK, DID YOU HEAR?
YEAH, THIRD-YEARS.
THAT'S FOUR NOW! IT'S GOTTA BE A CURSE!
MAN, THE MEDIA'S CRAWLING ALL OVER THE PLACE.
I'M SCARED! WHAT IF I'M NEXT?
HEH-HEH...
HEH-HEH-HEH...
THIS IS INCREDIBLE ......!
I CAN MAKE PEOPLE DIE WITHOUT ACTUALLY LIFTING A FINGER...!!

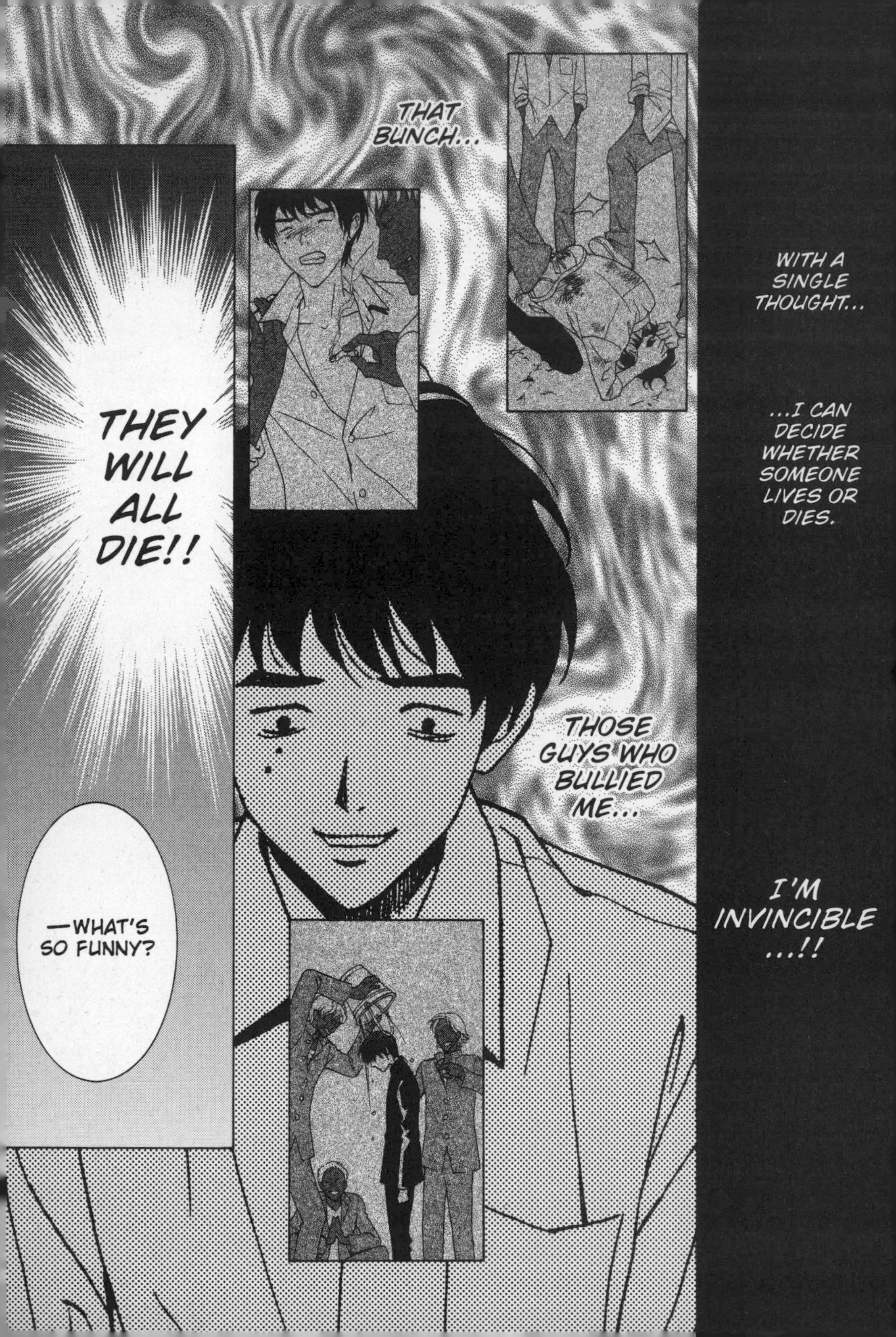
WITH A SINGLE THOUGHT...
...I CAN DECIDE WHETHER SOMEONE LIVES OR DIES.
I'M INVINCIBLE ...!!
THAT BUNCH...
THOSE GUYS WHO BULLIED ME...
THEY WILL ALL DIE!!
—WHAT'S SO FUNNY?

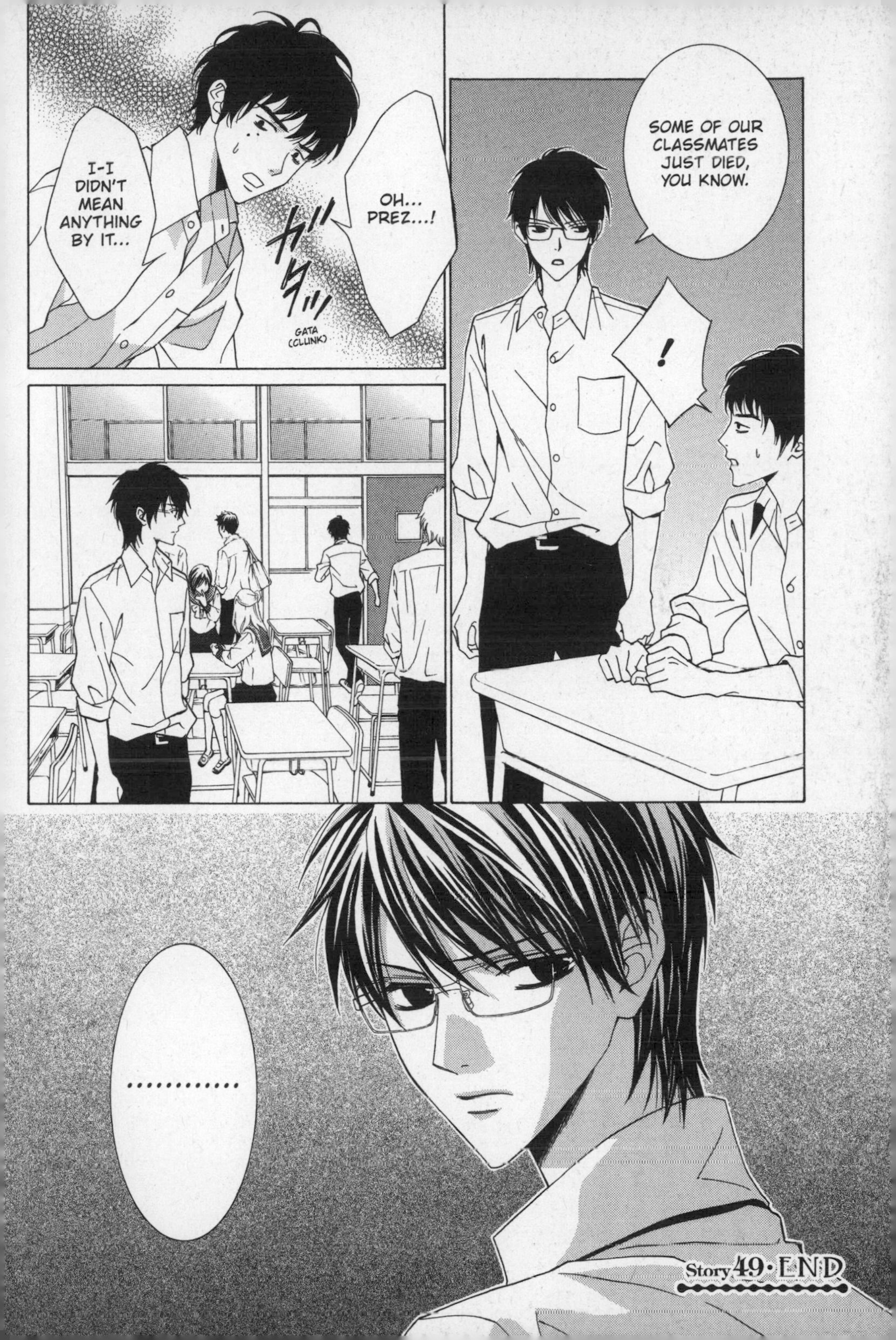
SOME OF OUR CLASSMATES JUST DIED, YOU KNOW.
!
OH... PREZ...!
GATA (CLUNK)
I-I DIDN'T MEAN ANYTHING BY IT...
....
Story 49 · END

THE
BETRAYAL
kNoWS MY NAME

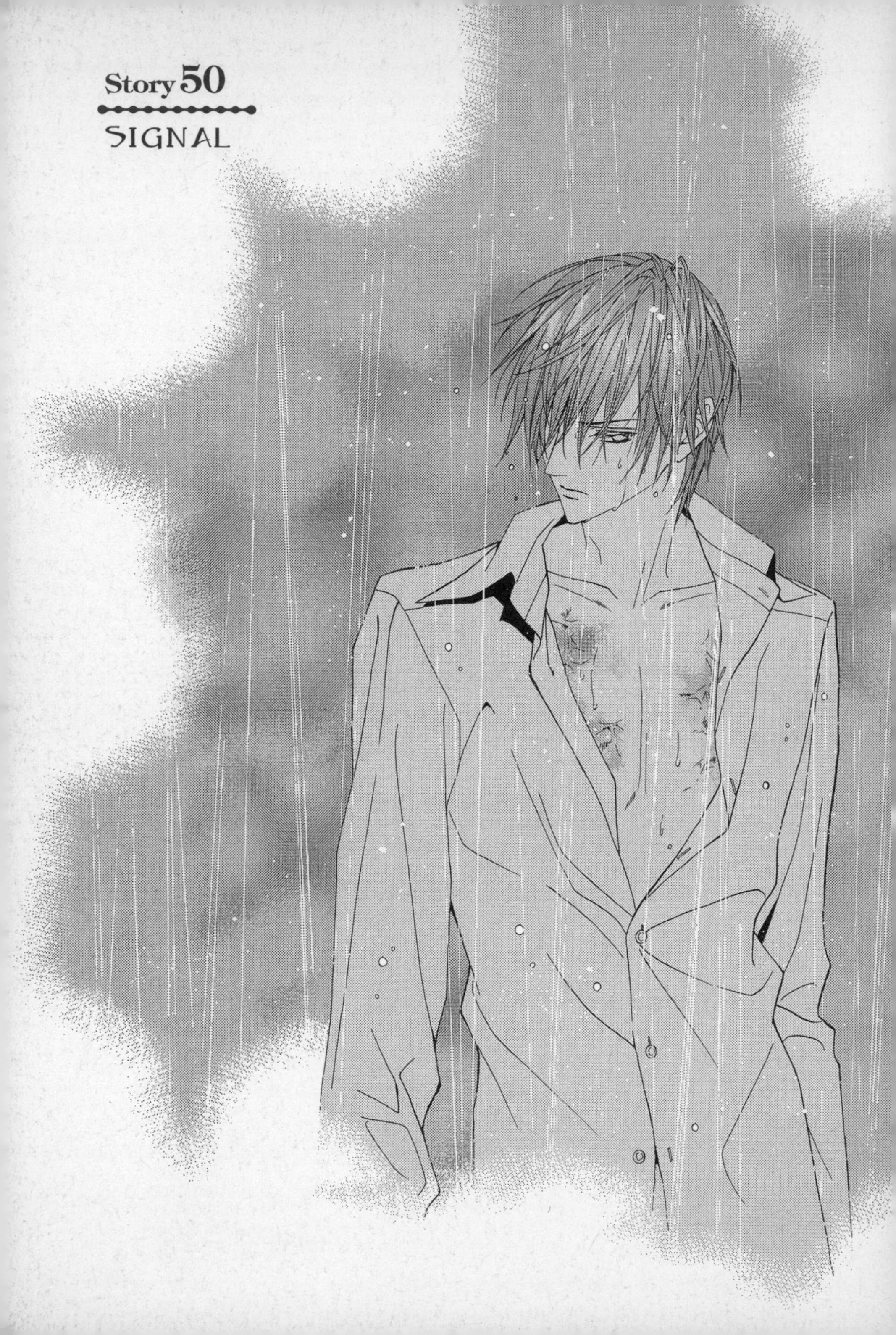
Story 50
SIGNAL

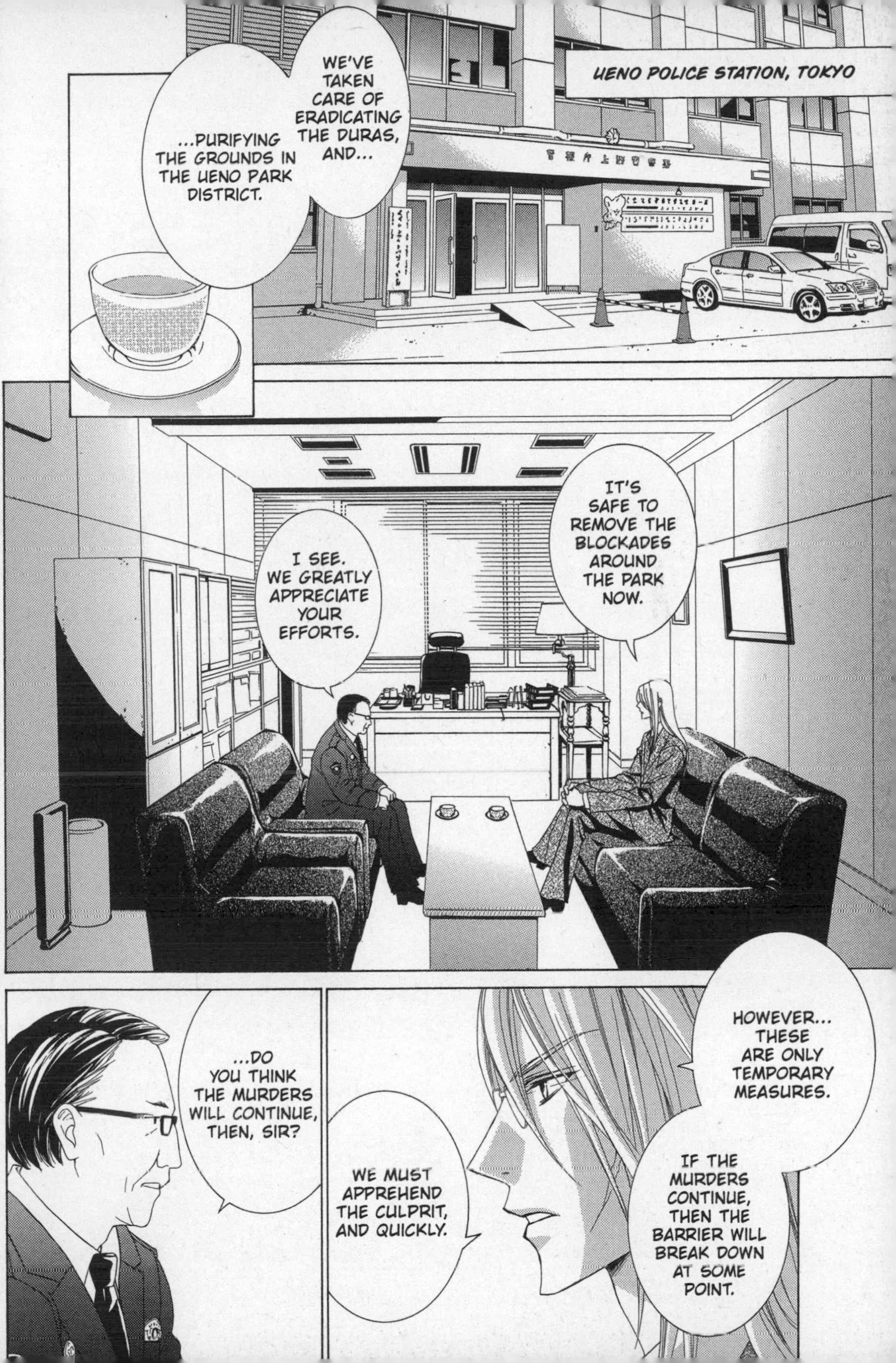
UENO POLICE STATION, TOKYO
WE'VE TAKEN CARE OF ERADICATING THE DURAS, AND...
...PURIFYING THE GROUNDS IN THE UENO PARK DISTRICT.
IT'S SAFE TO REMOVE THE BLOCKADES AROUND THE PARK NOW.
I SEE. WE GREATLY APPRECIATE YOUR EFFORTS.
HOWEVER... THESE ARE ONLY TEMPORARY MEASURES.
IF THE MURDERS CONTINUE, THEN THE BARRIER WILL BREAK DOWN AT SOME POINT.
WE MUST APPREHEND THE CULPRIT, AND QUICKLY.
...DO YOU THINK THE MURDERS WILL CONTINUE, THEN, SIR?

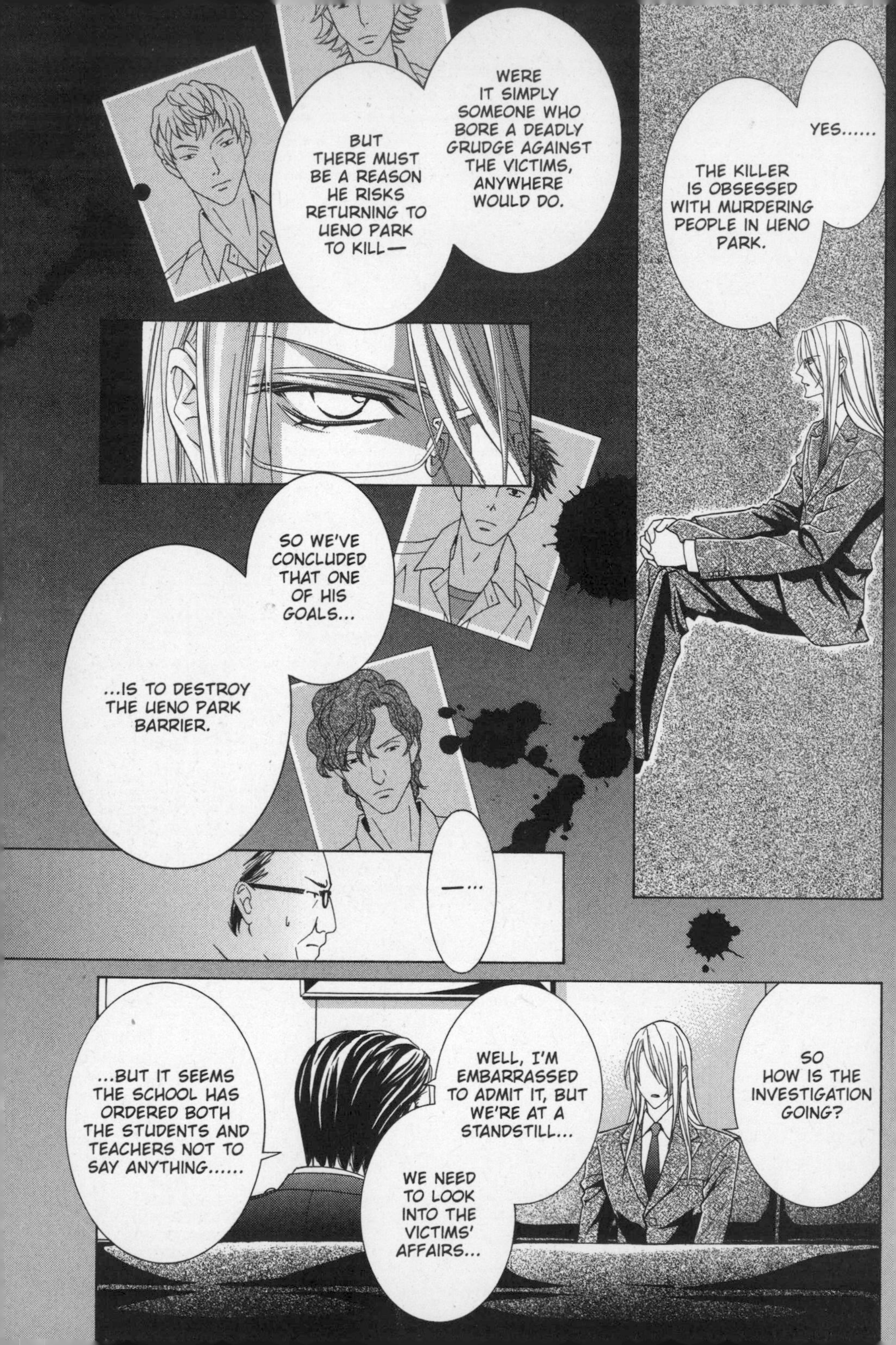
YES......
THE KILLER IS OBSESSED WITH MURDERING PEOPLE IN UENO PARK.
WERE IT SIMPLY SOMEONE WHO BORE A DEADLY GRUDGE AGAINST THE VICTIMS, ANYWHERE WOULD DO.
BUT THERE MUST BE A REASON HE RISKS RETURNING TO UENO PARK TO KILL—
SO WE'VE CONCLUDED THAT ONE OF HIS GOALS...
...IS TO DESTROY THE UENO PARK BARRIER.
—...
SO HOW IS THE INVESTIGATION GOING?
WELL, I'M EMBARRASSED TO ADMIT IT, BUT WE'RE AT A STANDSTILL...
WE NEED TO LOOK INTO THE VICTIMS' AFFAIRS...
...BUT IT SEEMS THE SCHOOL HAS ORDERED BOTH THE STUDENTS AND TEACHERS NOT TO SAY ANYTHING......

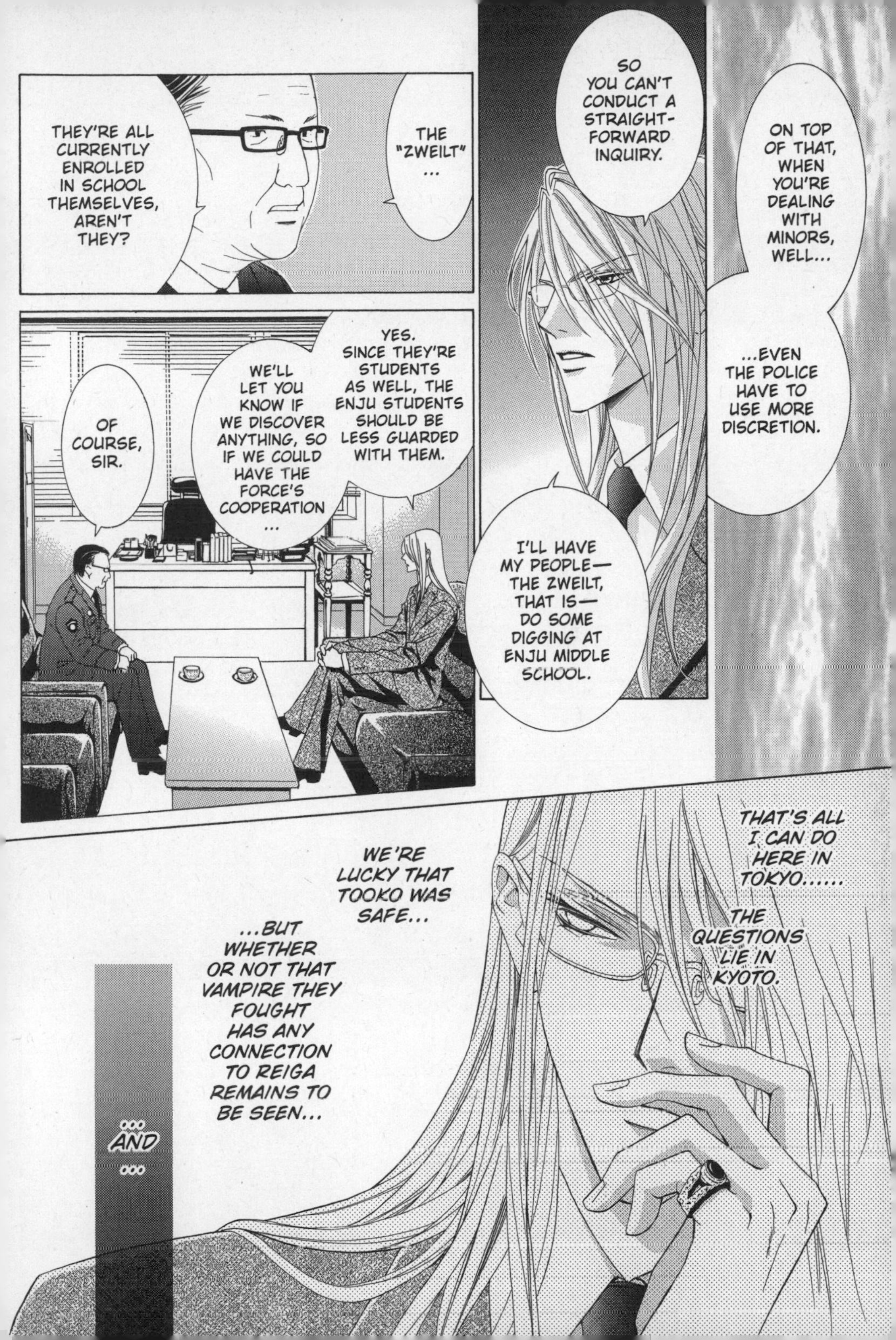
ON TOP OF THAT, WHEN YOU'RE DEALING WITH MINORS, WELL...
...EVEN THE POLICE HAVE TO USE MORE DISCRETION.
SO YOU CAN'T CONDUCT A STRAIGHT-FORWARD INQUIRY.
I'LL HAVE MY PEOPLE—THE ZWEILT, THAT IS—DO SOME DIGGING AT ENJU MIDDLE SCHOOL.
THE "ZWEILT"...
THEY'RE ALL CURRENTLY ENROLLED IN SCHOOL THEMSELVES, AREN'T THEY?
YES. SINCE THEY'RE STUDENTS AS WELL, THE ENJU STUDENTS SHOULD BE LESS GUARDED WITH THEM.
WE'LL LET YOU KNOW IF WE DISCOVER ANYTHING, SO IF WE COULD HAVE THE FORCE'S COOPERATION...
OF COURSE, SIR.
THAT'S ALL I CAN DO HERE IN TOKYO......
THE QUESTIONS LIE IN KYOTO.
WE'RE LUCKY THAT TOOKO WAS SAFE...
...BUT WHETHER OR NOT THAT VAMPIRE THEY FOUGHT HAS ANY CONNECTION TO REIGA REMAINS TO BE SEEN...
...AND...

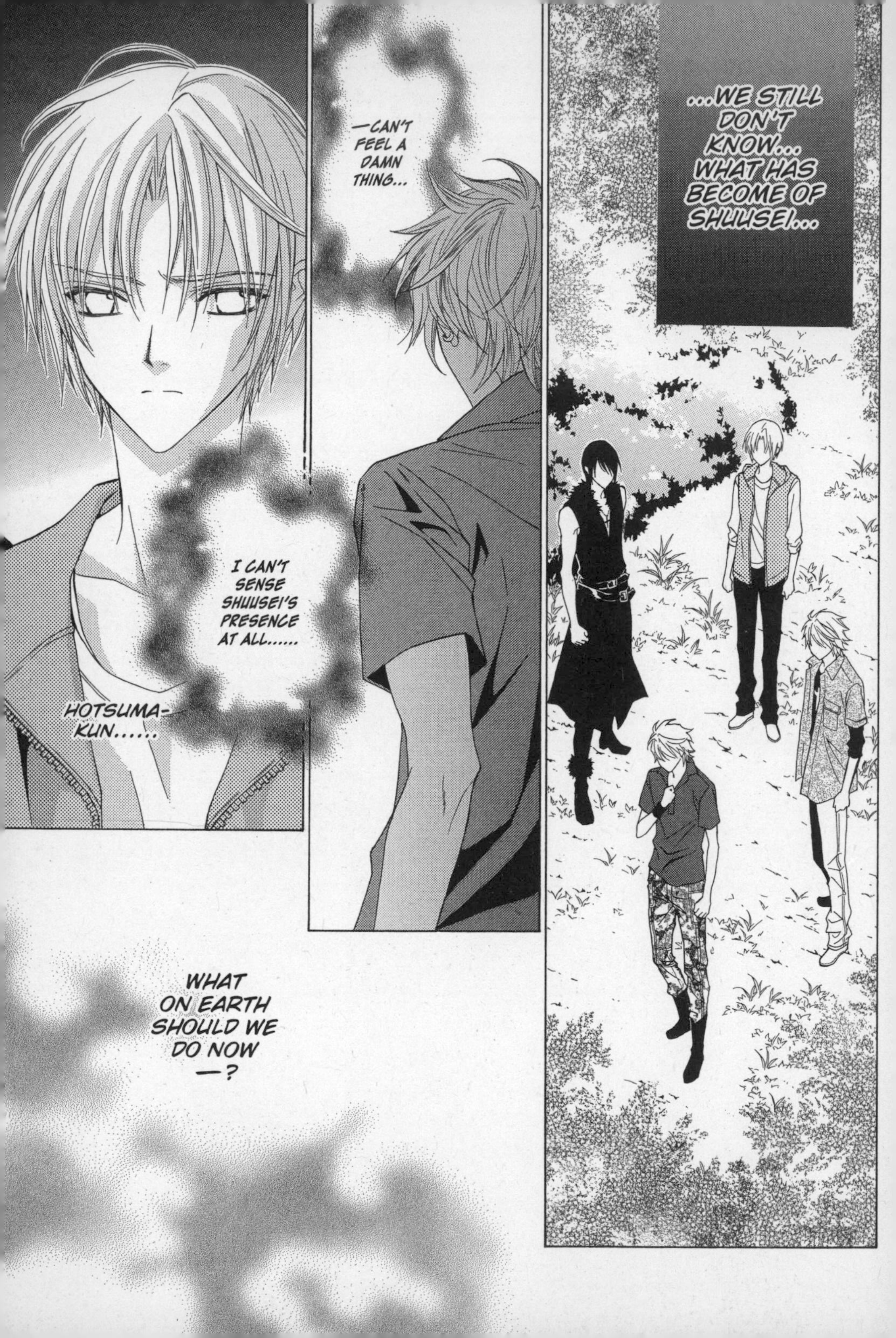
...WE STILL DON'T KNOW... WHAT HAS BECOME OF SHUUSEI...
—CAN'T FEEL A DAMN THING...
I CAN'T SENSE SHUUSEI'S PRESENCE AT ALL......
HOTSUMA-KUN......
WHAT ON EARTH SHOULD WE DO NOW —?

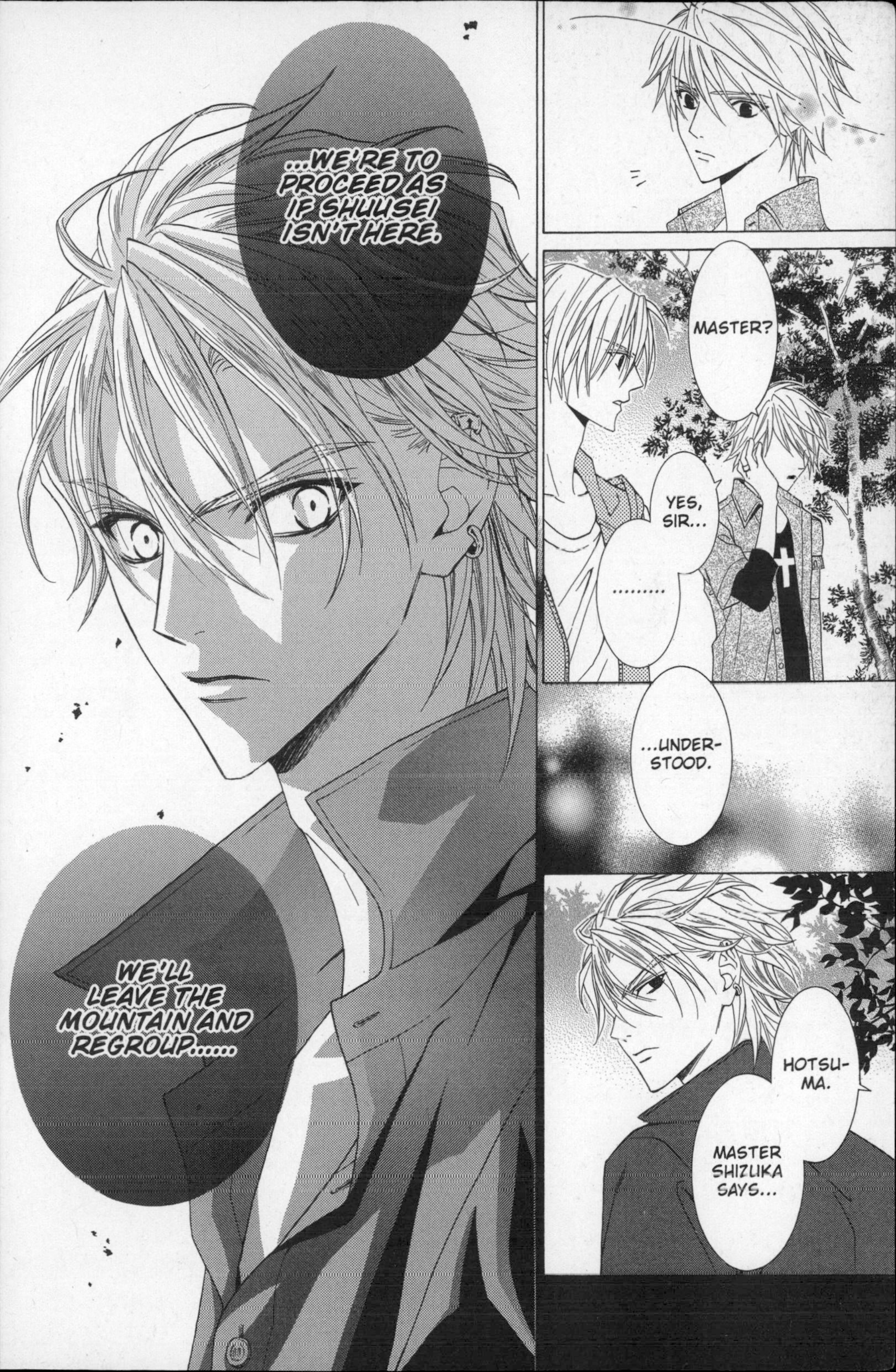
MASTER?
YES, SIR...
....
...UNDER-STOOD.
HOTSU-MA.
MASTER SHIZUKA SAYS...
...WE'RE TO PROCEED AS IF SHUUSEI ISN'T HERE.
WE'LL LEAVE THE MOUNTAIN AND REGROUP......

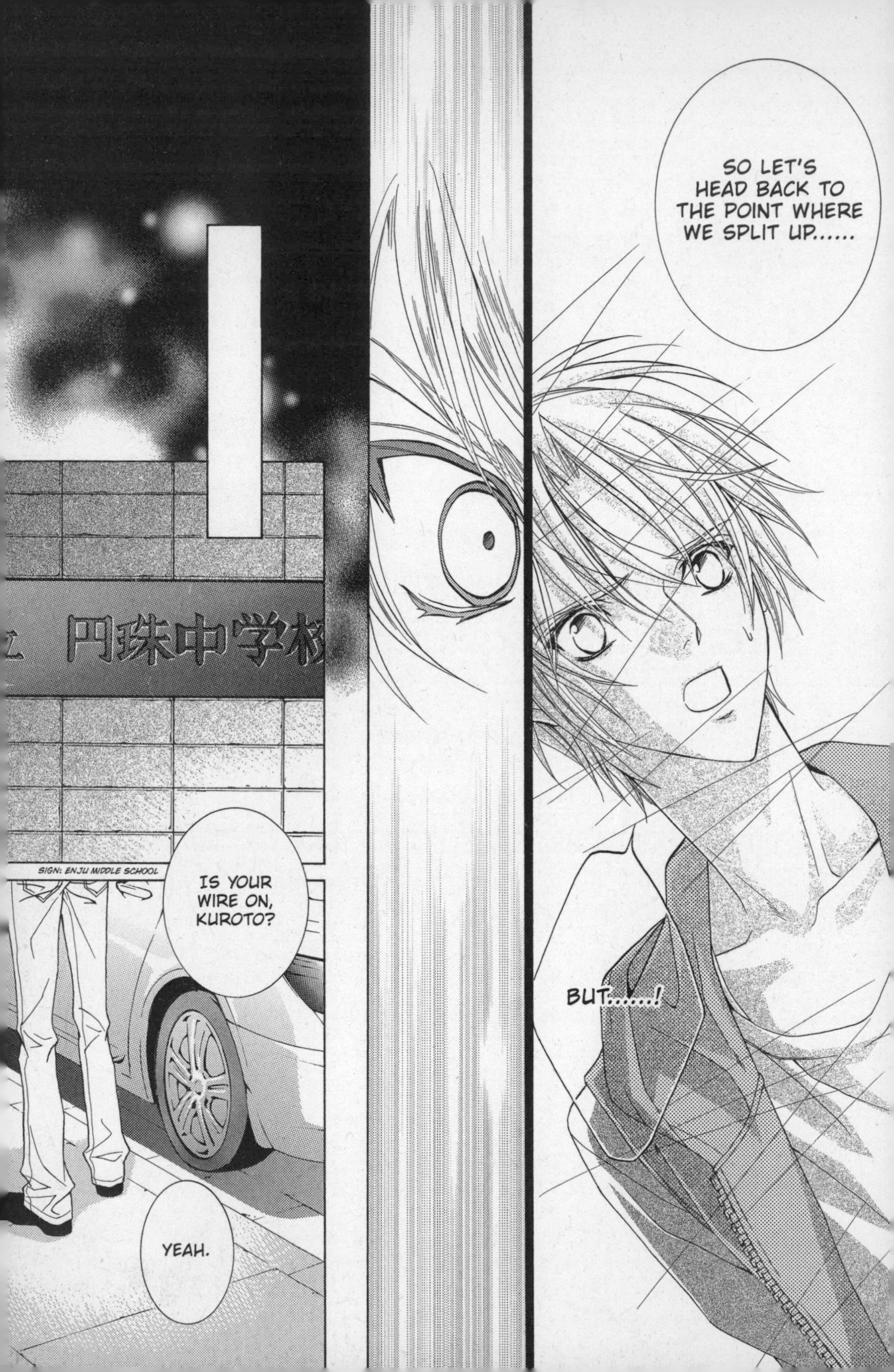
SO LET'S HEAD BACK TO THE POINT WHERE WE SPLIT UP......
BUT......!
円珠中学校
SIGN: ENJU MIDDLE SCHOOL
IS YOUR WIRE ON, KUROTO?
YEAH.

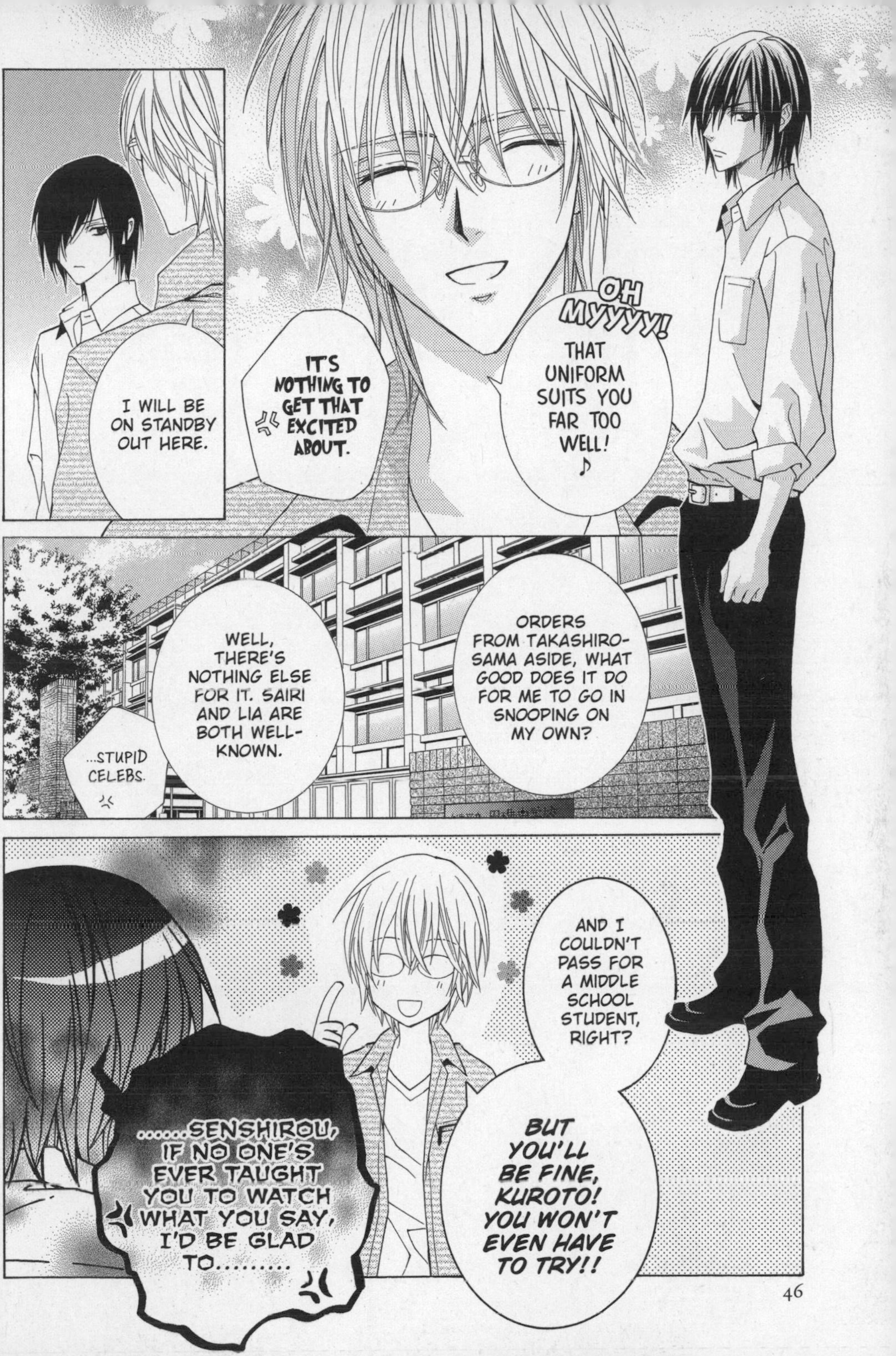
OH MYYYY!
THAT UNIFORM SUITS YOU FAR TOO WELL! ♪
IT'S NOTHING TO GET THAT EXCITED ABOUT.
I WILL BE ON STANDBY OUT HERE.
ORDERS FROM TAKASHIRO-SAMA ASIDE, WHAT GOOD DOES IT DO FOR ME TO GO IN SNOOPING ON MY OWN?
WELL, THERE'S NOTHING ELSE FOR IT. SAIRI AND LIA ARE BOTH WELL-KNOWN.
...STUPID CELEBS.
AND I COULDN'T PASS FOR A MIDDLE SCHOOL STUDENT, RIGHT?
BUT YOU'LL BE FINE, KUROTO! YOU WON'T EVEN HAVE TO TRY!!
......SENSHIROU, IF NO ONE'S EVER TAUGHT YOU TO WATCH WHAT YOU SAY, I'D BE GLAD TO.........

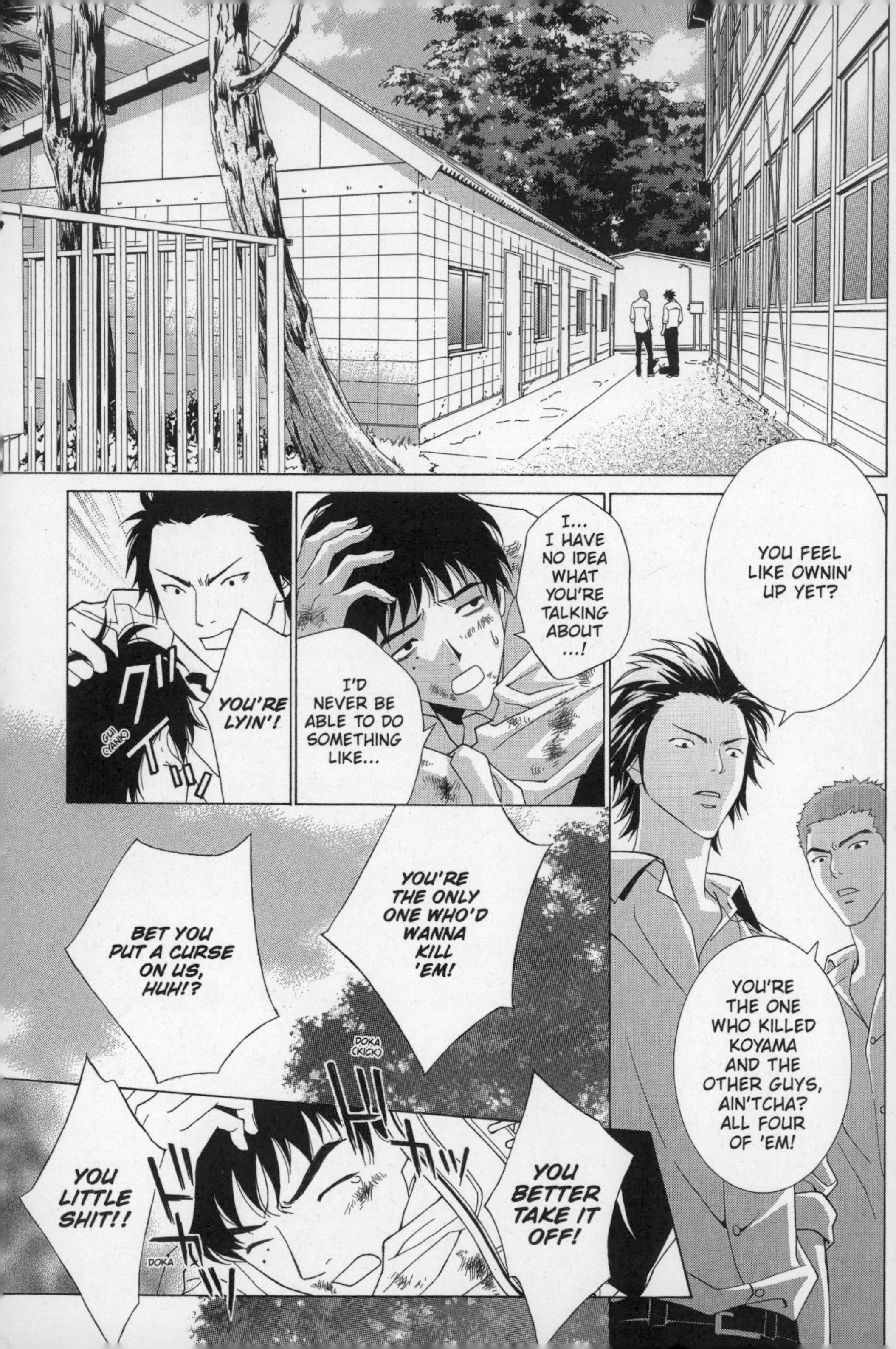

YOU FEEL LIKE OWNIN' UP YET?
YOU'RE THE ONE WHO KILLED KOYAMA AND THE OTHER GUYS, AIN'TCHA? ALL FOUR OF 'EM!
I... I HAVE NO IDEA WHAT YOU'RE TALKING ABOUT ...!
I'D NEVER BE ABLE TO DO SOMETHING LIKE...
YOU'RE LYIN'!
GUI (YANK)
YOU'RE THE ONLY ONE WHO'D WANNA KILL 'EM!
BET YOU PUT A CURSE ON US, HUH!?
DOKA (KICK)
YOU BETTER TAKE IT OFF!
YOU LITTLE SHIT!!
DOKA

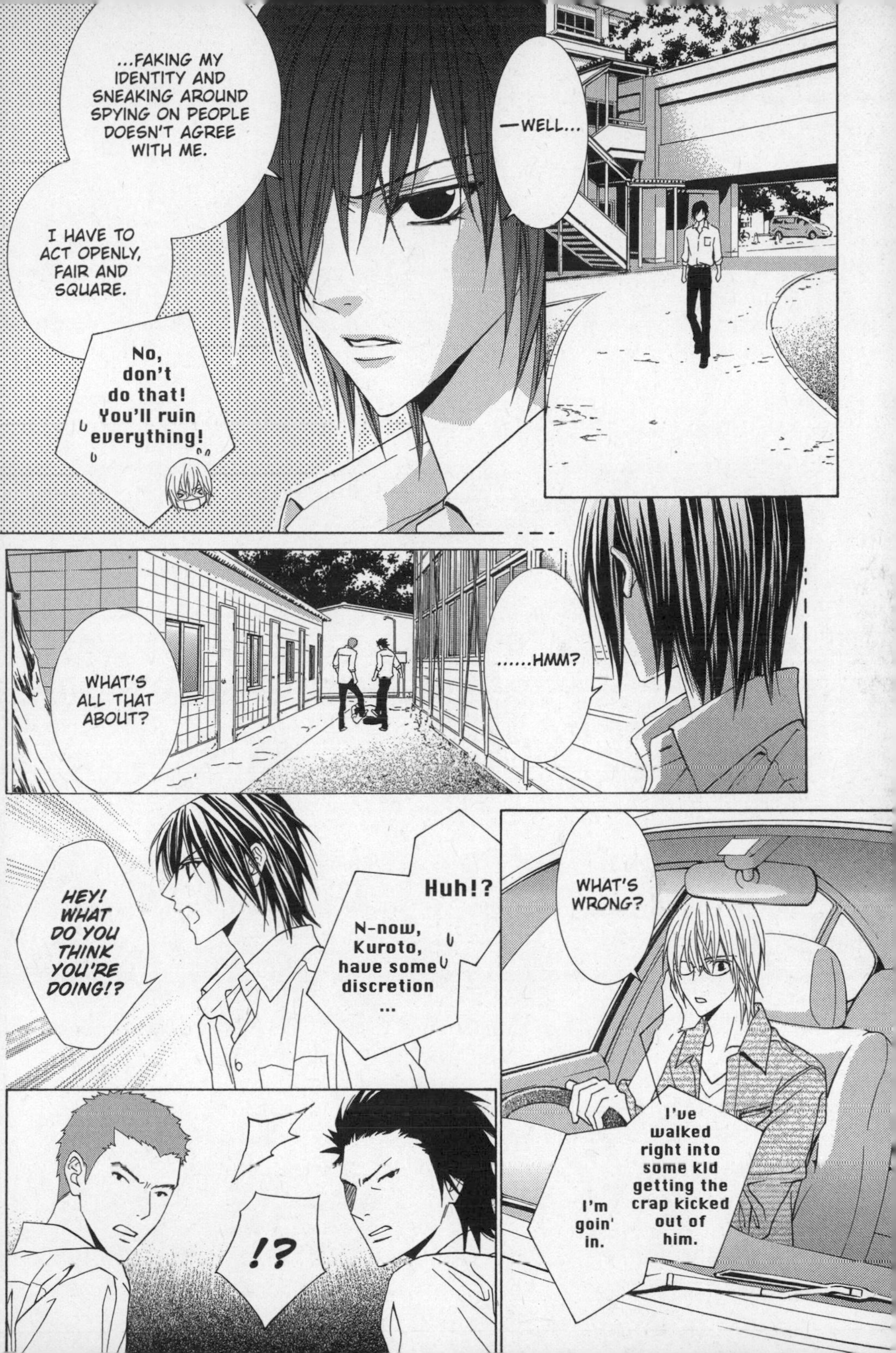
—WELL...
...FAKING MY IDENTITY AND SNEAKING AROUND SPYING ON PEOPLE DOESN'T AGREE WITH ME.
I HAVE TO ACT OPENLY, FAIR AND SQUARE.
No, don't do that! You'll ruin everything!
......HMM?
WHAT'S ALL THAT ABOUT?
WHAT'S WRONG?
I've walked right into some kid getting the crap kicked out of him.
I'm goin' in.
Huh!?
N-now, Kuroto, have some discretion ...
HEY! WHAT DO YOU THINK YOU'RE DOING!?
!?

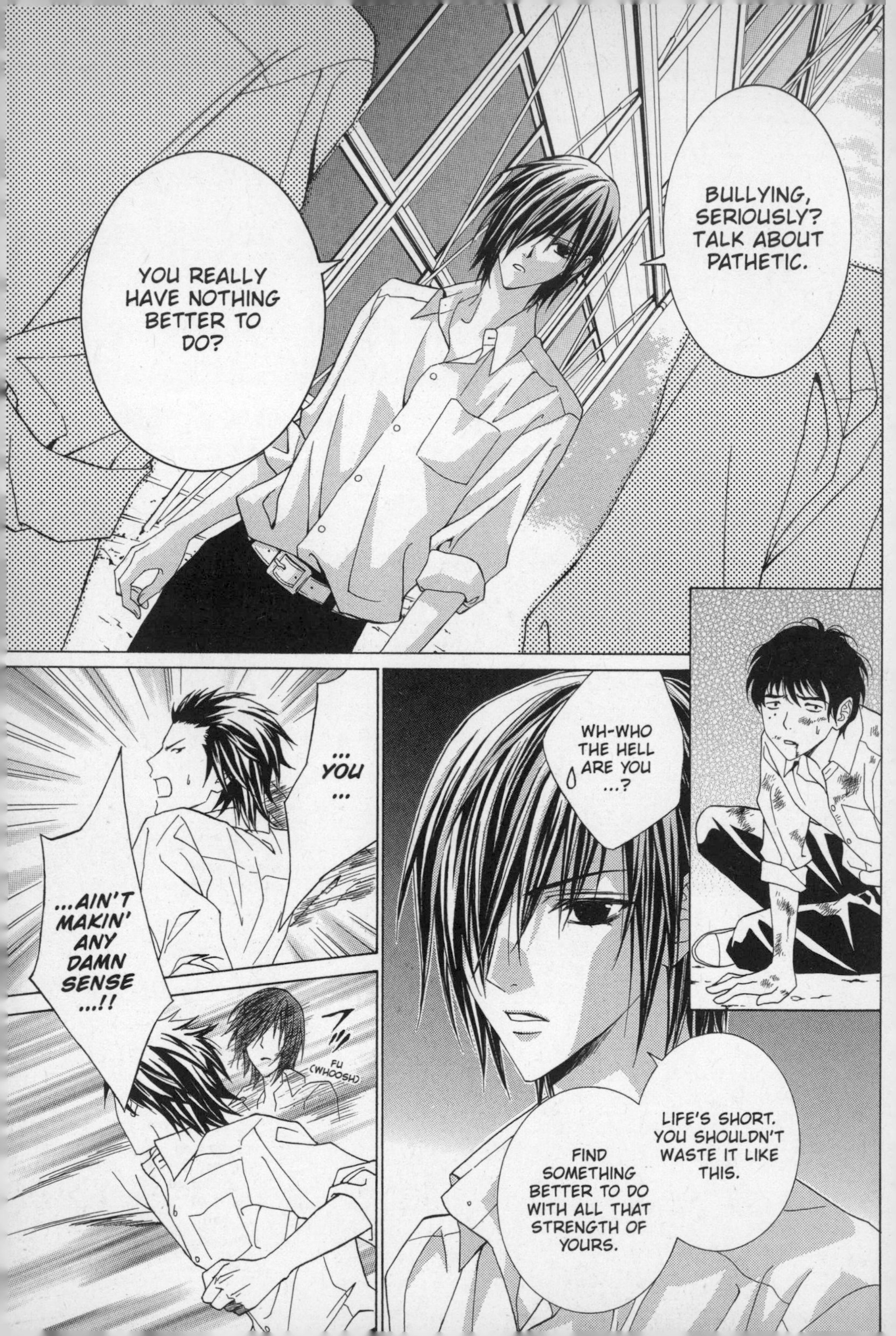
BULLYING, SERIOUSLY? TALK ABOUT PATHETIC.
YOU REALLY HAVE NOTHING BETTER TO DO?
WH-WHO THE HELL ARE YOU ...?
LIFE'S SHORT. YOU SHOULDN'T WASTE IT LIKE THIS.
FIND SOMETHING BETTER TO DO WITH ALL THAT STRENGTH OF YOURS.
... YOU ...
...AIN'T MAKIN' ANY DAMN SENSE ...!!
FU (WHOOSH)

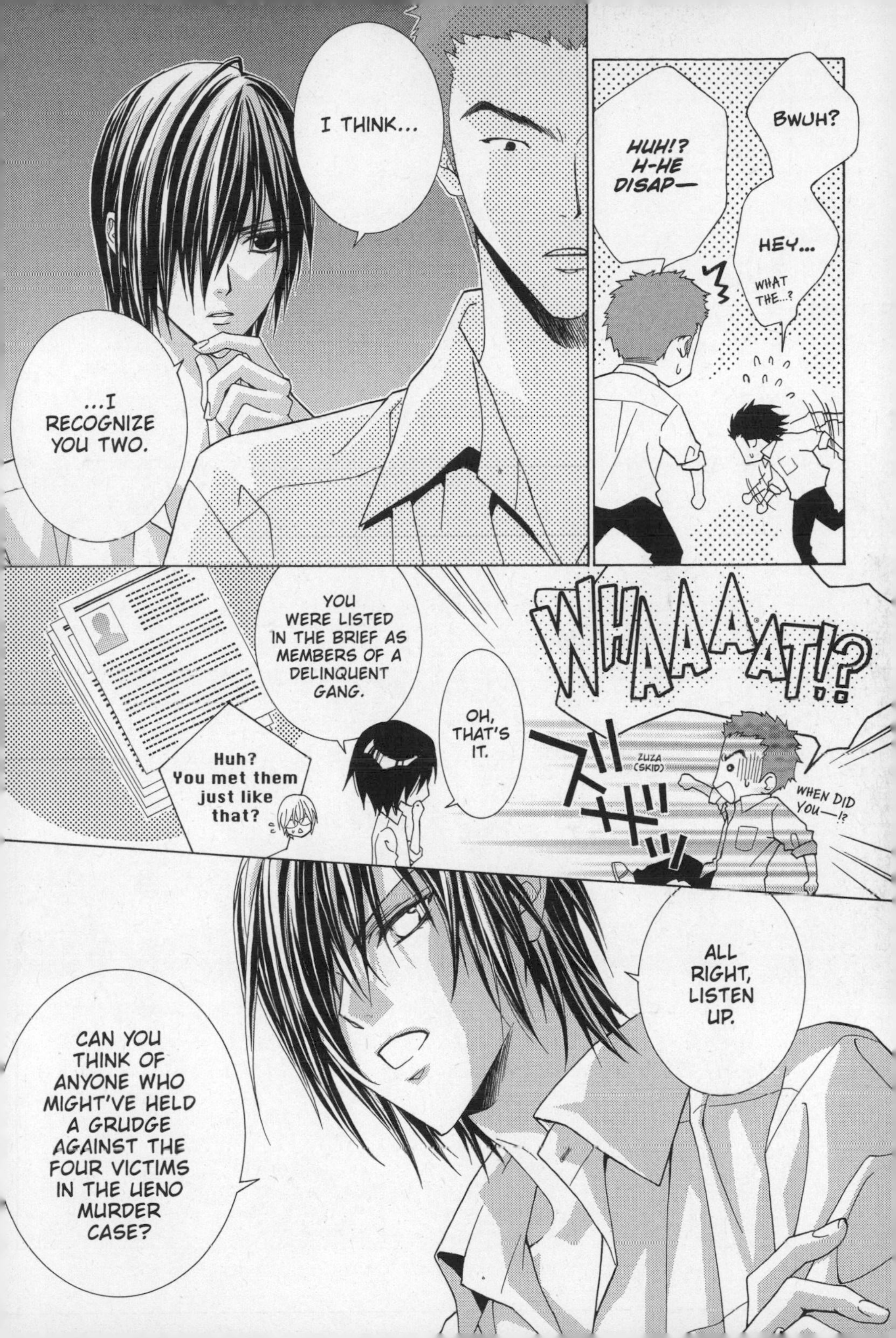
BWUH?
HUH!? H-HE DISAP—
HEY...
WHAT THE...?
I THINK...
...I RECOGNIZE YOU TWO.
WHAAAAT!?
WHEN DID YOU—!?
ZUZA (SKID)
YOU WERE LISTED IN THE BRIEF AS MEMBERS OF A DELINQUENT GANG.
OH, THAT'S IT.
Huh? You met them just like that?
ALL RIGHT, LISTEN UP.
CAN YOU THINK OF ANYONE WHO MIGHT'VE HELD A GRUDGE AGAINST THE FOUR VICTIMS IN THE UENO MURDER CASE?

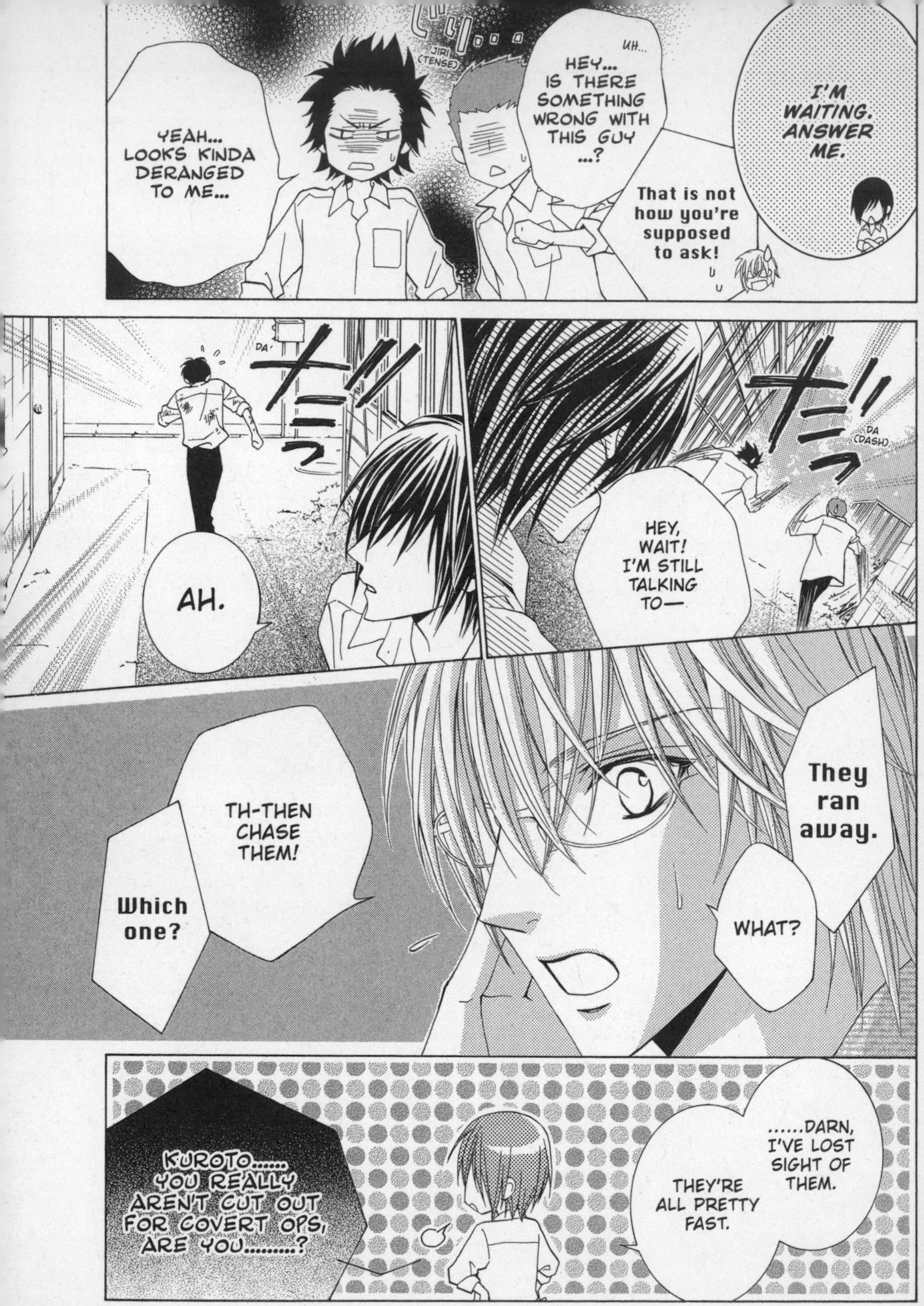
I'M WAITING. ANSWER ME.
That is not how you're supposed to ask!
UH...
HEY... IS THERE SOMETHING WRONG WITH THIS GUY ...?
JIRI (TENSE)
YEAH... LOOKS KINDA DERANGED TO ME...
DA (DASH)
HEY, WAIT! I'M STILL TALKING TO—
DA
AH.
They ran away.
WHAT?
TH-THEN CHASE THEM!
Which one?
......DARN, I'VE LOST SIGHT OF THEM.
THEY'RE ALL PRETTY FAST.
KUROTO...... YOU REALLY AREN'T CUT OUT FOR COVERT OPS, ARE YOU.........?

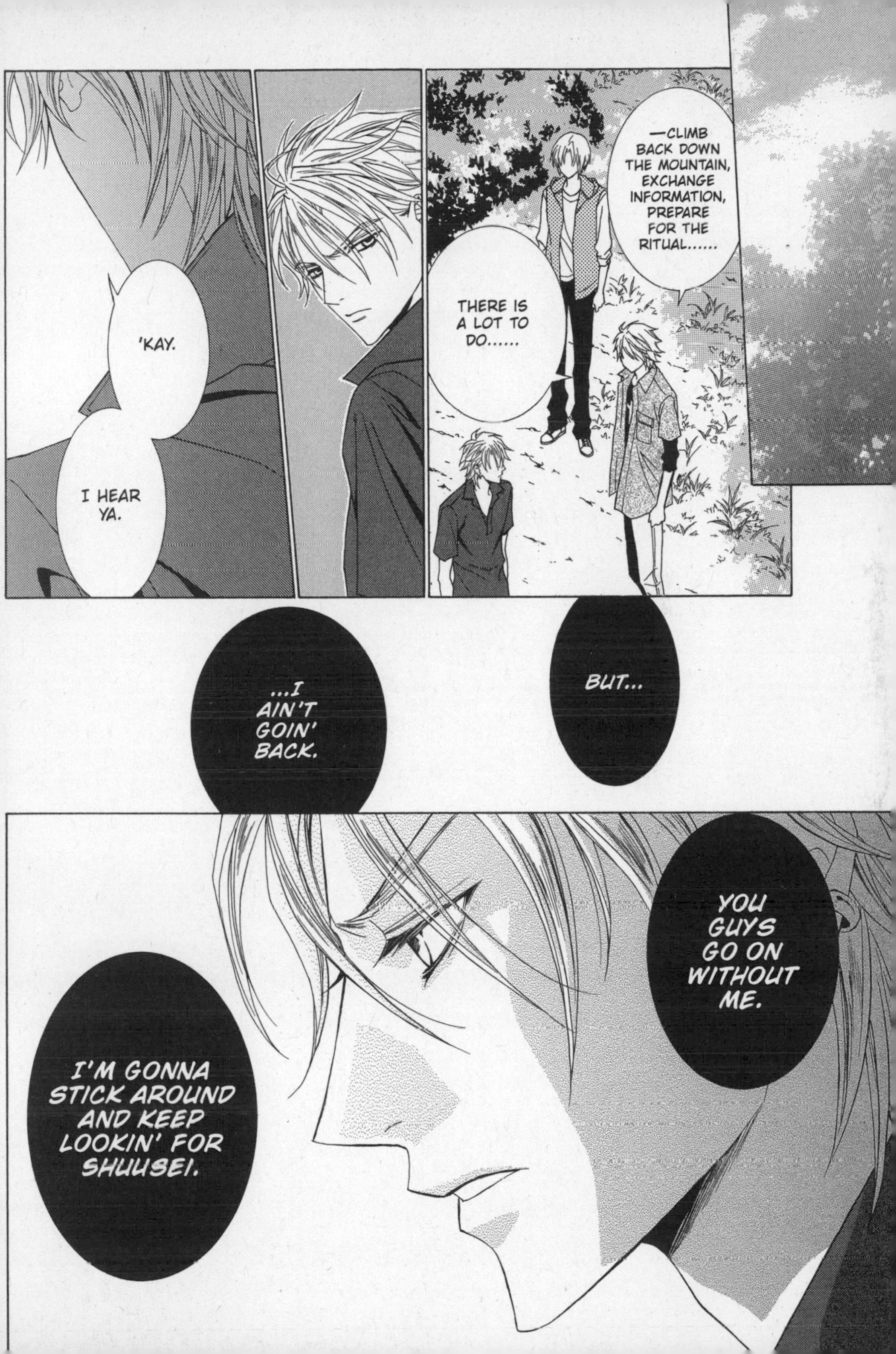
—CLIMB BACK DOWN THE MOUNTAIN, EXCHANGE INFORMATION, PREPARE FOR THE RITUAL......
THERE IS A LOT TO DO......
'KAY.
I HEAR YA.
BUT...
...I AIN'T GOIN' BACK.
YOU GUYS GO ON WITHOUT ME.
I'M GONNA STICK AROUND AND KEEP LOOKIN' FOR SHUUSEI.

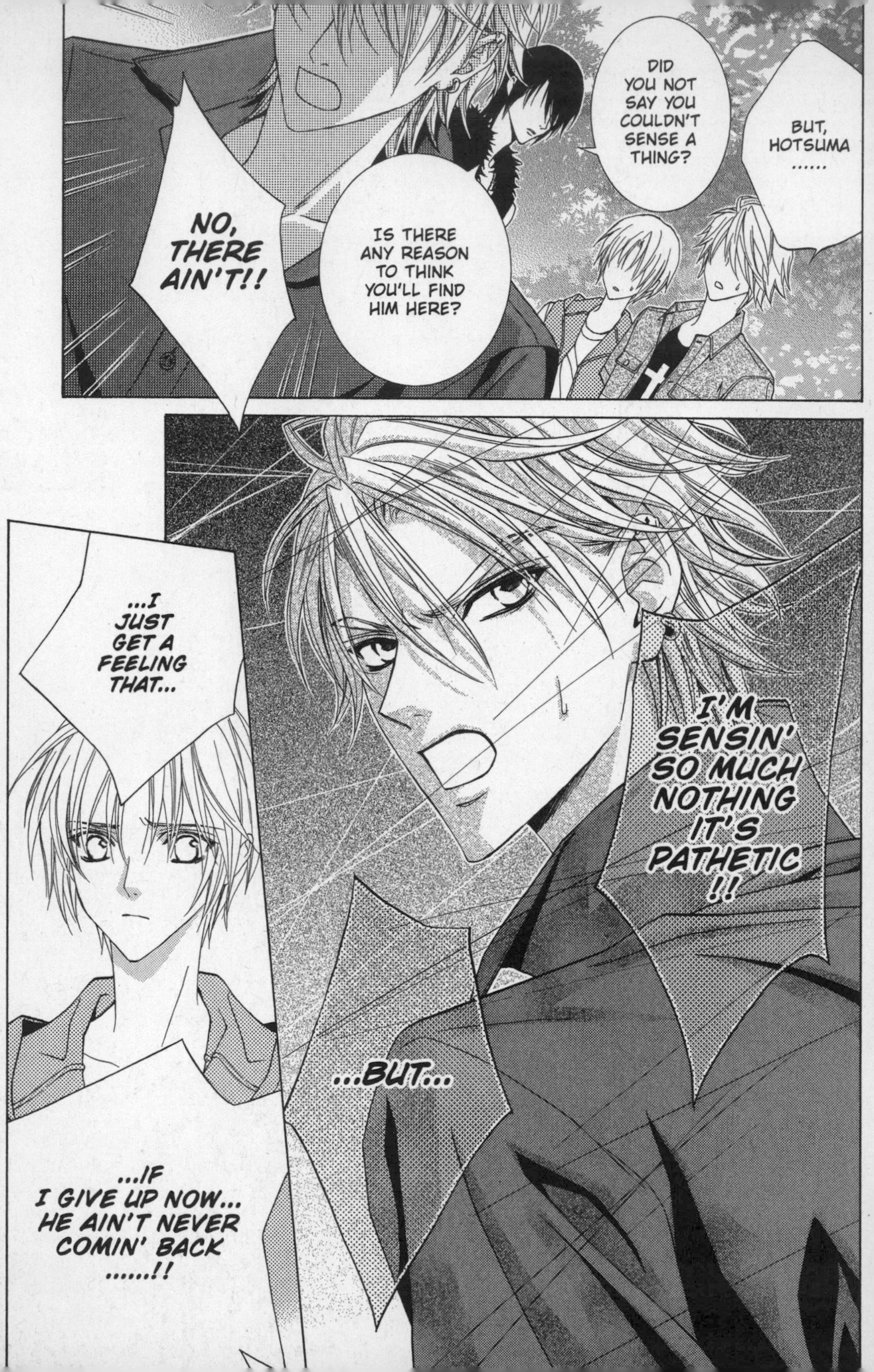
BUT, HOTSUMA ......
DID YOU NOT SAY YOU COULDN'T SENSE A THING?
IS THERE ANY REASON TO THINK YOU'LL FIND HIM HERE?
NO, THERE AIN'T!!
I'M SENSIN' SO MUCH NOTHING IT'S PATHETIC !!
...BUT...
...I JUST GET A FEELING THAT...
...IF I GIVE UP NOW... HE AIN'T NEVER COMIN' BACK ......!!

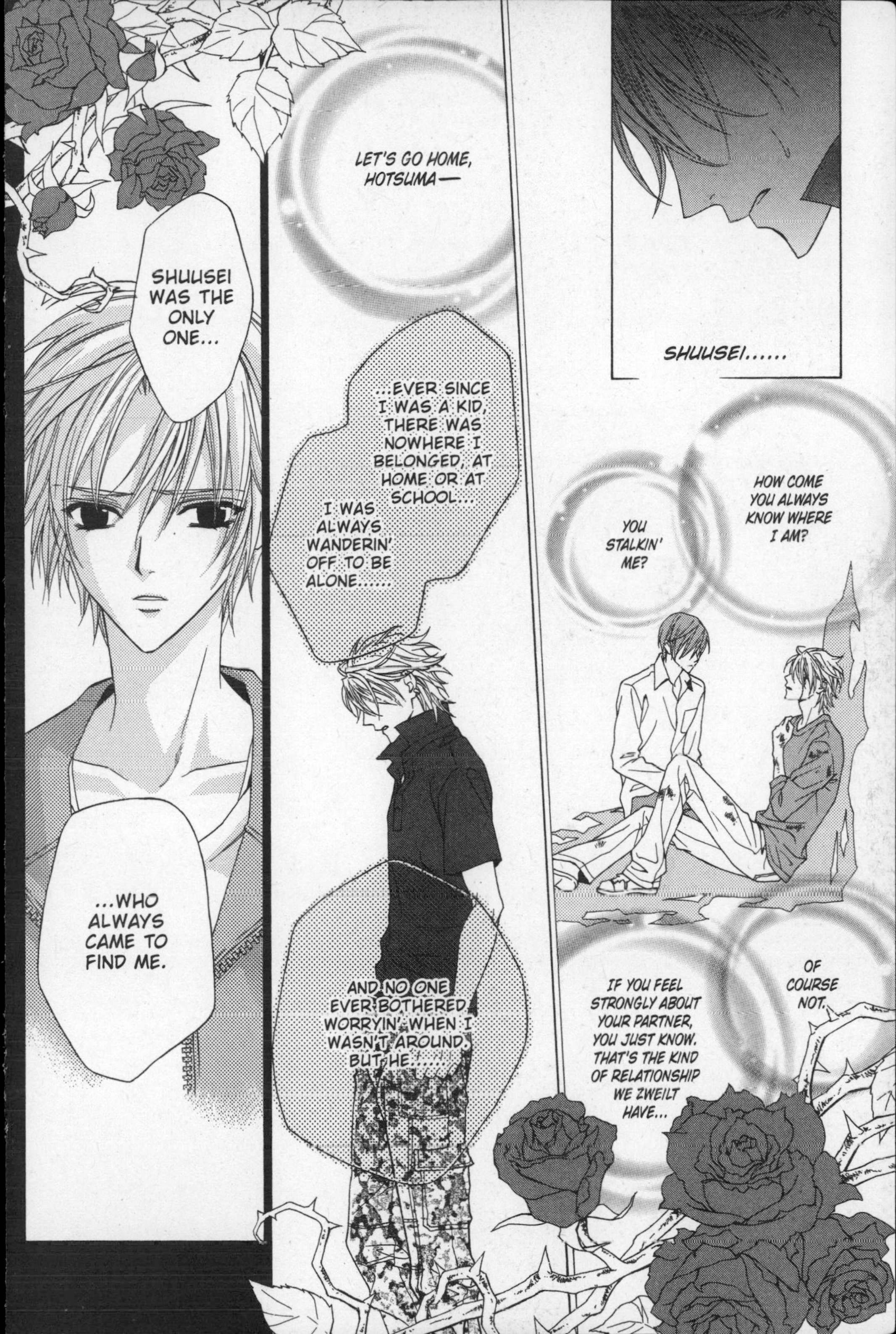
SHUUSEI......
HOW COME YOU ALWAYS KNOW WHERE I AM?
YOU STALKIN' ME?
OF COURSE NOT.
IF YOU FEEL STRONGLY ABOUT YOUR PARTNER, YOU JUST KNOW. THAT'S THE KIND OF RELATIONSHIP WE ZWEILT HAVE...
LET'S GO HOME, HOTSUMA—
...EVER SINCE I WAS A KID, THERE WAS NOWHERE I BELONGED, AT HOME OR AT SCHOOL...
I WAS ALWAYS WANDERIN' OFF TO BE ALONE.....
AND NO ONE EVER BOTHERED WORRYIN' WHEN I WASN'T AROUND. BUT HE......
SHUUSEI WAS THE ONLY ONE...
...WHO ALWAYS CAME TO FIND ME.

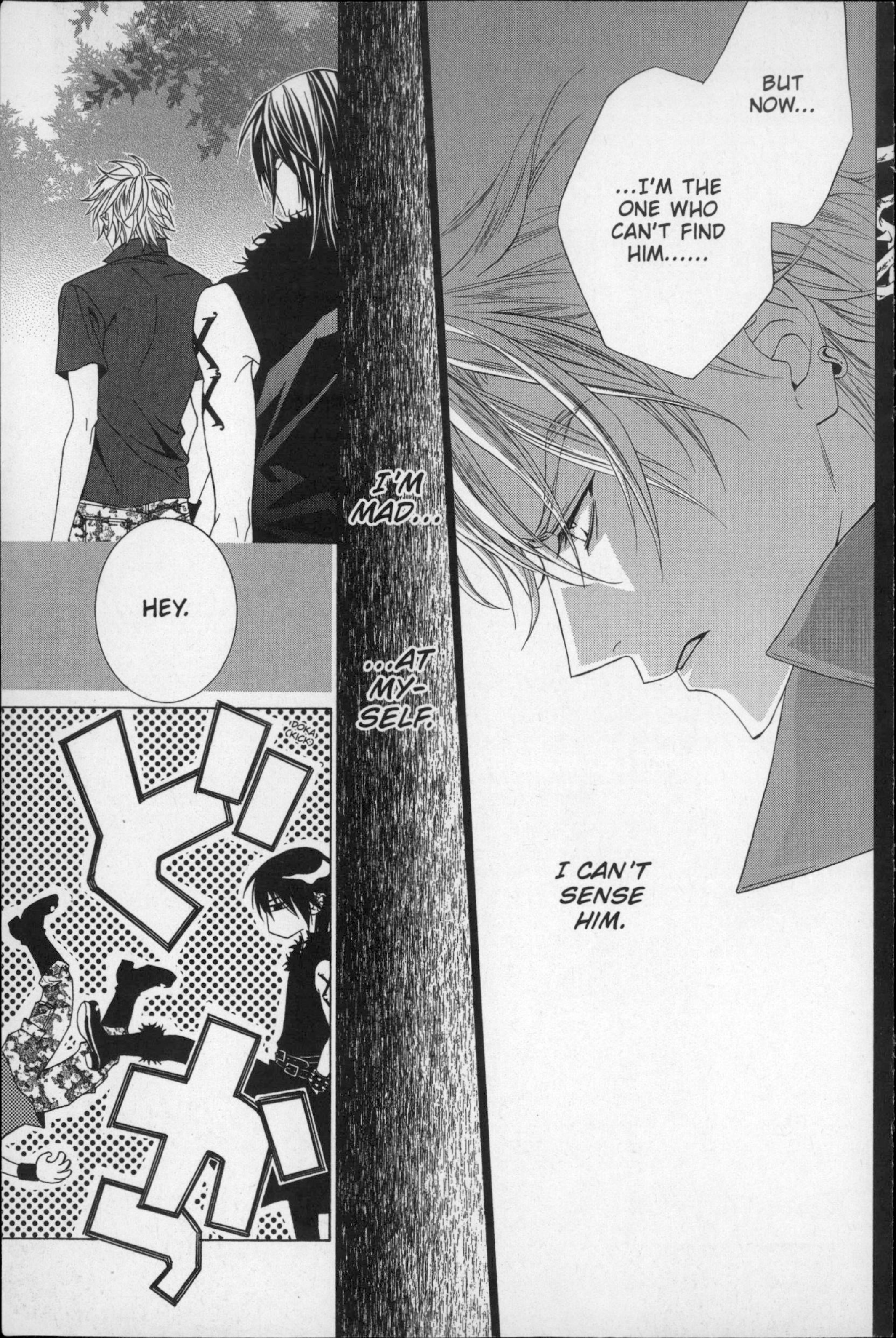
BUT NOW...
...I'M THE ONE WHO CAN'T FIND HIM......
I CAN'T SENSE HIM.
I'M MAD...
...AT MY-SELF.
HEY.
DOKA (KICK)

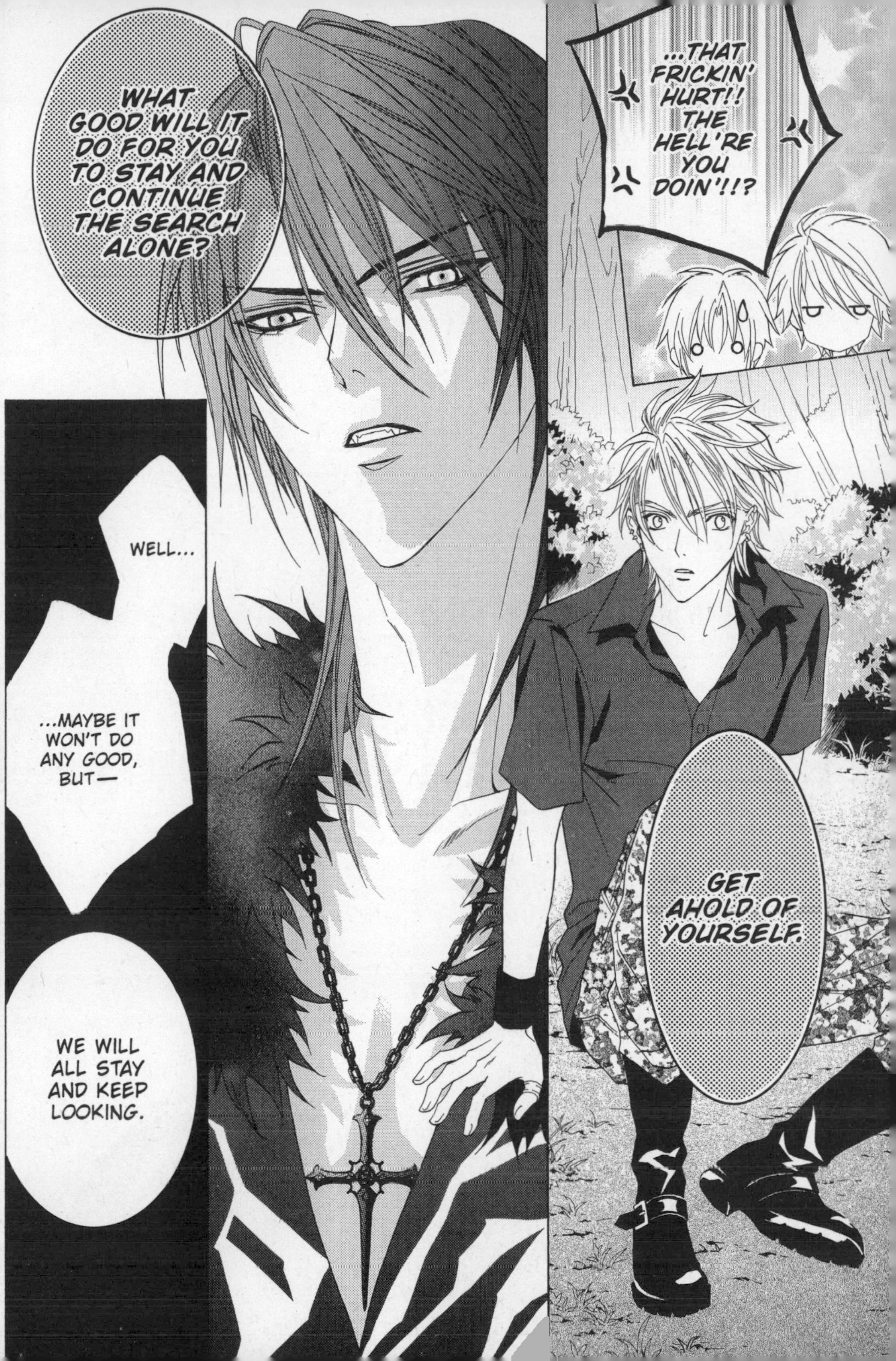
...THAT FRICKIN' HURT!! THE HELL'RE YOU DOIN'!!?
GET AHOLD OF YOURSELF.
WHAT GOOD WILL IT DO FOR YOU TO STAY AND CONTINUE THE SEARCH ALONE?
WELL...
...MAYBE IT WON'T DO ANY GOOD, BUT—
WE WILL ALL STAY AND KEEP LOOKING.

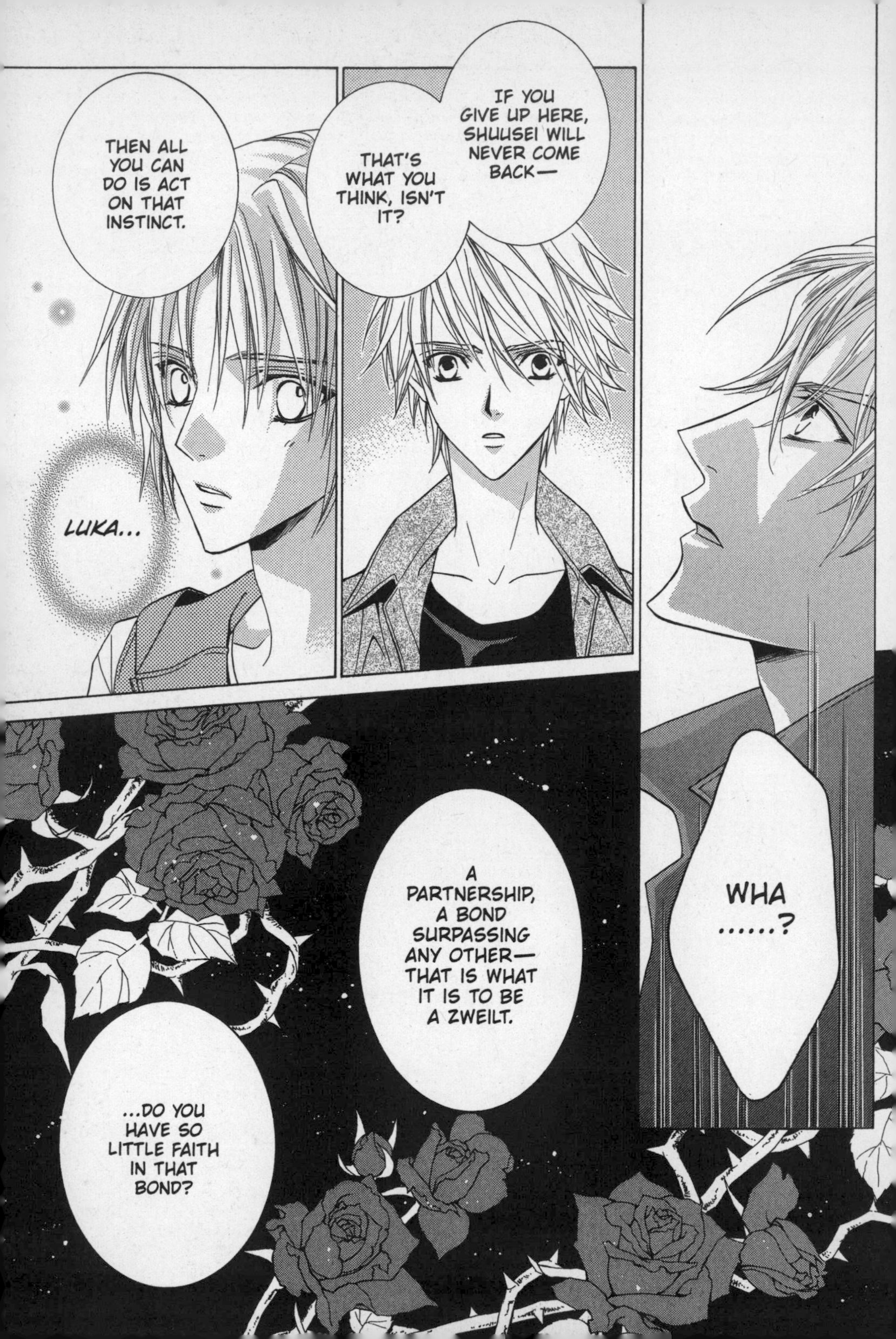
IF YOU GIVE UP HERE, SHUUSEI WILL NEVER COME BACK—
THAT'S WHAT YOU THINK, ISN'T IT?
THEN ALL YOU CAN DO IS ACT ON THAT INSTINCT.
LUKA...
A PARTNERSHIP, A BOND SURPASSING ANY OTHER— THAT IS WHAT IT IS TO BE A ZWEILT.
...DO YOU HAVE SO LITTLE FAITH IN THAT BOND?
WHA ......?

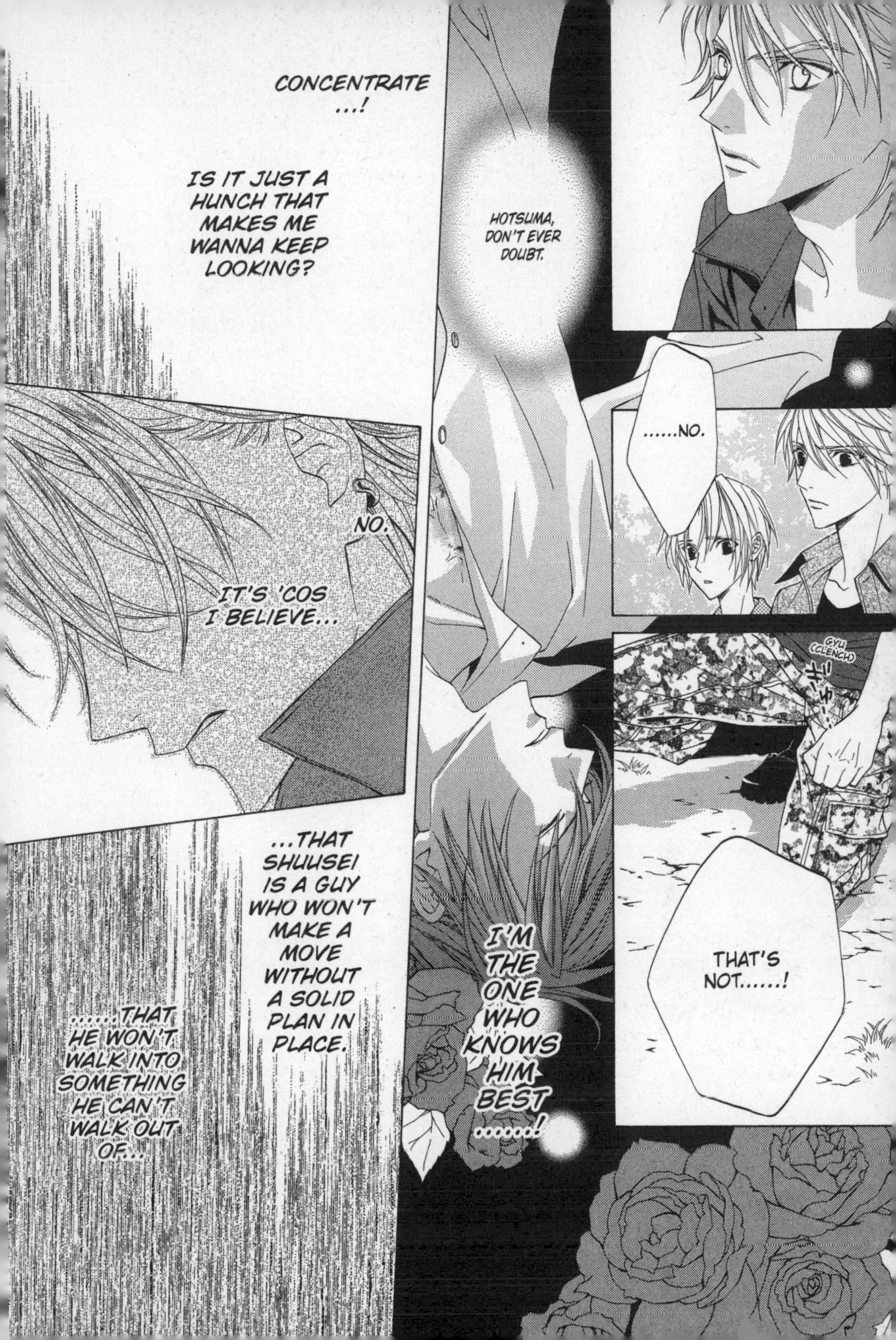
......NO.
GYU (CLENCH)
THAT'S NOT......!
HOTSUMA, DON'T EVER DOUBT.
CONCENTRATE ...!
IS IT JUST A HUNCH THAT MAKES ME WANNA KEEP LOOKING?
NO.
IT'S 'COS I BELIEVE...
...THAT SHUUSEI IS A GUY WHO WON'T MAKE A MOVE WITHOUT A SOLID PLAN IN PLACE.
......THAT HE WON'T WALK INTO SOMETHING HE CAN'T WALK OUT OF...
I'M THE ONE WHO KNOWS HIM BEST......!

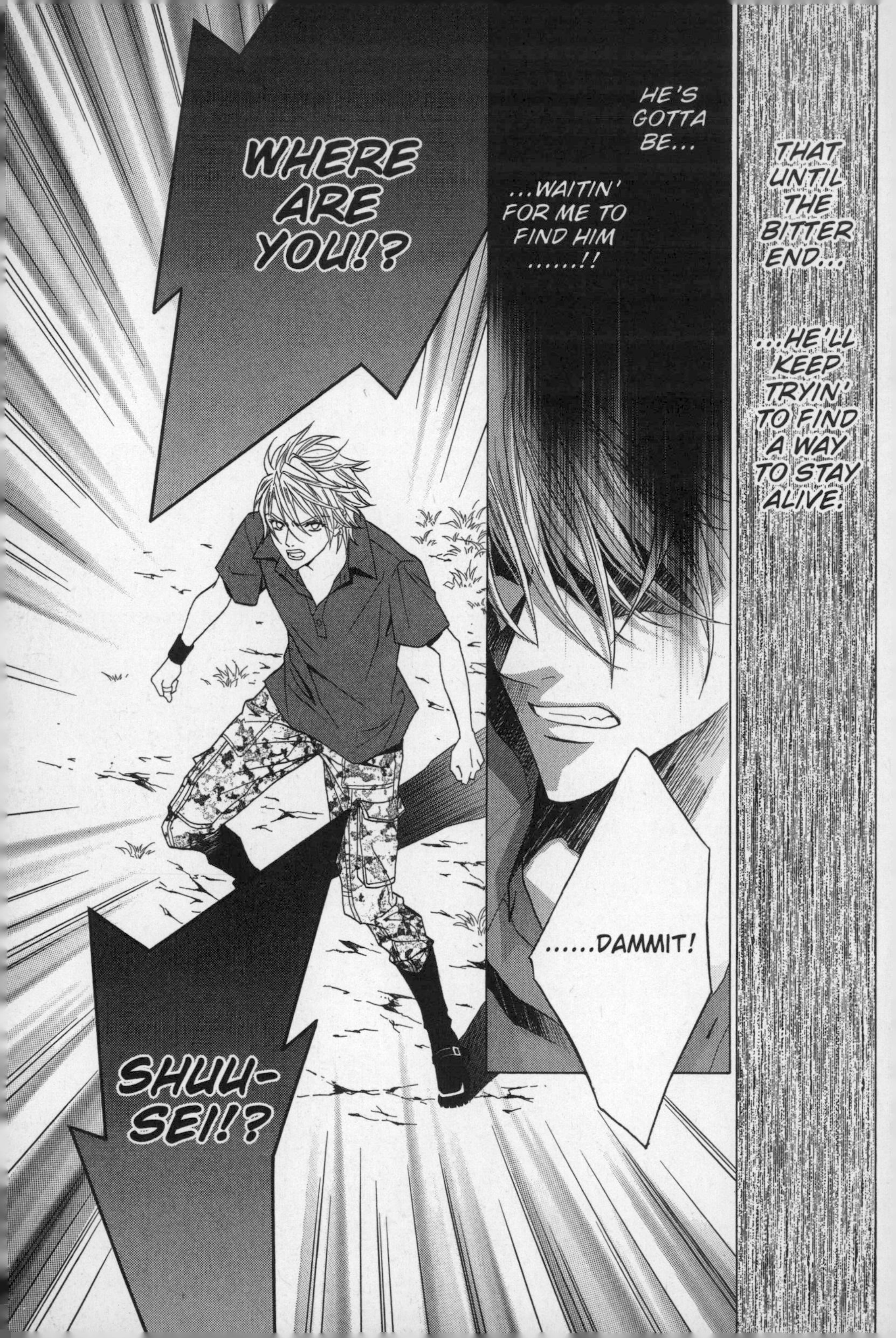
THAT UNTIL THE BITTER END...
...HE'LL KEEP TRYIN' TO FIND A WAY TO STAY ALIVE.
HE'S GOTTA BE...
...WAITIN' FOR ME TO FIND HIM ......!!
......DAMMIT!
WHERE ARE YOU!?
SHUU-SEI!?

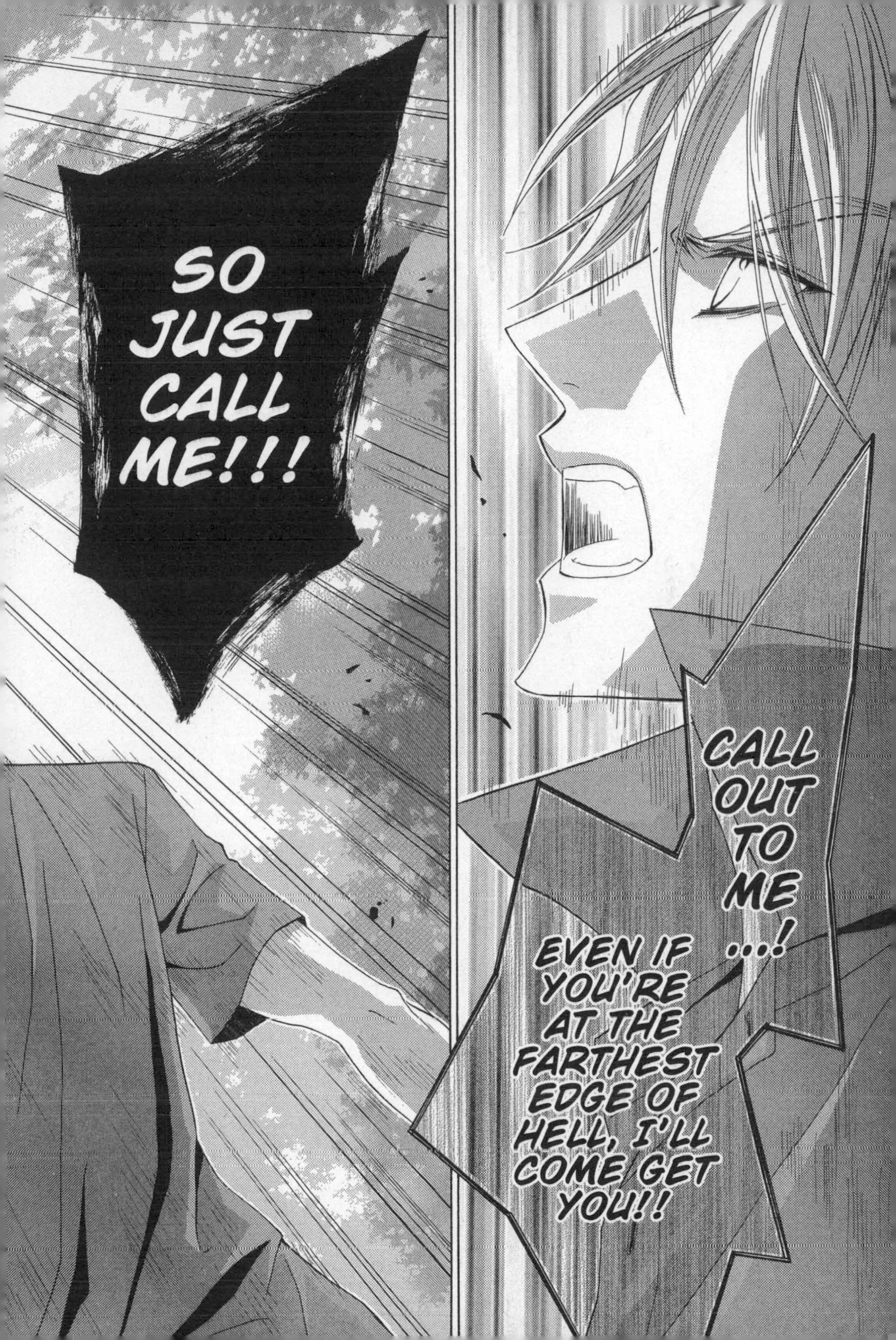
CALL OUT TO ME ...!
EVEN IF YOU'RE AT THE FARTHEST EDGE OF HELL, I'LL COME GET YOU!!
SO JUST CALL ME!!!

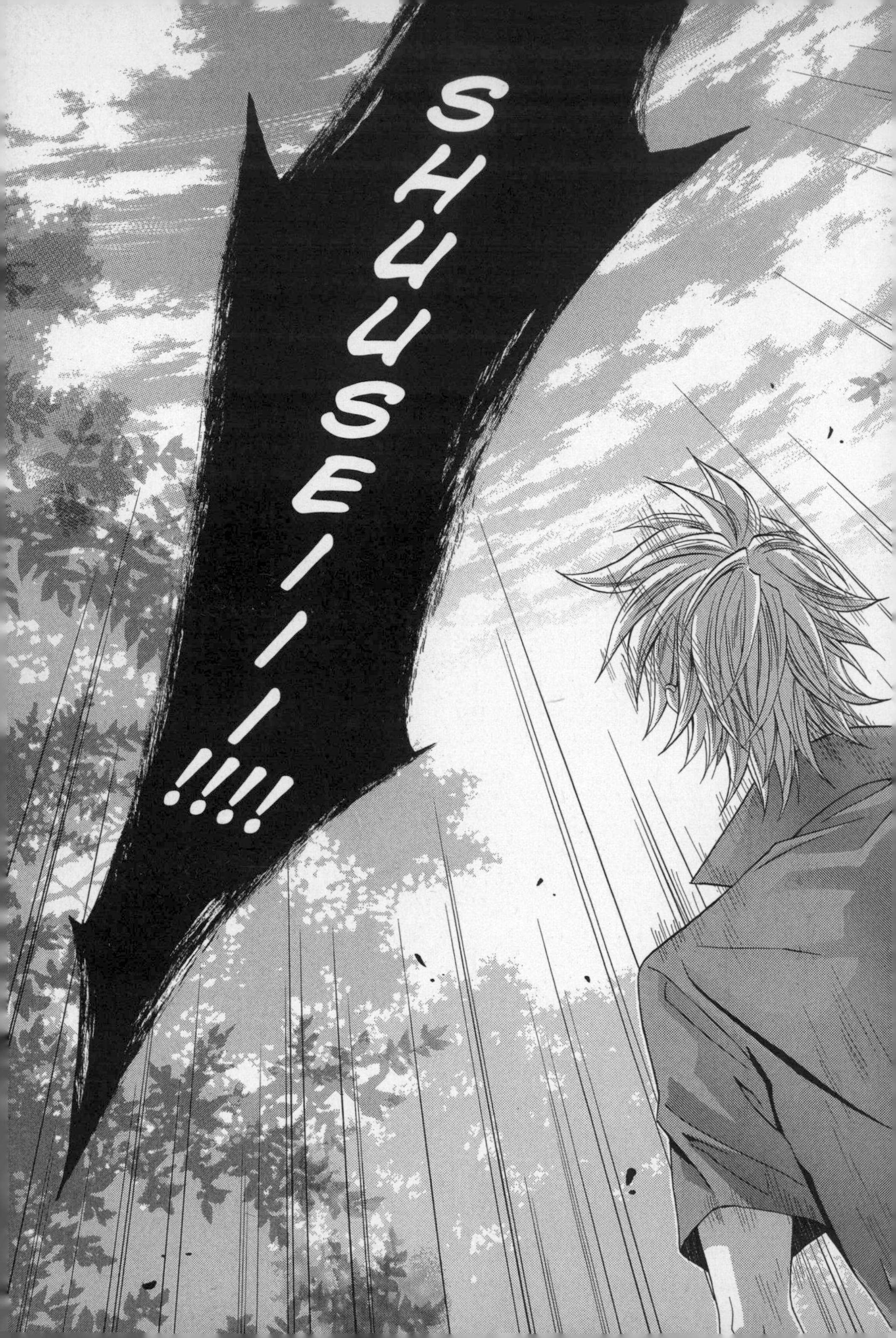
SHUUSEI---!!!!

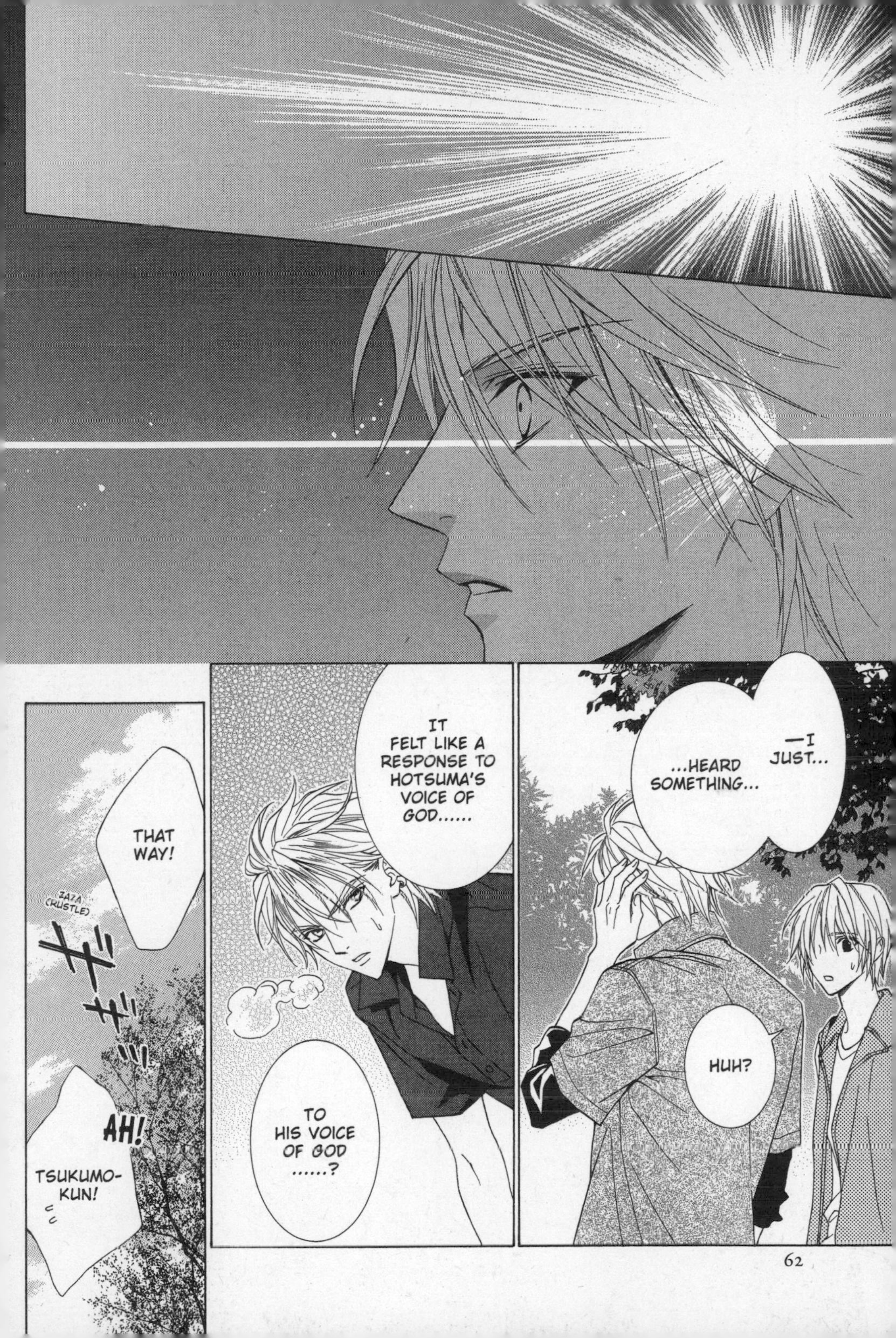
—I JUST...
...HEARD SOMETHING...
HUH?
IT FELT LIKE A RESPONSE TO HOTSUMA'S VOICE OF GOD......
TO HIS VOICE OF GOD ......?
THAT WAY!
ZAZA (RUSTLE)
AH!
TSUKUMO-KUN!

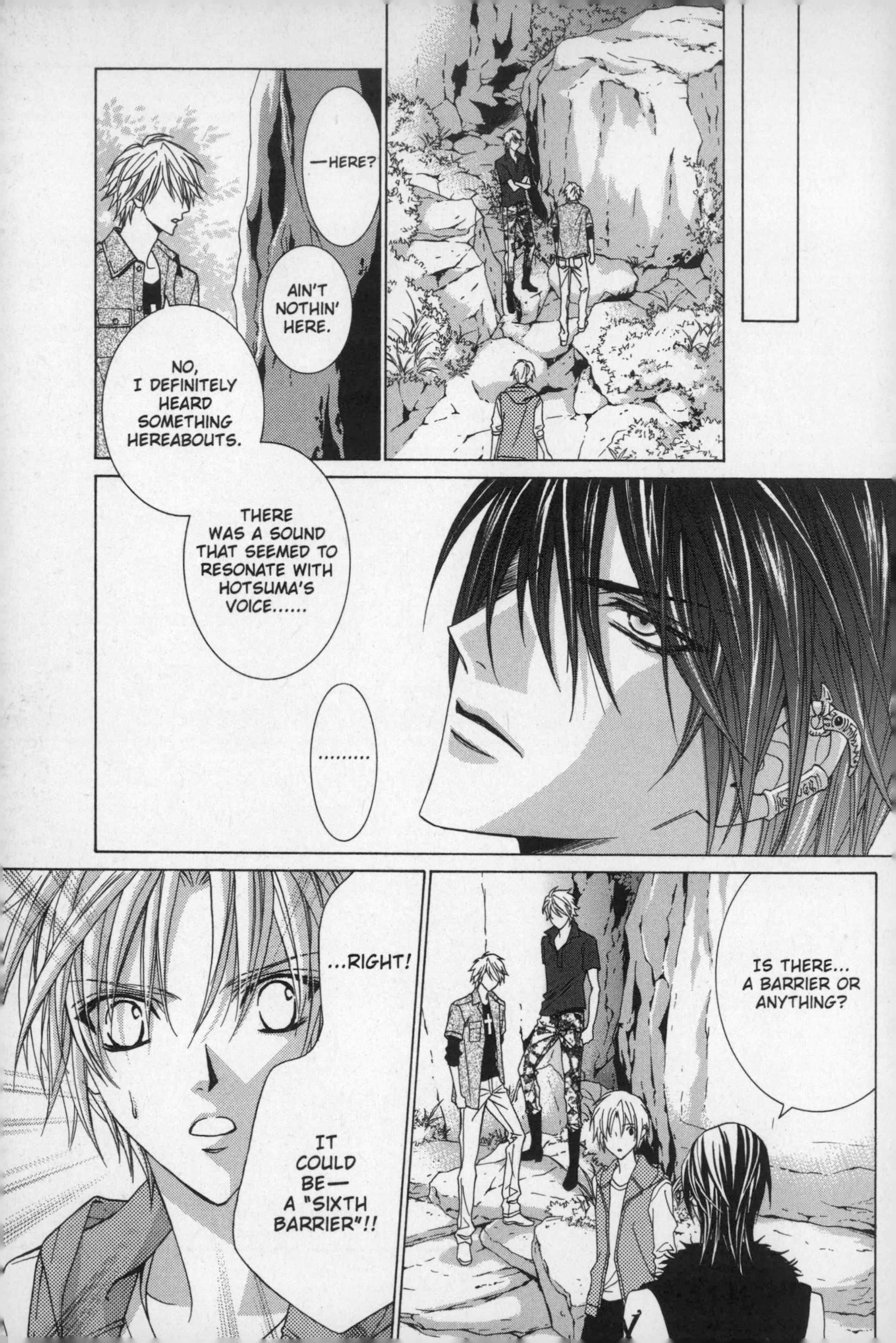
—HERE?
AIN'T NOTHIN' HERE.
NO, I DEFINITELY HEARD SOMETHING HEREABOUTS.
THERE WAS A SOUND THAT SEEMED TO RESONATE WITH HOTSUMA'S VOICE......
....
IS THERE... A BARRIER OR ANYTHING?
...RIGHT!
IT COULD BE— A "SIXTH BARRIER"!!

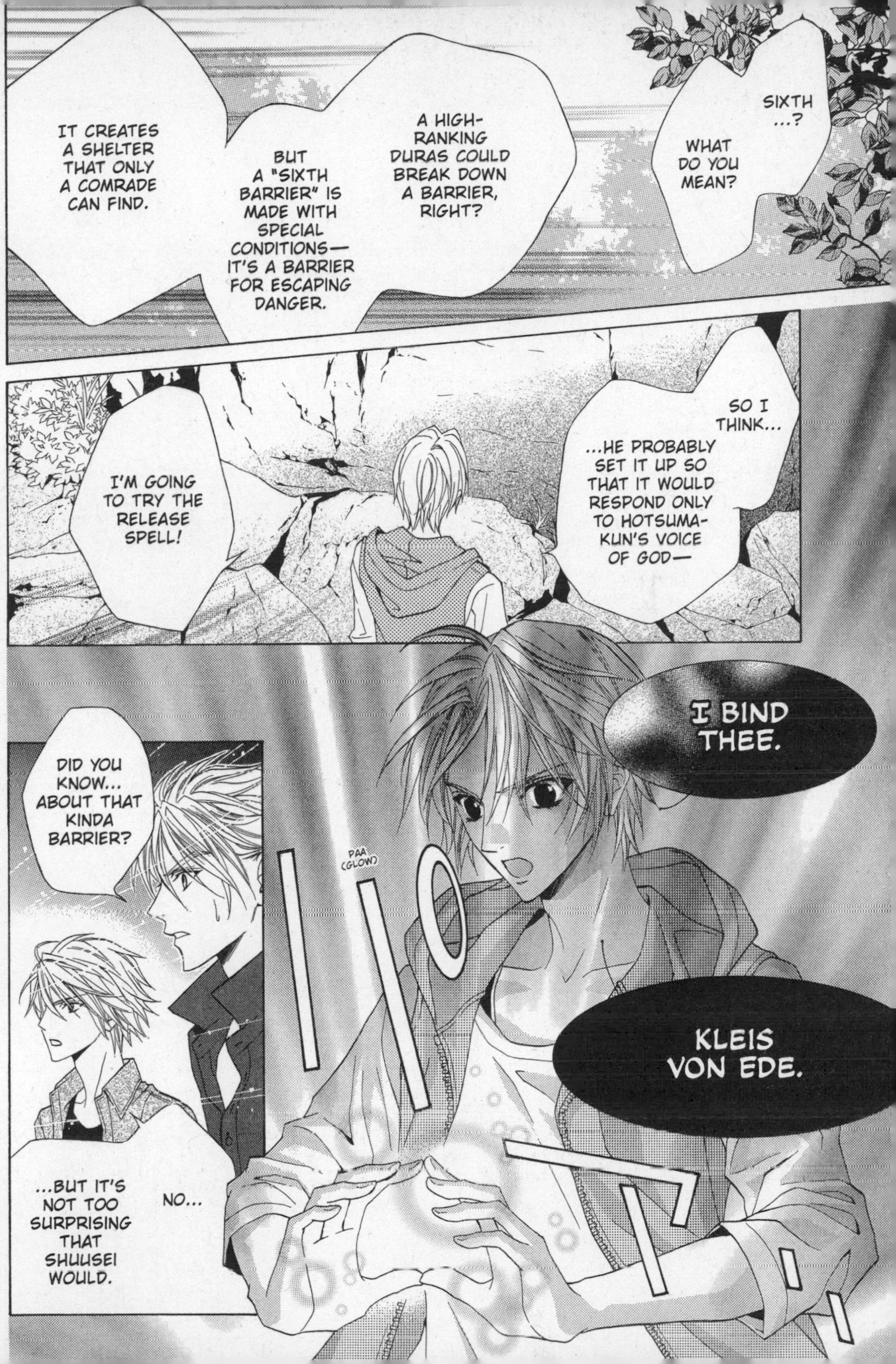
SIXTH ...?
WHAT DO YOU MEAN?
A HIGH-RANKING DURAS COULD BREAK DOWN A BARRIER, RIGHT?
BUT A "SIXTH BARRIER" IS MADE WITH SPECIAL CONDITIONS— IT'S A BARRIER FOR ESCAPING DANGER.
IT CREATES A SHELTER THAT ONLY A COMRADE CAN FIND.
SO I THINK...
...HE PROBABLY SET IT UP SO THAT IT WOULD RESPOND ONLY TO HOTSUMA-KUN'S VOICE OF GOD—
I'M GOING TO TRY THE RELEASE SPELL!
I BIND THEE.
KLEIS VON EDE.
PAA (GLOW)
DID YOU KNOW... ABOUT THAT KINDA BARRIER?
NO...
...BUT IT'S NOT TOO SURPRISING THAT SHUUSEI WOULD.

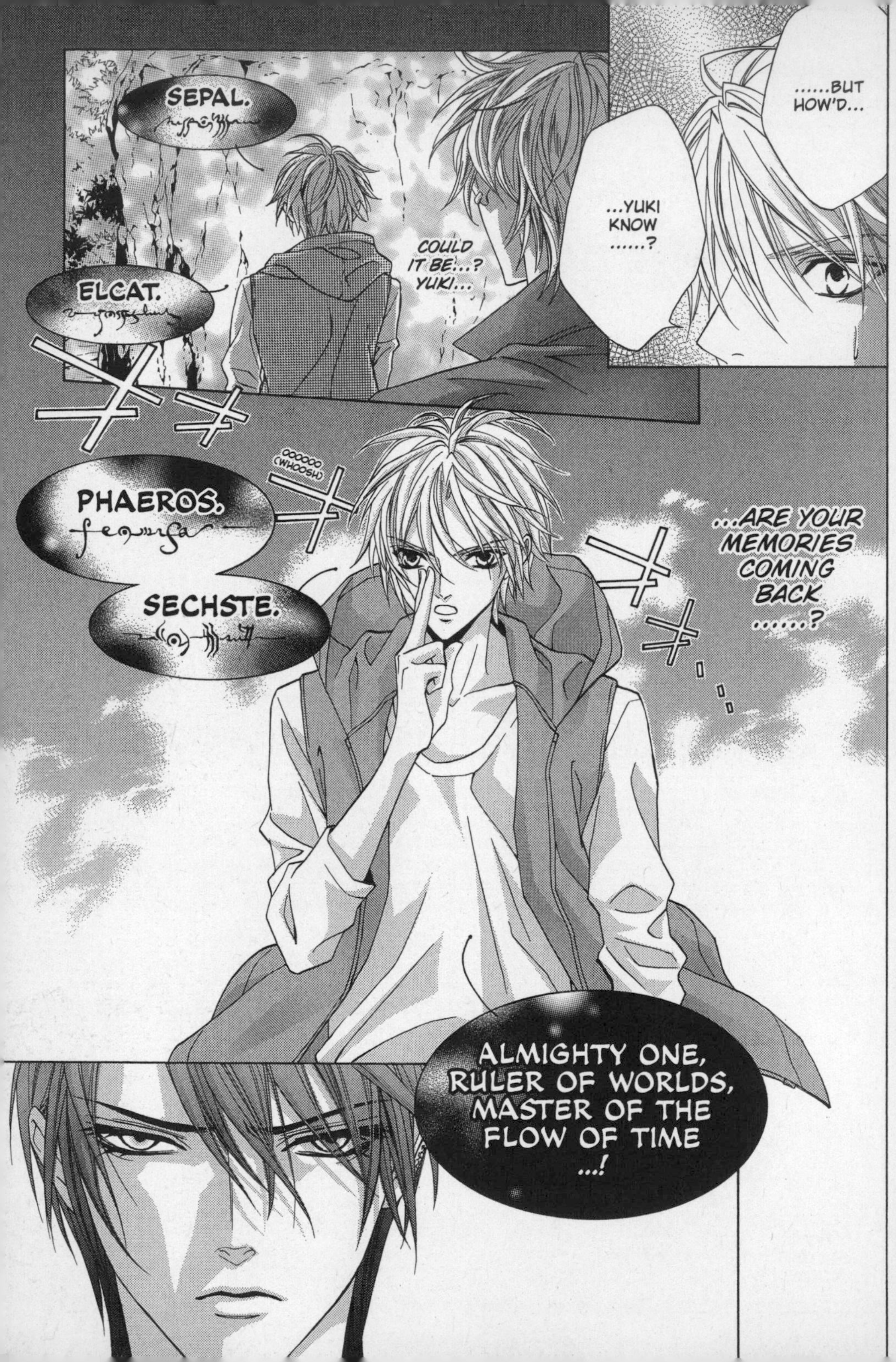
......BUT HOW'D...
...YUKI KNOW ......?
SEPAL.
COULD IT BE...? YUKI...
ELCAT.
(WHOOSH)
...ARE YOUR MEMORIES COMING BACK ......?
PHAEROS.
SECHSTE.
ALMIGHTY ONE, RULER OF WORLDS, MASTER OF THE FLOW OF TIME ...!

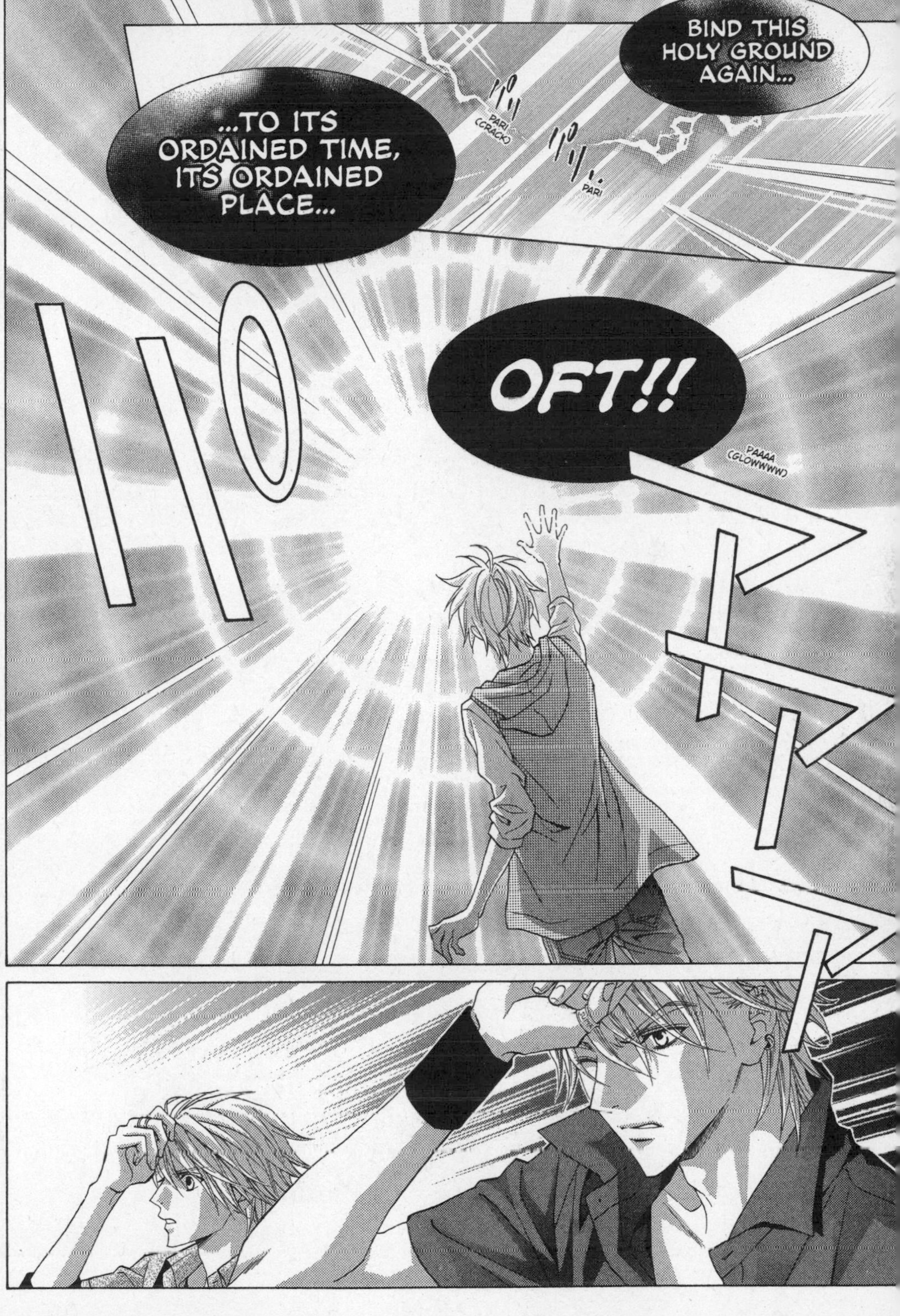
BIND THIS HOLY GROUND AGAIN...
PARI (CRACK)
PARI
...TO ITS ORDAINED TIME, ITS ORDAINED PLACE...
OFT!!
PAAAA (GLOWWWW)

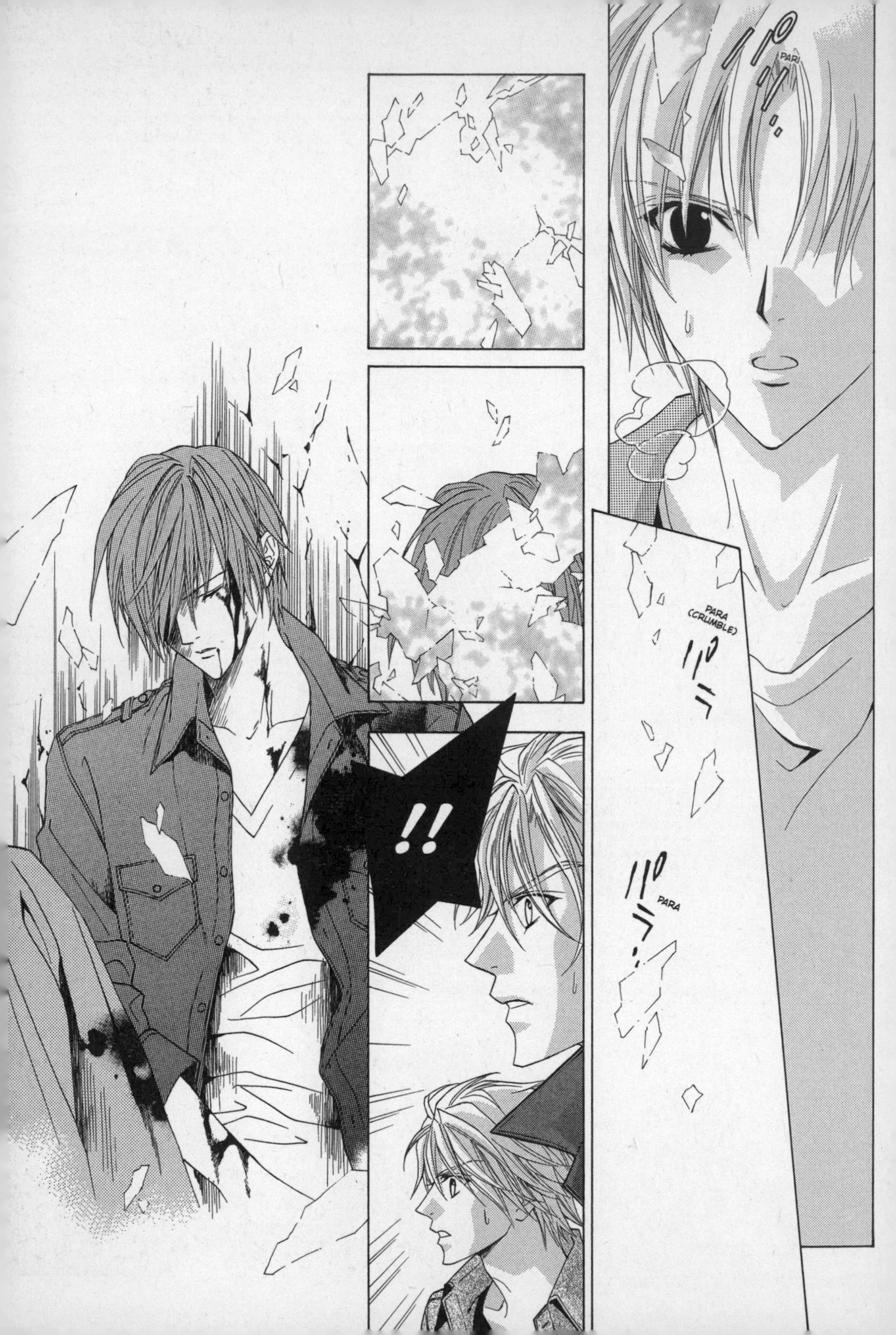

PARI
PARA (CRUMBLE)
PARA
!!

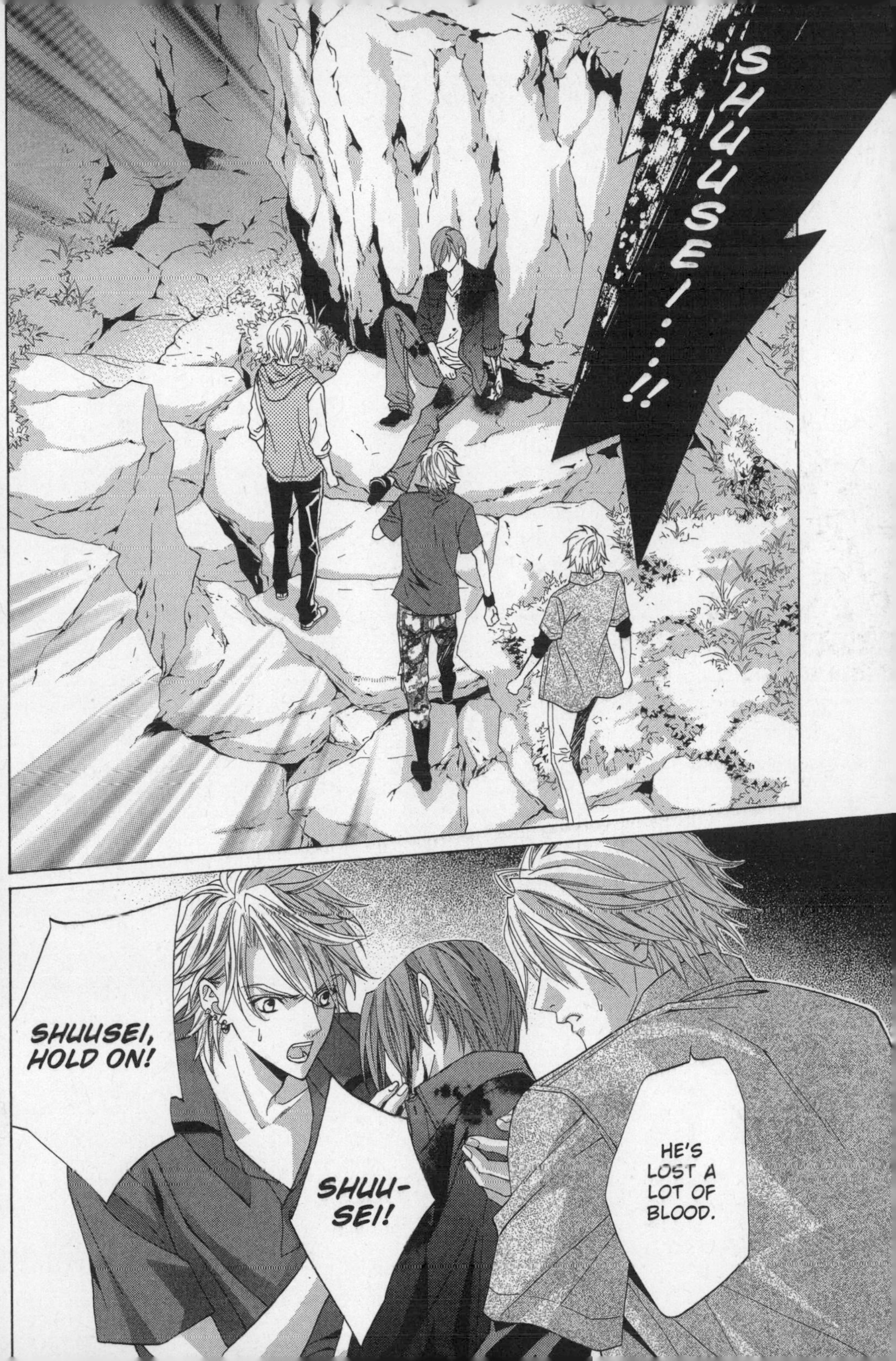
SHUUSEI...!!
HE'S LOST A LOT OF BLOOD.
SHUU-SEI!
SHUUSEI, HOLD ON!

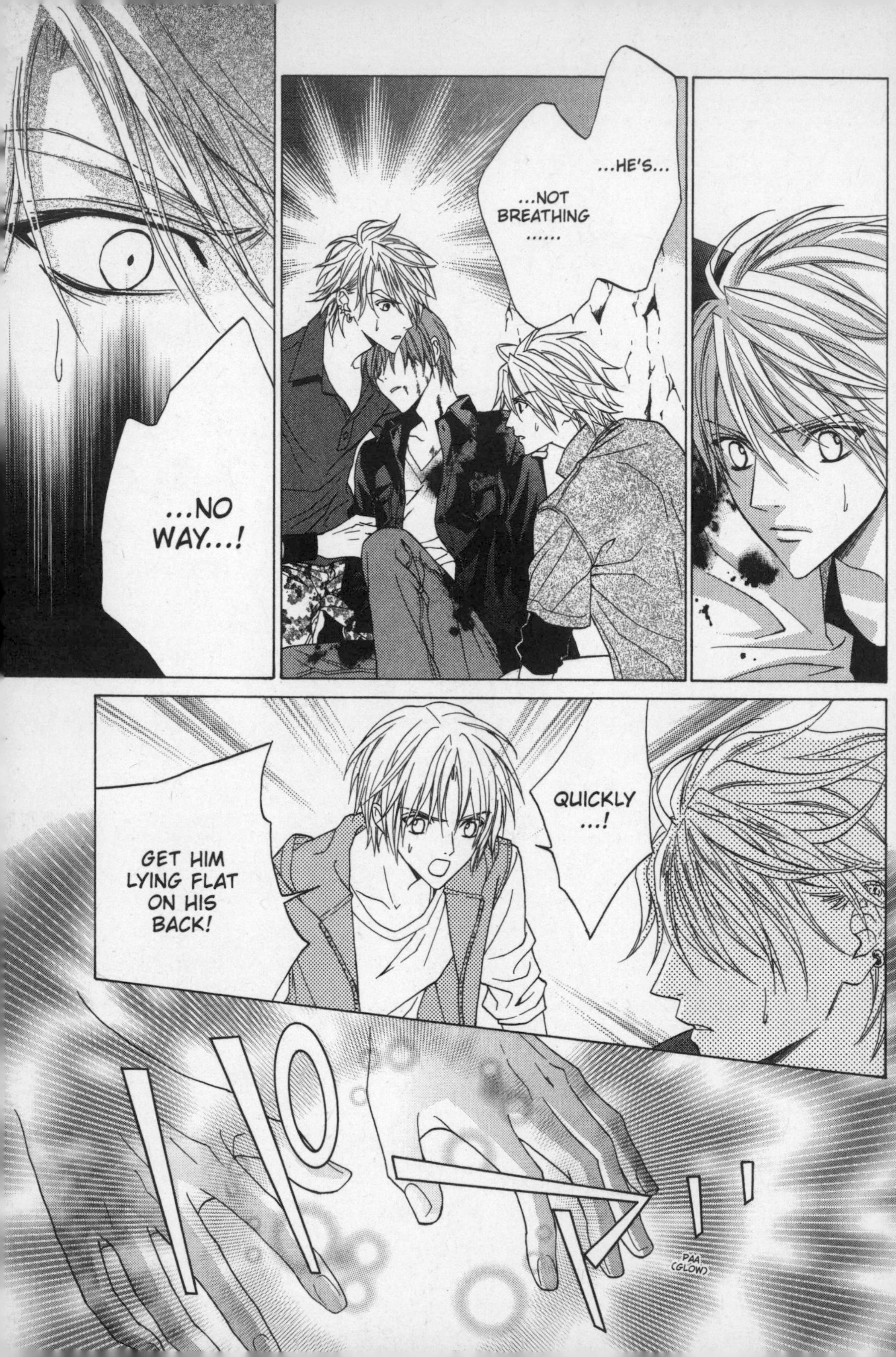
...HE'S...
...NOT BREATHING ......
...NO WAY...!
QUICKLY ...!
GET HIM LYING FLAT ON HIS BACK!
PAA (GLOW)

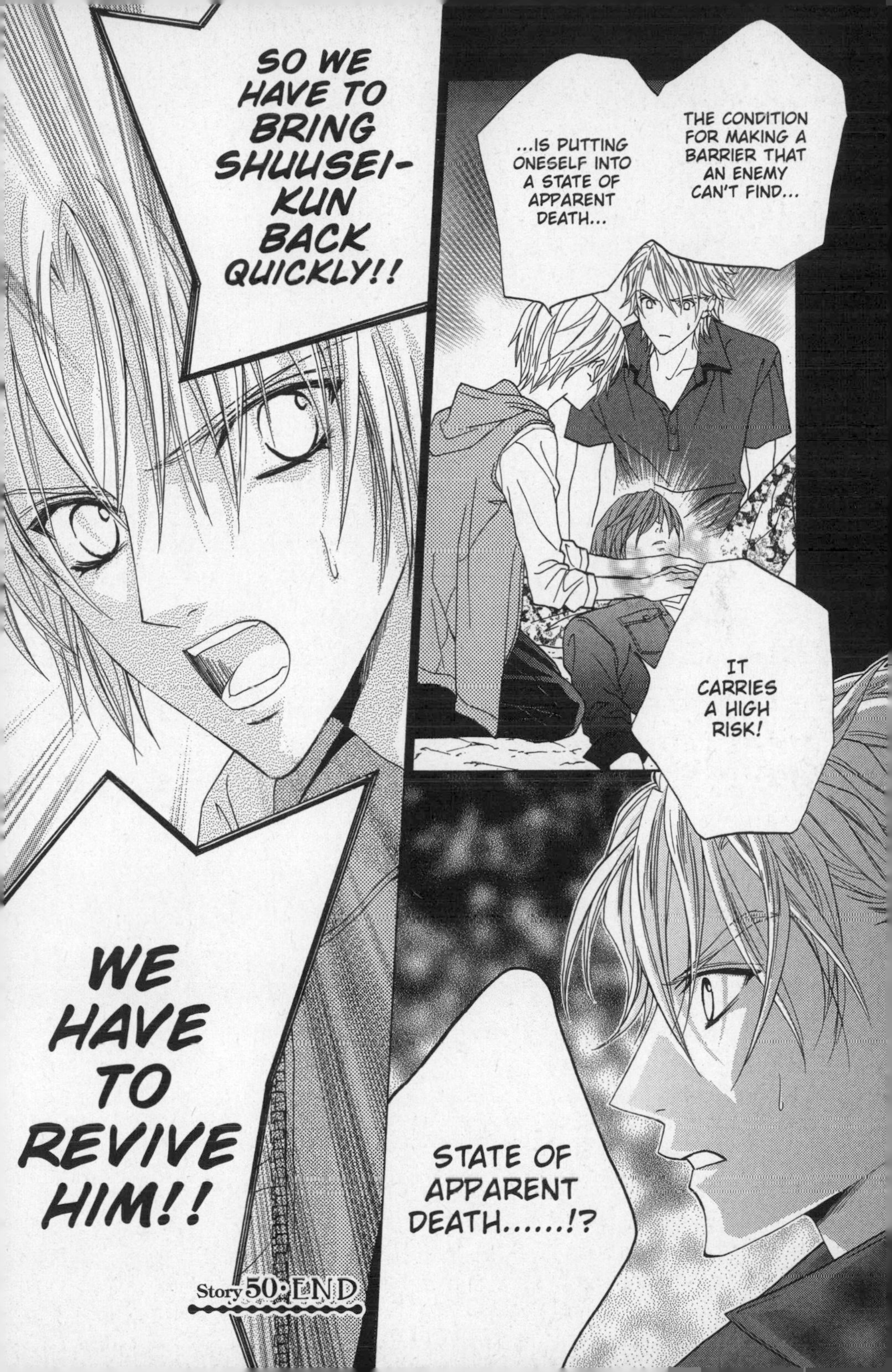
THE CONDITION FOR MAKING A BARRIER THAT AN ENEMY CAN'T FIND...
...IS PUTTING ONESELF INTO A STATE OF APPARENT DEATH...
IT CARRIES A HIGH RISK!
STATE OF APPARENT DEATH......!?
SO WE HAVE TO BRING SHUUSEI-KUN BACK QUICKLY!!
WE HAVE TO REVIVE HIM!!
Story 50: END

The Betrayal Knows My Name

Story 51

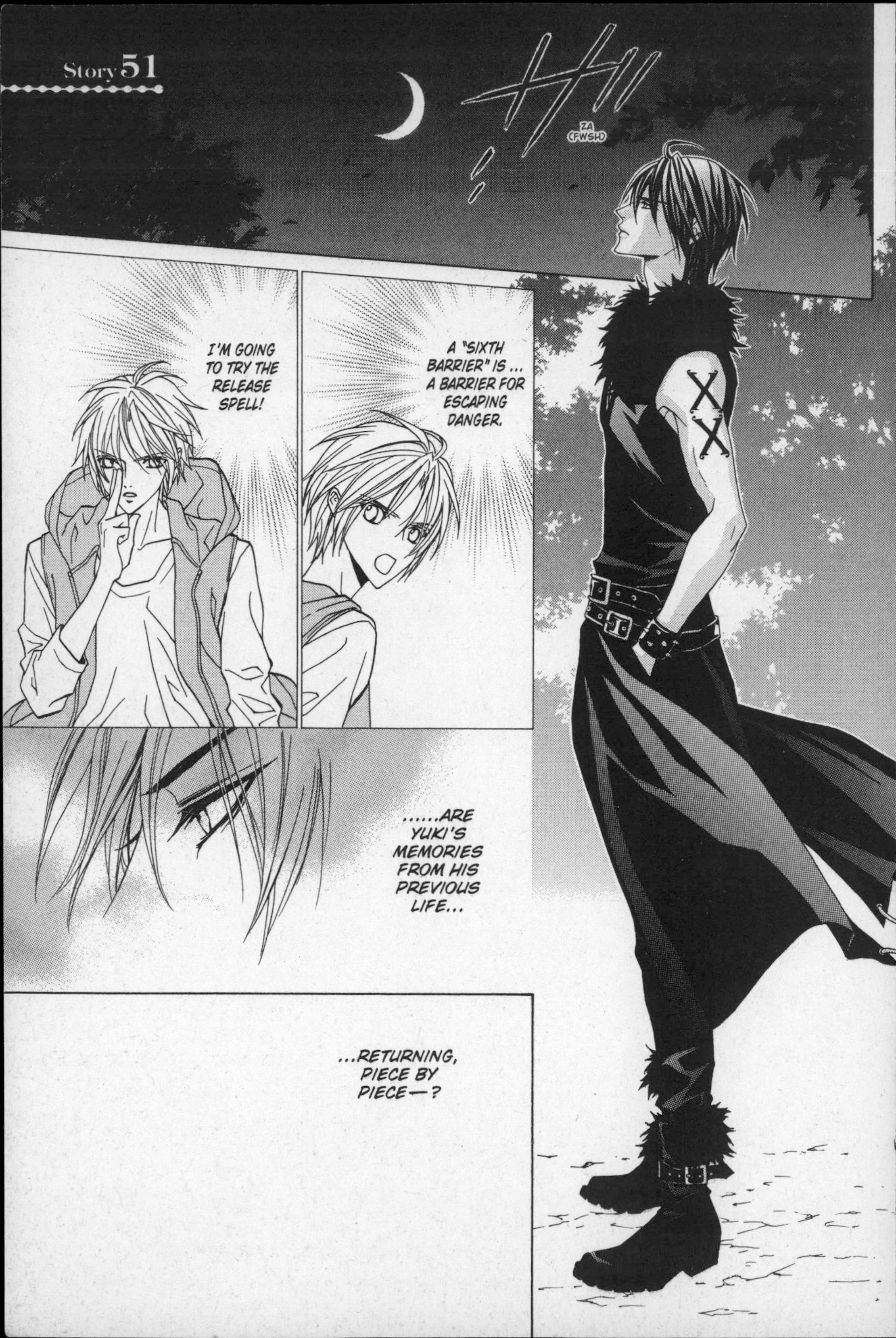
ZA (FWSH)
A "SIXTH BARRIER" IS ... A BARRIER FOR ESCAPING DANGER.
I'M GOING TO TRY THE RELEASE SPELL!
......ARE YUKI'S MEMORIES FROM HIS PREVIOUS LIFE...
...RETURNING, PIECE BY PIECE—?

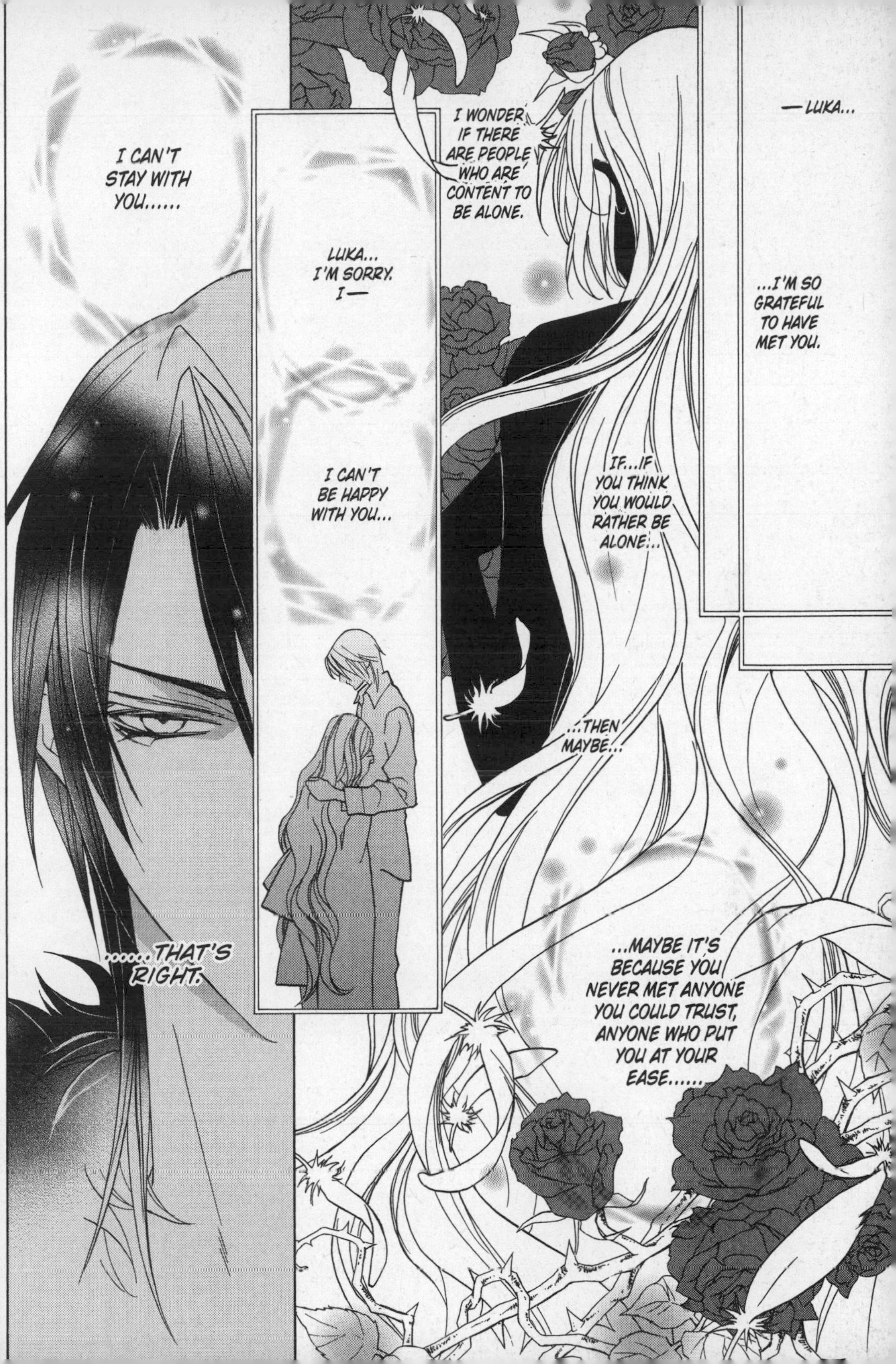
—LUKA...
...I'M SO GRATEFUL TO HAVE MET YOU.
I WONDER IF THERE ARE PEOPLE WHO ARE CONTENT TO BE ALONE.
IF...IF YOU THINK YOU WOULD RATHER BE ALONE...
...THEN MAYBE...
...MAYBE IT'S BECAUSE YOU NEVER MET ANYONE YOU COULD TRUST, ANYONE WHO PUT YOU AT YOUR EASE......
LUKA... I'M SORRY. I—
I CAN'T BE HAPPY WITH YOU...
I CAN'T STAY WITH YOU......
......THAT'S RIGHT.

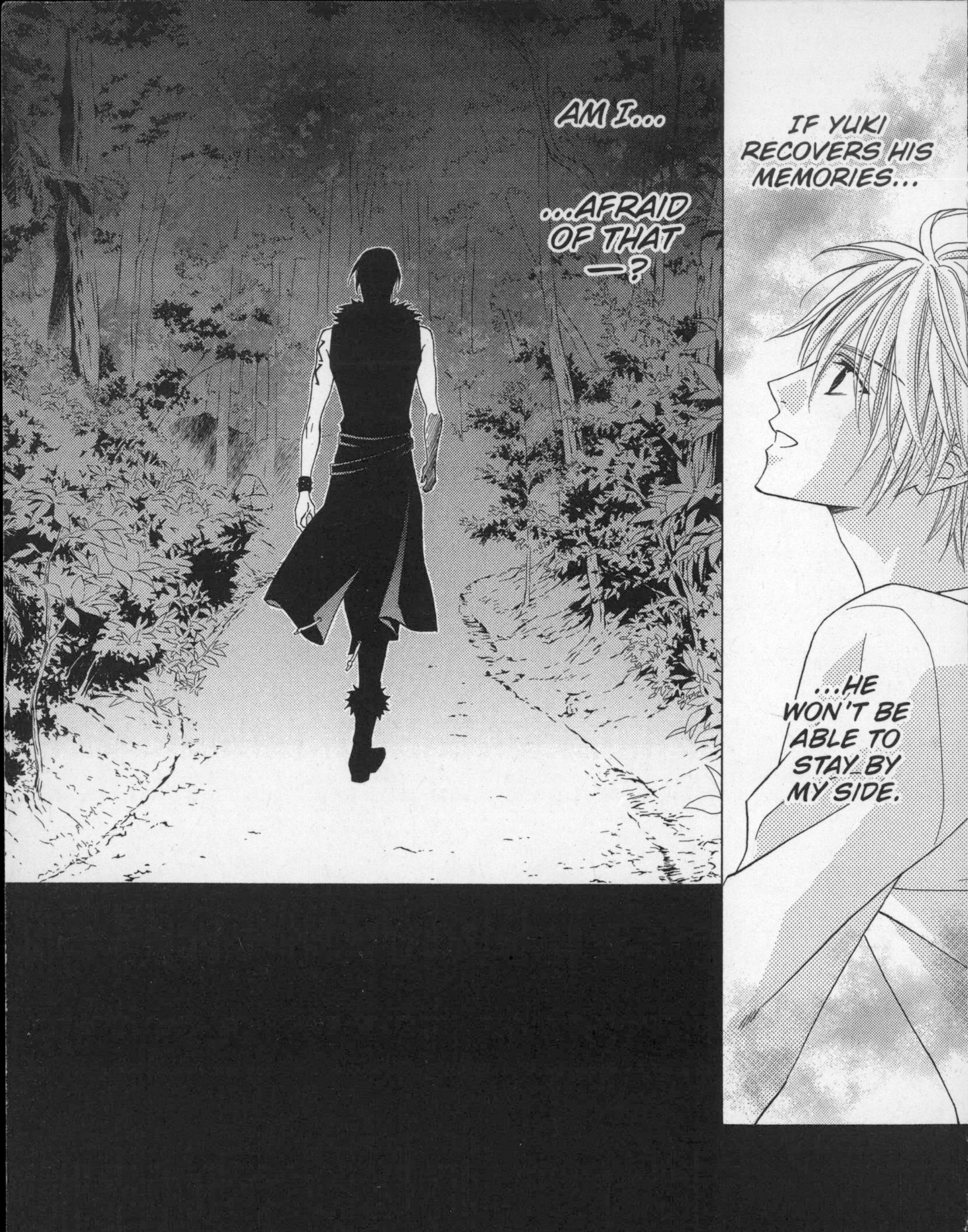
IF YUKI RECOVERS HIS MEMORIES...
...HE WON'T BE ABLE TO STAY BY MY SIDE.
AM I...
...AFRAID OF THAT —?

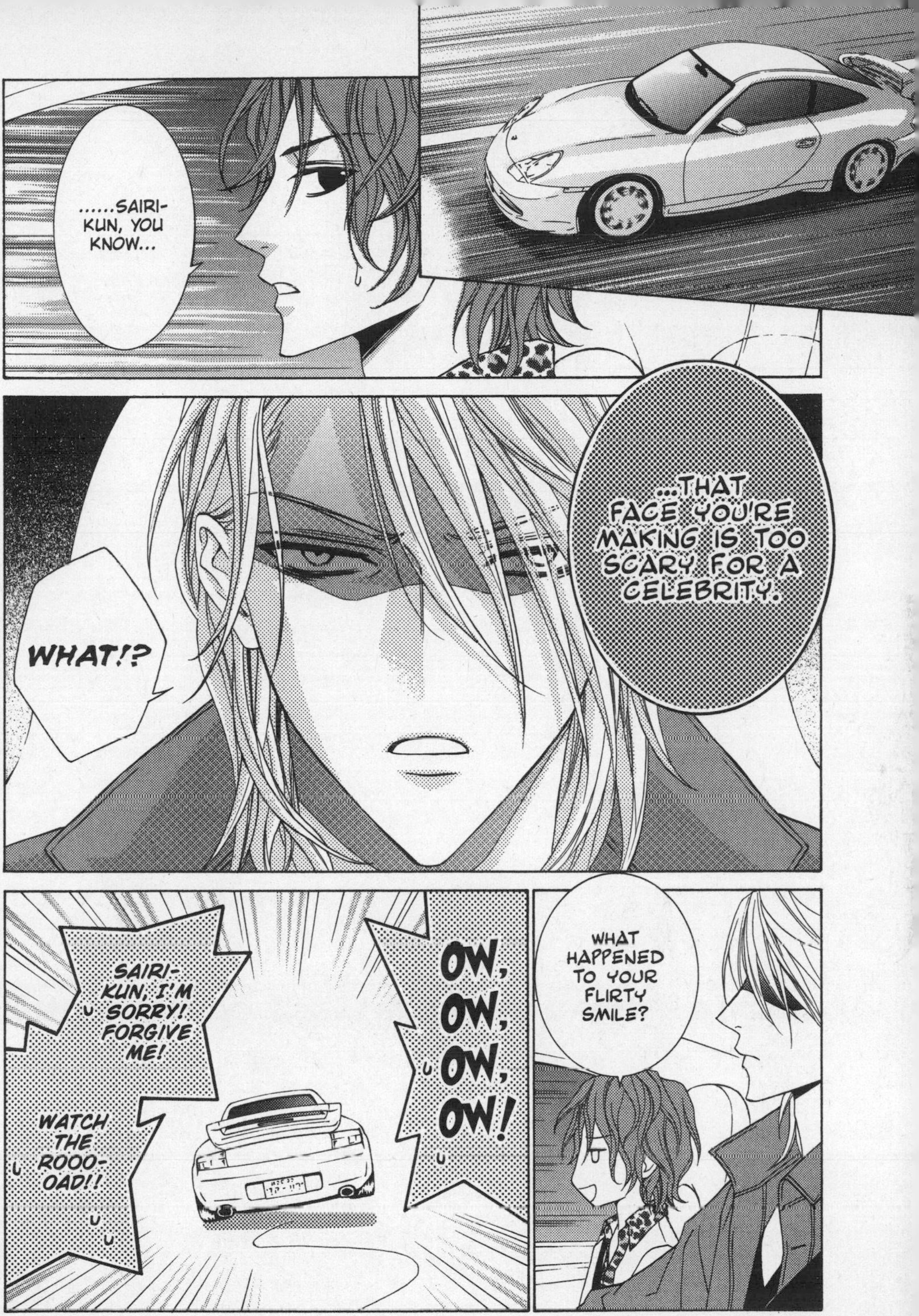
......SAIRI-KUN, YOU KNOW...
...THAT FACE YOU'RE MAKING IS TOO SCARY FOR A CELEBRITY.
WHAT!?
WHAT HAPPENED TO YOUR FLIRTY SMILE?
OW, OW, OW, OW!
SAIRI-KUN, I'M SORRY! FORGIVE ME!
WATCH THE ROOO-OAD!!

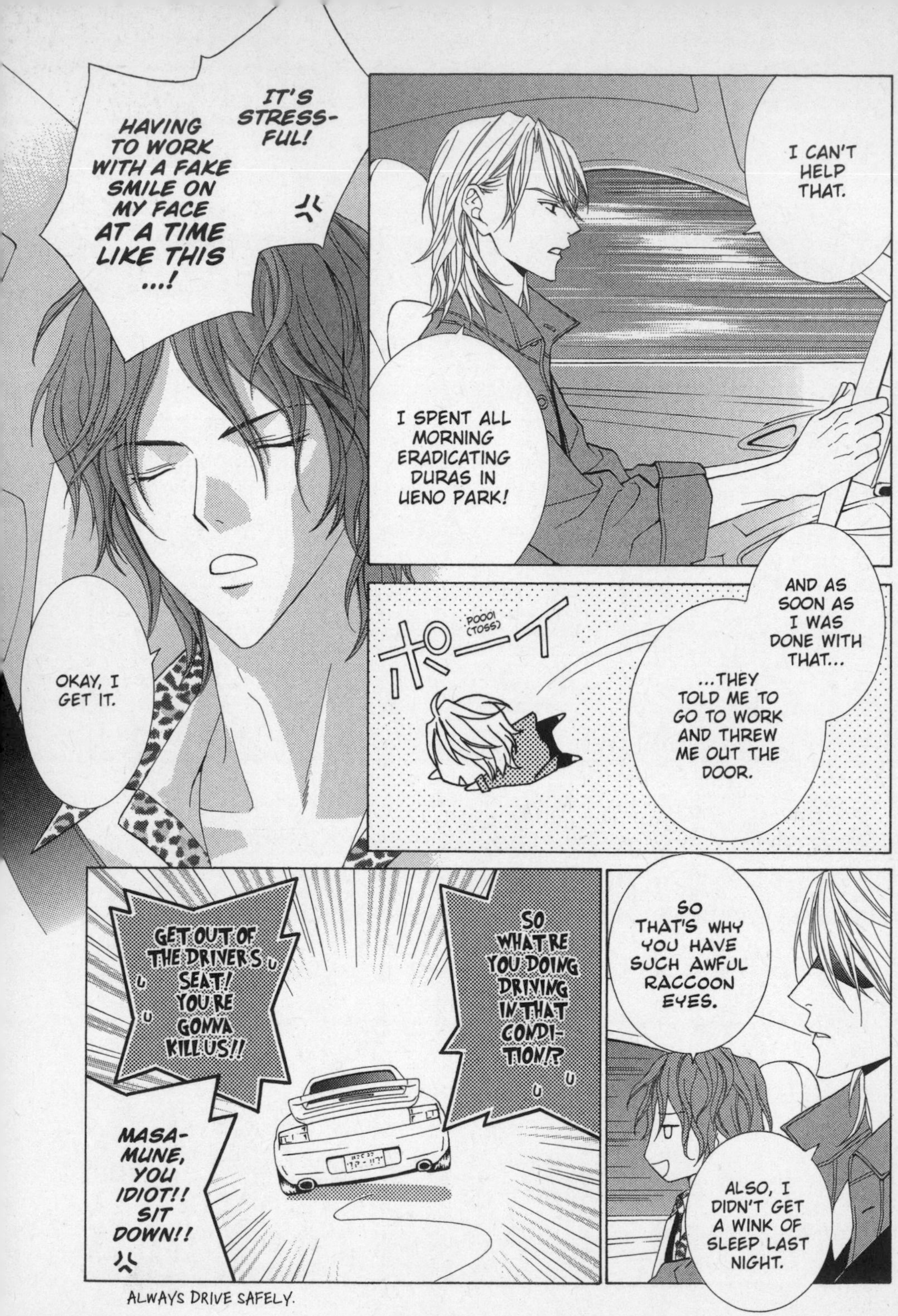
I CAN'T HELP THAT.
I SPENT ALL MORNING ERADICATING DURAS IN UENO PARK!
AND AS SOON AS I WAS DONE WITH THAT...
POOOI (TOSS)
...THEY TOLD ME TO GO TO WORK AND THREW ME OUT THE DOOR.
IT'S STRESS-FUL!
HAVING TO WORK WITH A FAKE SMILE ON MY FACE AT A TIME LIKE THIS ...!
OKAY, I GET IT.
SO THAT'S WHY YOU HAVE SUCH AWFUL RACCOON EYES.
ALSO, I DIDN'T GET A WINK OF SLEEP LAST NIGHT.
SO WHAT'RE YOU DOING DRIVING IN THAT CONDITION!?
GET OUT OF THE DRIVER'S SEAT! YOU'RE GONNA KILL US!!
MASA-MUNE, YOU IDIOT!! SIT DOWN!!

ALWAYS DRIVE SAFELY.

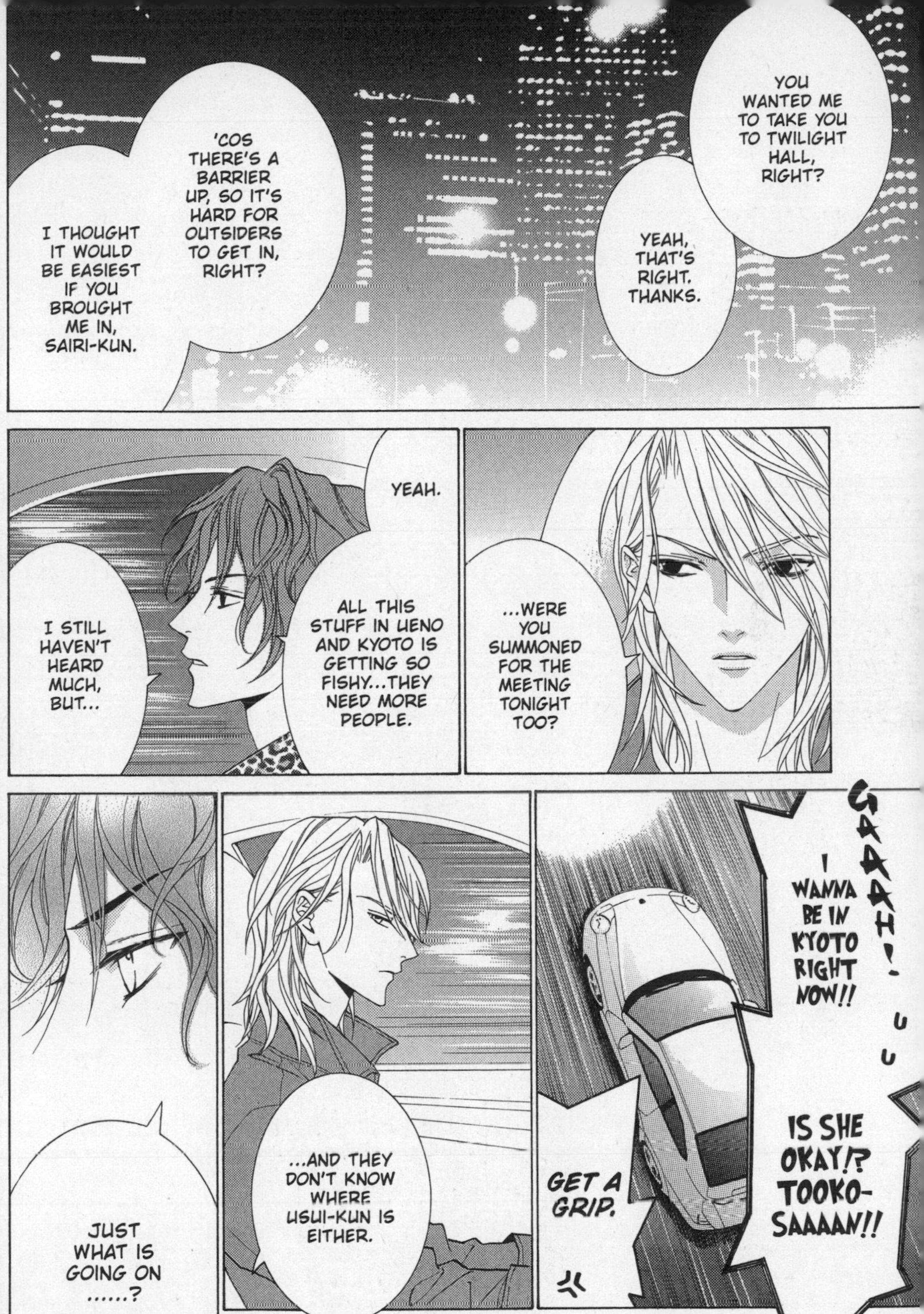
YOU WANTED ME TO TAKE YOU TO TWILIGHT HALL, RIGHT?
YEAH, THAT'S RIGHT. THANKS.
'COS THERE'S A BARRIER UP, SO IT'S HARD FOR OUTSIDERS TO GET IN, RIGHT?
I THOUGHT IT WOULD BE EASIEST IF YOU BROUGHT ME IN, SAIRI-KUN.
...WERE YOU SUMMONED FOR THE MEETING TONIGHT TOO?
YEAH.
ALL THIS STUFF IN UENO AND KYOTO IS GETTING SO FISHY...THEY NEED MORE PEOPLE.
I STILL HAVEN'T HEARD MUCH, BUT...
GAAAAH!
I WANNA BE IN KYOTO RIGHT NOW!!
UU
IS SHE OKAY!? TOOKO-SAAAAN!!
GET A GRIP.
...AND THEY DON'T KNOW WHERE USUI-KUN IS EITHER.
JUST WHAT IS GOING ON ......?

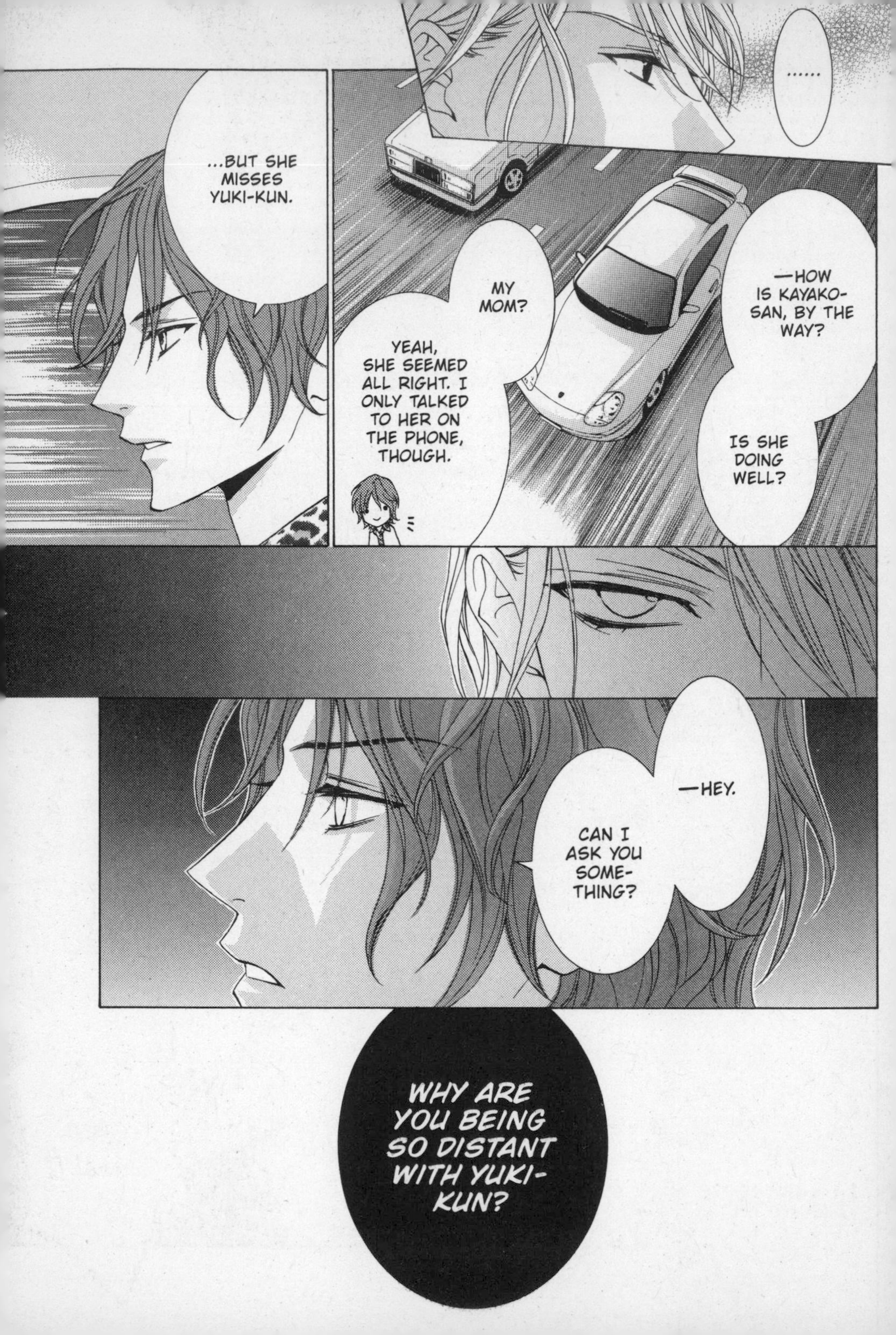
......
—HOW IS KAYAKO-SAN, BY THE WAY?
IS SHE DOING WELL?
MY MOM?
YEAH, SHE SEEMED ALL RIGHT. I ONLY TALKED TO HER ON THE PHONE, THOUGH.
...BUT SHE MISSES YUKI-KUN.
—HEY.
CAN I ASK YOU SOMETHING?
WHY ARE YOU BEING SO DISTANT WITH YUKI-KUN?

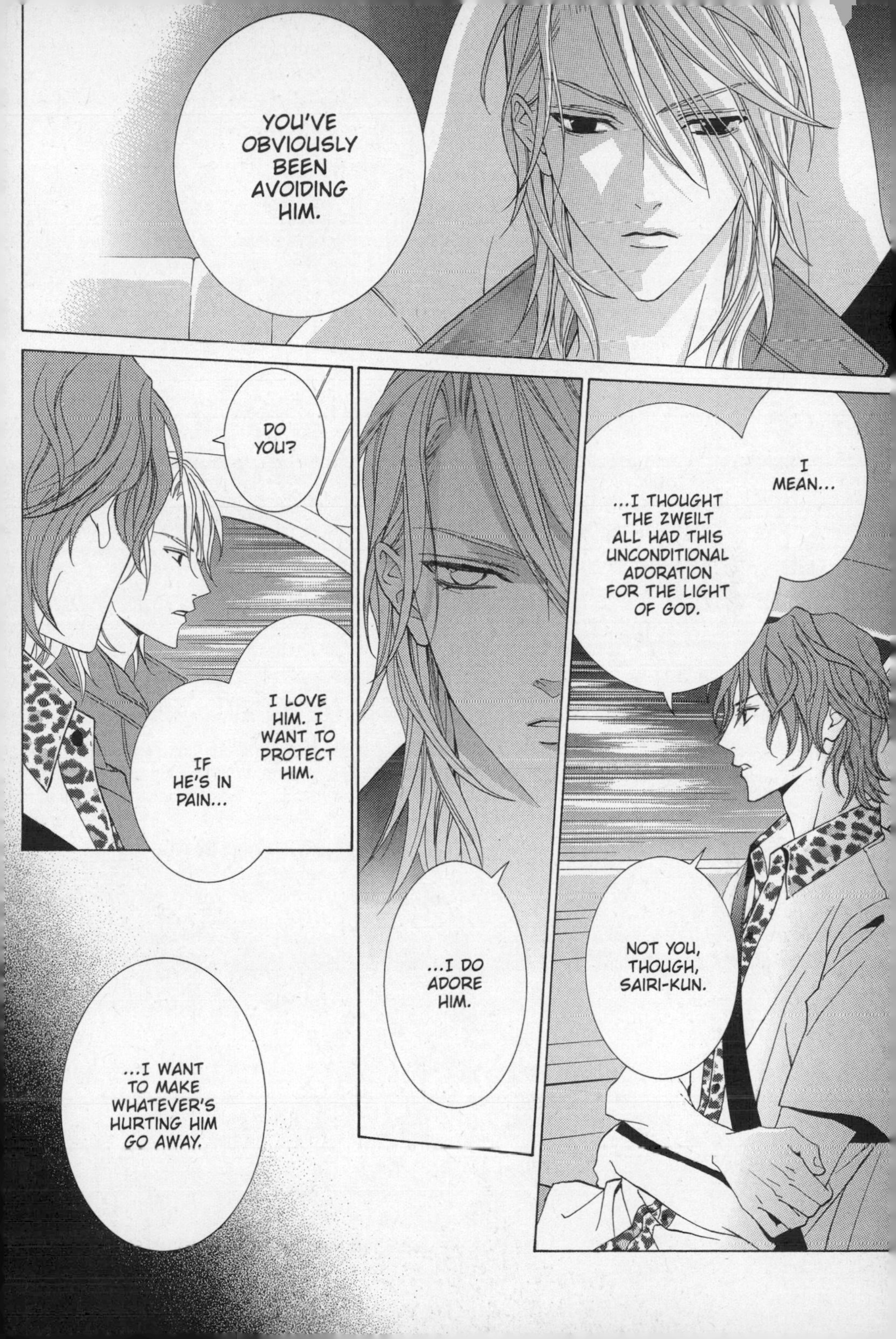

YOU'VE OBVIOUSLY BEEN AVOIDING HIM.
I MEAN...
...I THOUGHT THE ZWEILT ALL HAD THIS UNCONDITIONAL ADORATION FOR THE LIGHT OF GOD.
NOT YOU, THOUGH, SAIRI-KUN.
...I DO ADORE HIM.
DO YOU?
I LOVE HIM. I WANT TO PROTECT HIM.
IF HE'S IN PAIN...
...I WANT TO MAKE WHATEVER'S HURTING HIM GO AWAY.

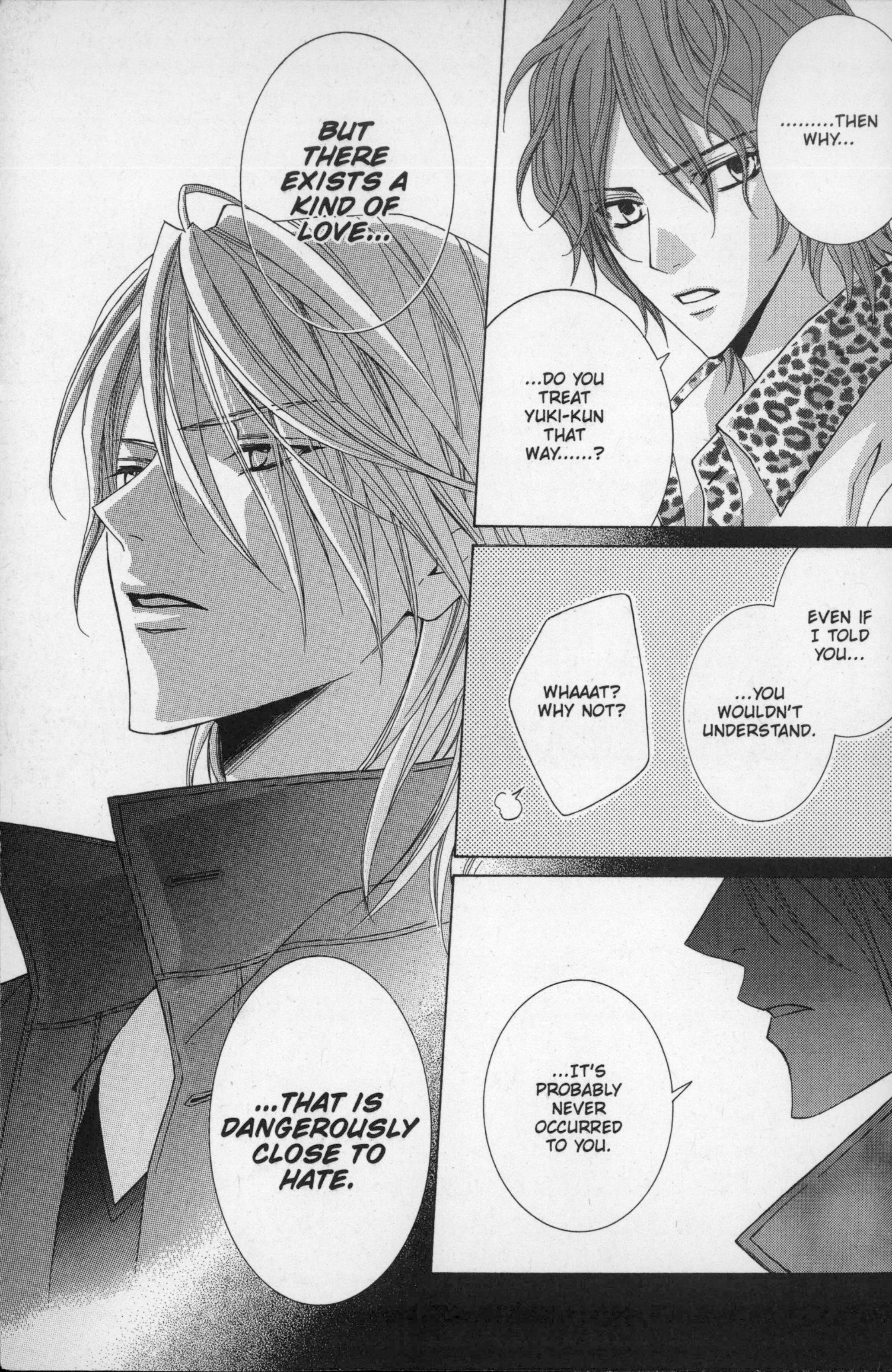
.........THEN WHY...
...DO YOU TREAT YUKI-KUN THAT WAY......?
EVEN IF I TOLD YOU...
...YOU WOULDN'T UNDERSTAND.
WHAAAT? WHY NOT?
...IT'S PROBABLY NEVER OCCURRED TO YOU.
BUT THERE EXISTS A KIND OF LOVE...
...THAT IS DANGEROUSLY CLOSE TO HATE.

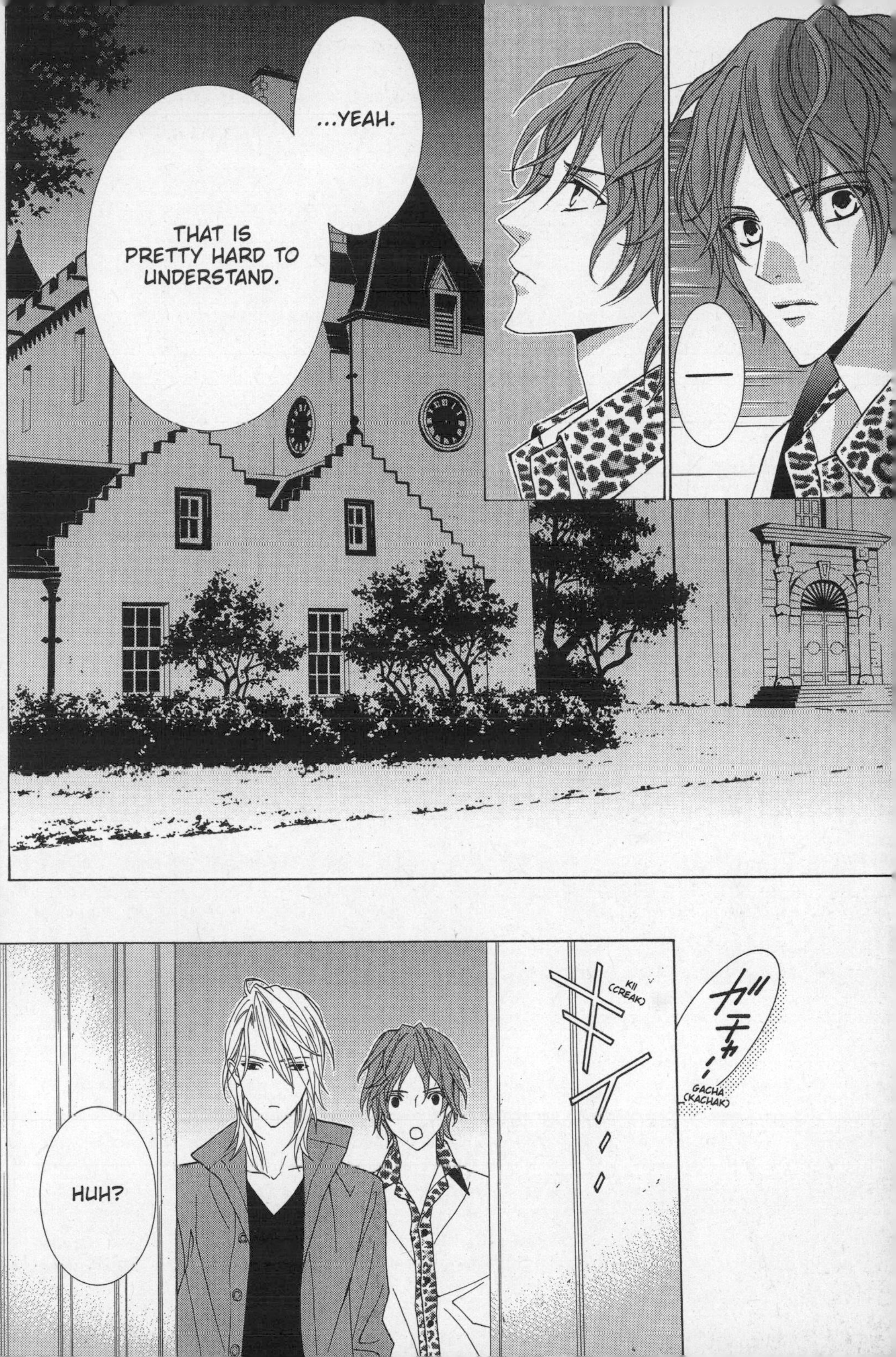
—
...YEAH.
THAT IS PRETTY HARD TO UNDERSTAND.
ガチャ!
GACHA (KACHAK)
キィ...
KII (CREAK)
HUH?

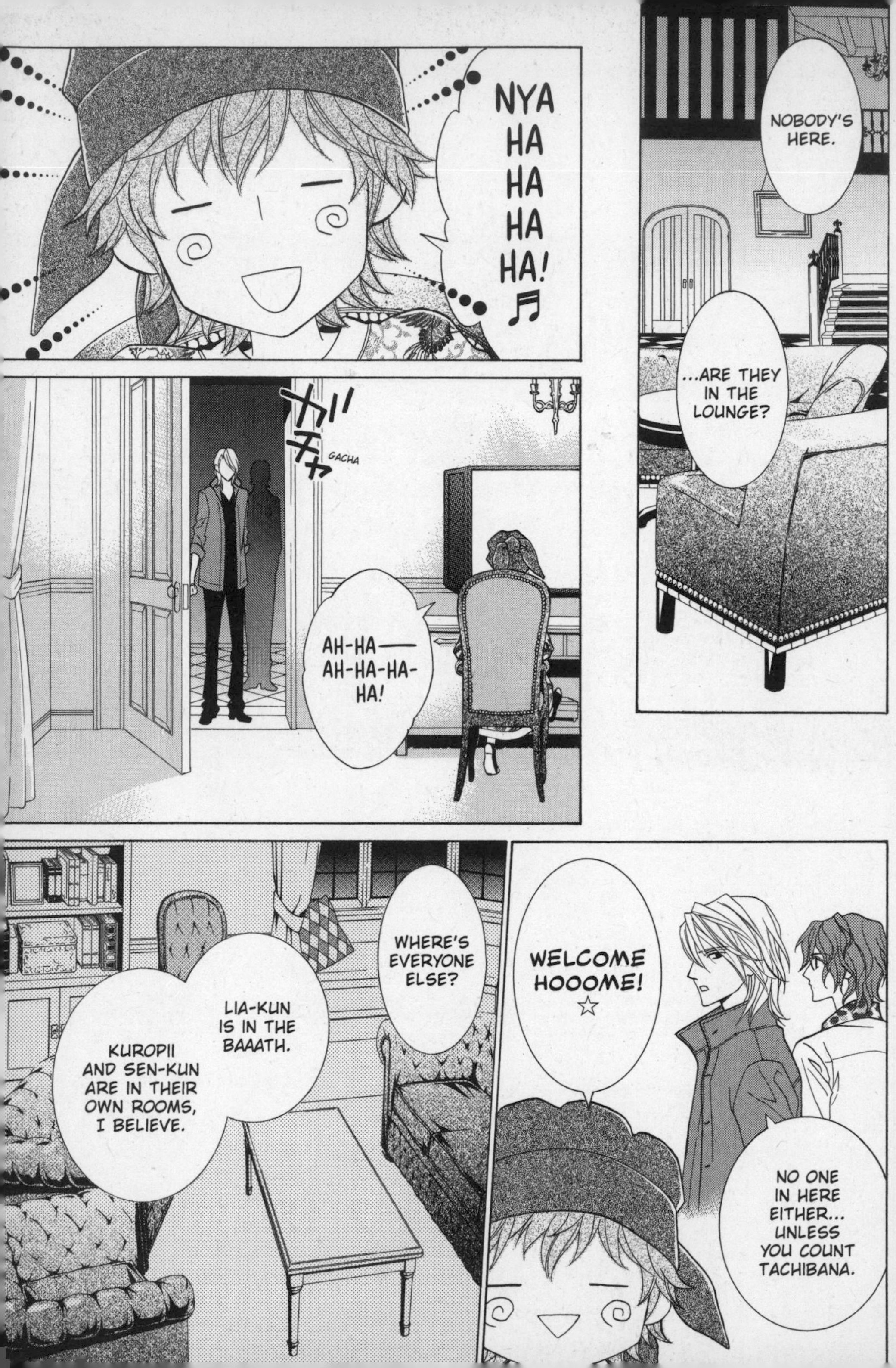
NOBODY'S HERE.
...ARE THEY IN THE LOUNGE?
NYA HA HA HA HA! ♬
GACHA
AH-HA— AH-HA-HA-HA!
WELCOME HOOOME! ☆
NO ONE IN HERE EITHER... UNLESS YOU COUNT TACHIBANA.
WHERE'S EVERYONE ELSE?
LIA-KUN IS IN THE BAAATH.
KUROPII AND SEN-KUN ARE IN THEIR OWN ROOMS, I BELIEVE.

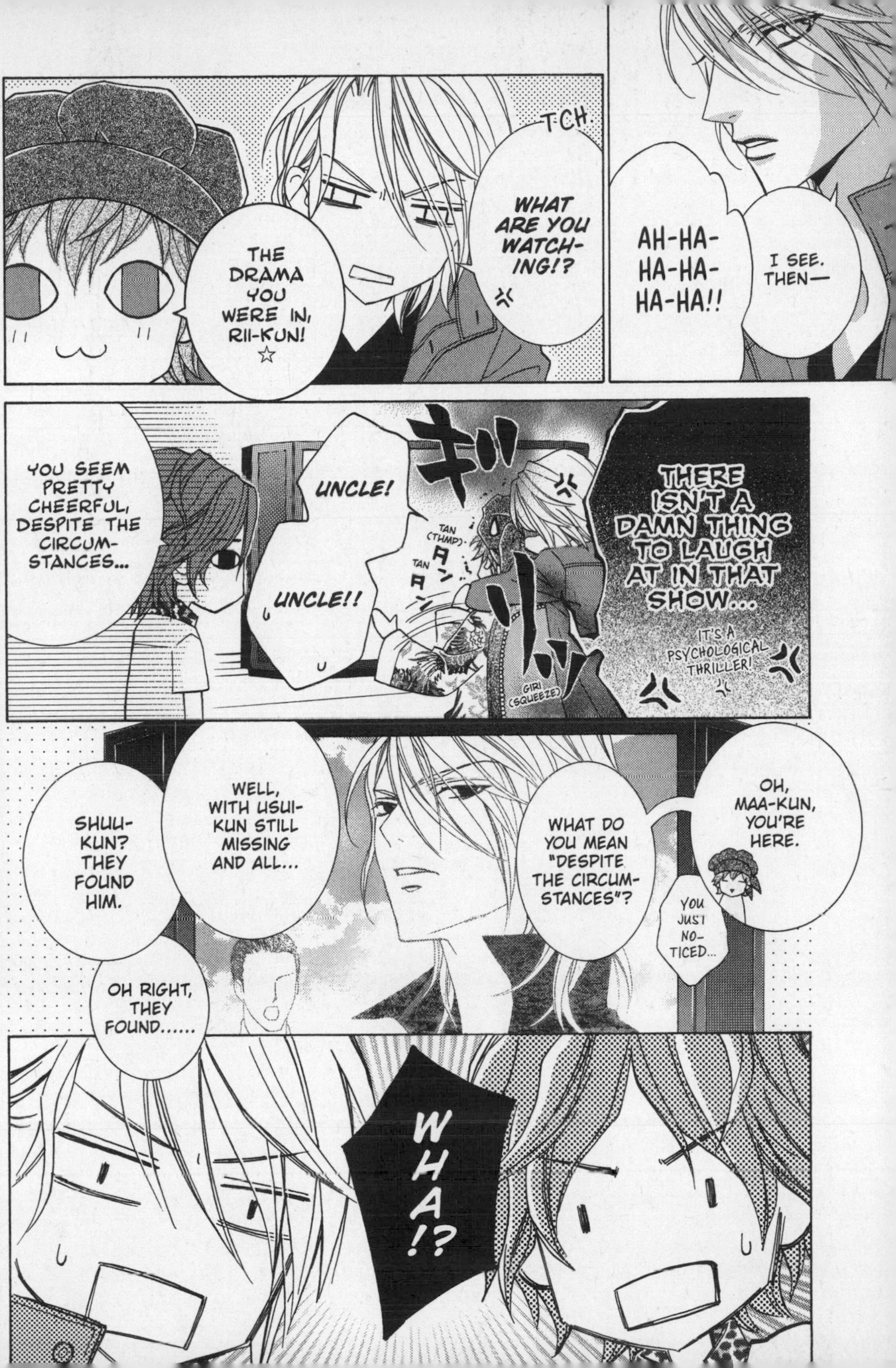
I SEE. THEN—
AH-HA-HA-HA-HA-HA!!
TCH
WHAT ARE YOU WATCHING!?
THE DRAMA YOU WERE IN, RII-KUN! ☆
THERE ISN'T A DAMN THING TO LAUGH AT IN THAT SHOW...
IT'S A PSYCHOLOGICAL THRILLER!
ギリッ
GIRI (SQUEEZE)
UNCLE!
UNCLE!!
TAN (THMP) TAN
タンタン
YOU SEEM PRETTY CHEERFUL, DESPITE THE CIRCUMSTANCES...
OH, MAA-KUN, YOU'RE HERE.
YOU JUST NOTICED...
WHAT DO YOU MEAN "DESPITE THE CIRCUMSTANCES"?
WELL, WITH USUI-KUN STILL MISSING AND ALL...
SHUU-KUN? THEY FOUND HIM.
OH RIGHT, THEY FOUND......
WHA!?

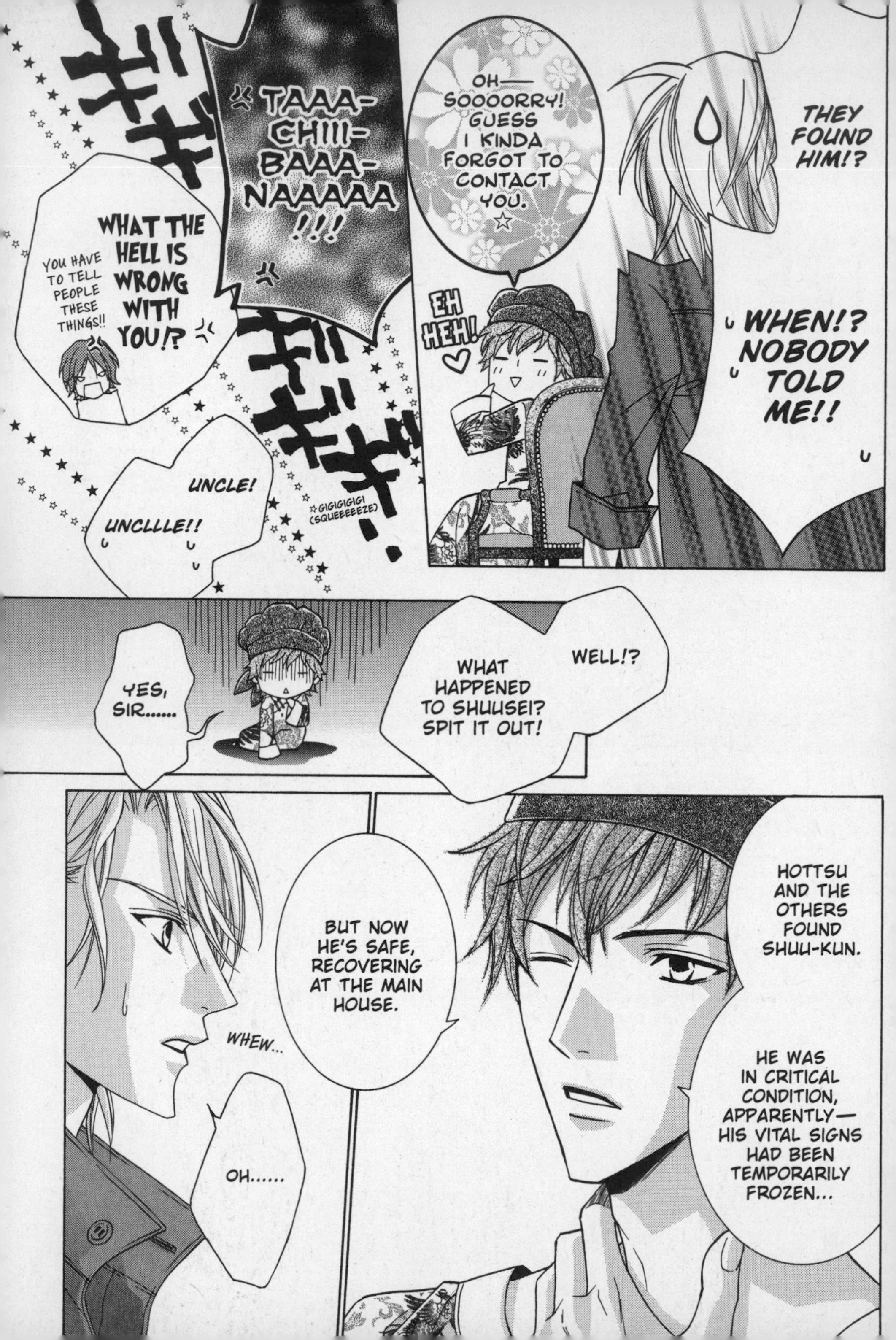
THEY FOUND HIM!?
WHEN!? NOBODY TOLD ME!!
OH— SOOOORRY! GUESS I KINDA FORGOT TO CONTACT YOU. ☆
EH HEH! ♥
TAAA-CHIII-BAAA-NAAAAAA!!!
WHAT THE HELL IS WRONG WITH YOU!?
YOU HAVE TO TELL PEOPLE THESE THINGS!!
☆GIGIGIGIGI (SQUEEEEEZE)
UNCLE!
UNCLLLE!!
WELL!?
WHAT HAPPENED TO SHUUSEI? SPIT IT OUT!
YES, SIR......
HOTTSU AND THE OTHERS FOUND SHUU-KUN.
HE WAS IN CRITICAL CONDITION, APPARENTLY— HIS VITAL SIGNS HAD BEEN TEMPORARILY FROZEN...
BUT NOW HE'S SAFE, RECOVERING AT THE MAIN HOUSE.
WHEW...
OH......

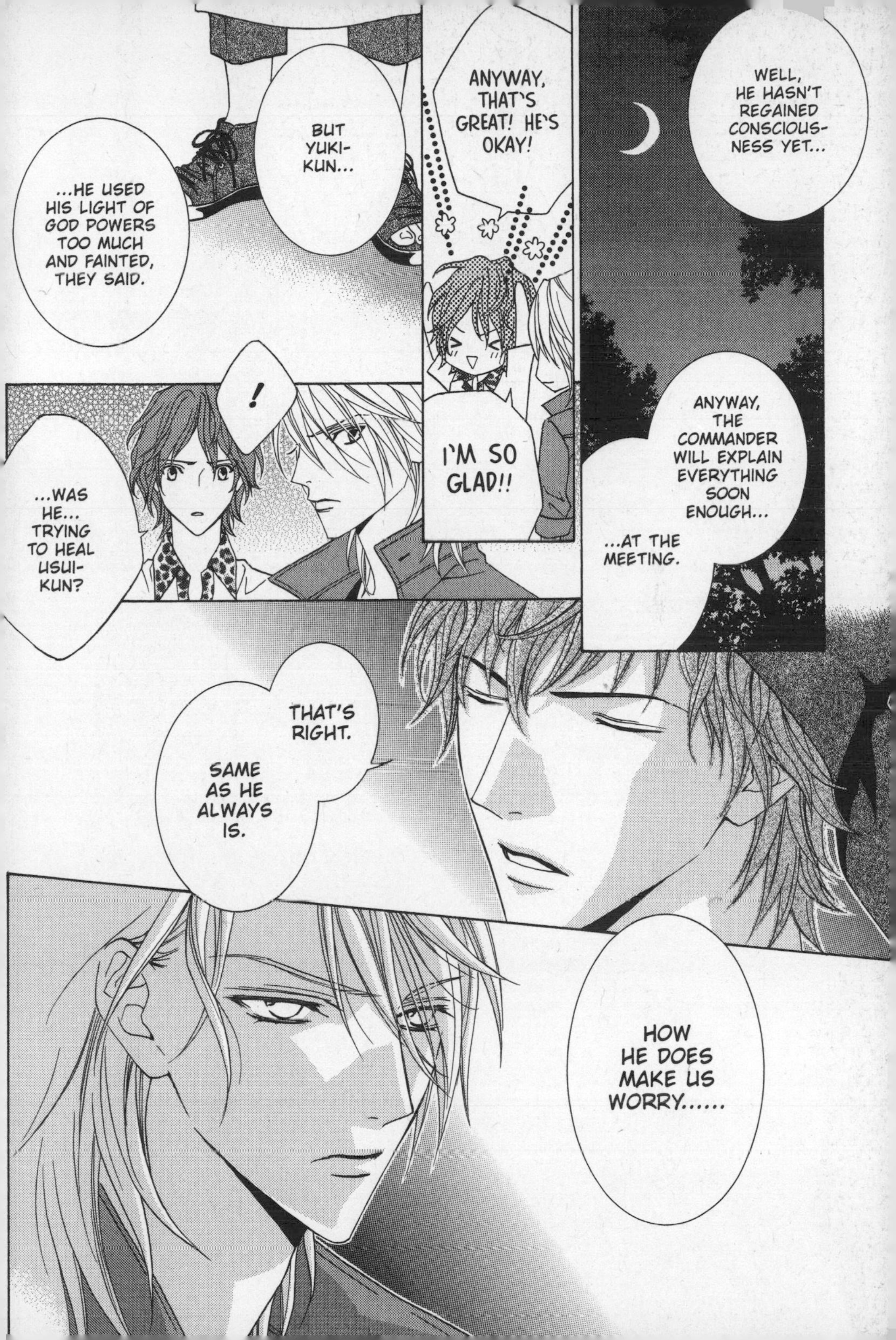
WELL, HE HASN'T REGAINED CONSCIOUSNESS YET...
ANYWAY, THE COMMANDER WILL EXPLAIN EVERYTHING SOON ENOUGH...
...AT THE MEETING.
ANYWAY, THAT'S GREAT! HE'S OKAY!
I'M SO GLAD!!
BUT YUKI-KUN...
...HE USED HIS LIGHT OF GOD POWERS TOO MUCH AND FAINTED, THEY SAID.
!
...WAS HE... TRYING TO HEAL USUI-KUN?
THAT'S RIGHT.
SAME AS HE ALWAYS IS.
HOW HE DOES MAKE US WORRY......

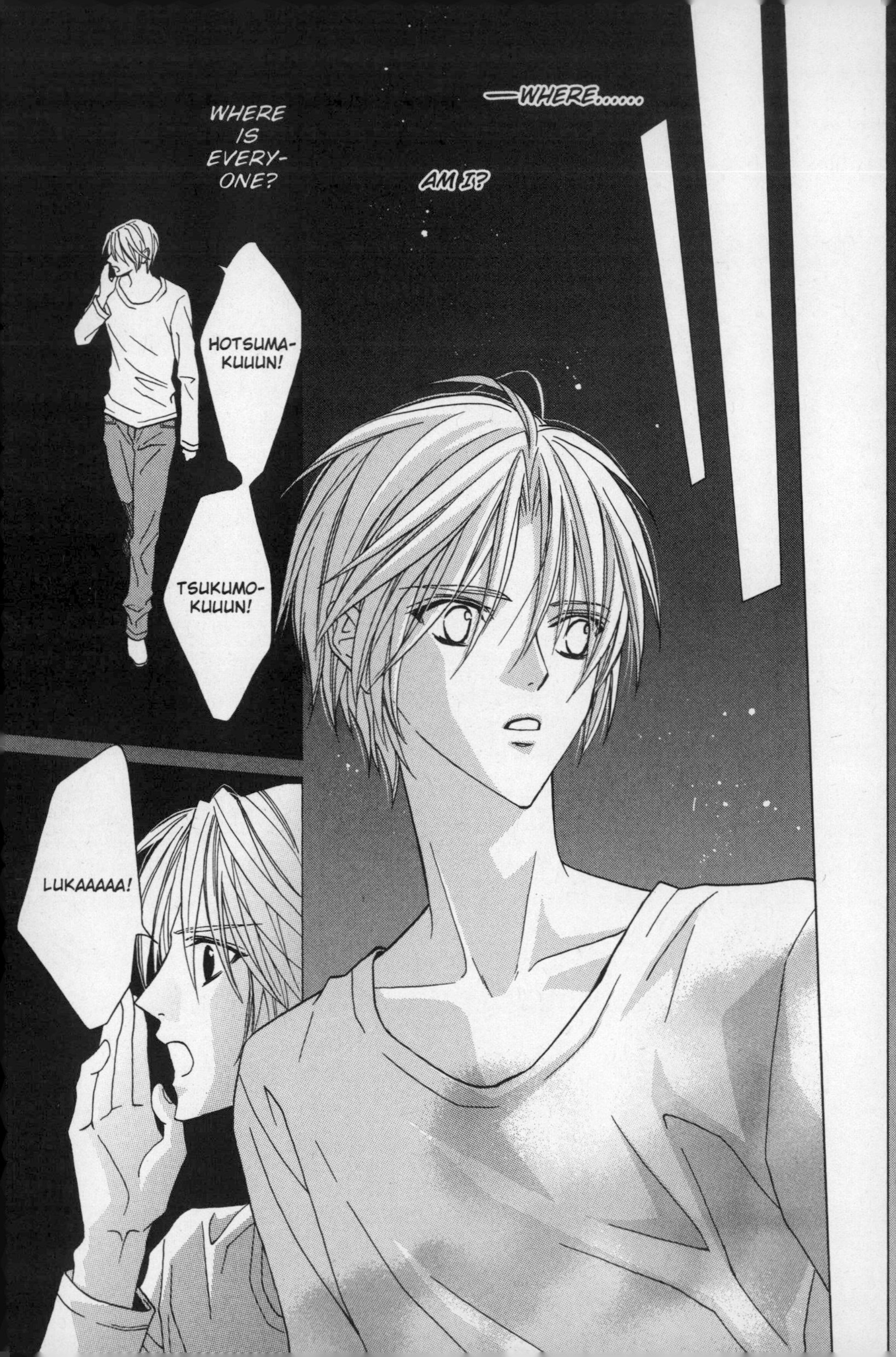
—WHERE......
AM I?
WHERE IS EVERYONE?
HOTSUMA-KUUUN!
TSUKUMO-KUUUN!
LUKAAAAA!

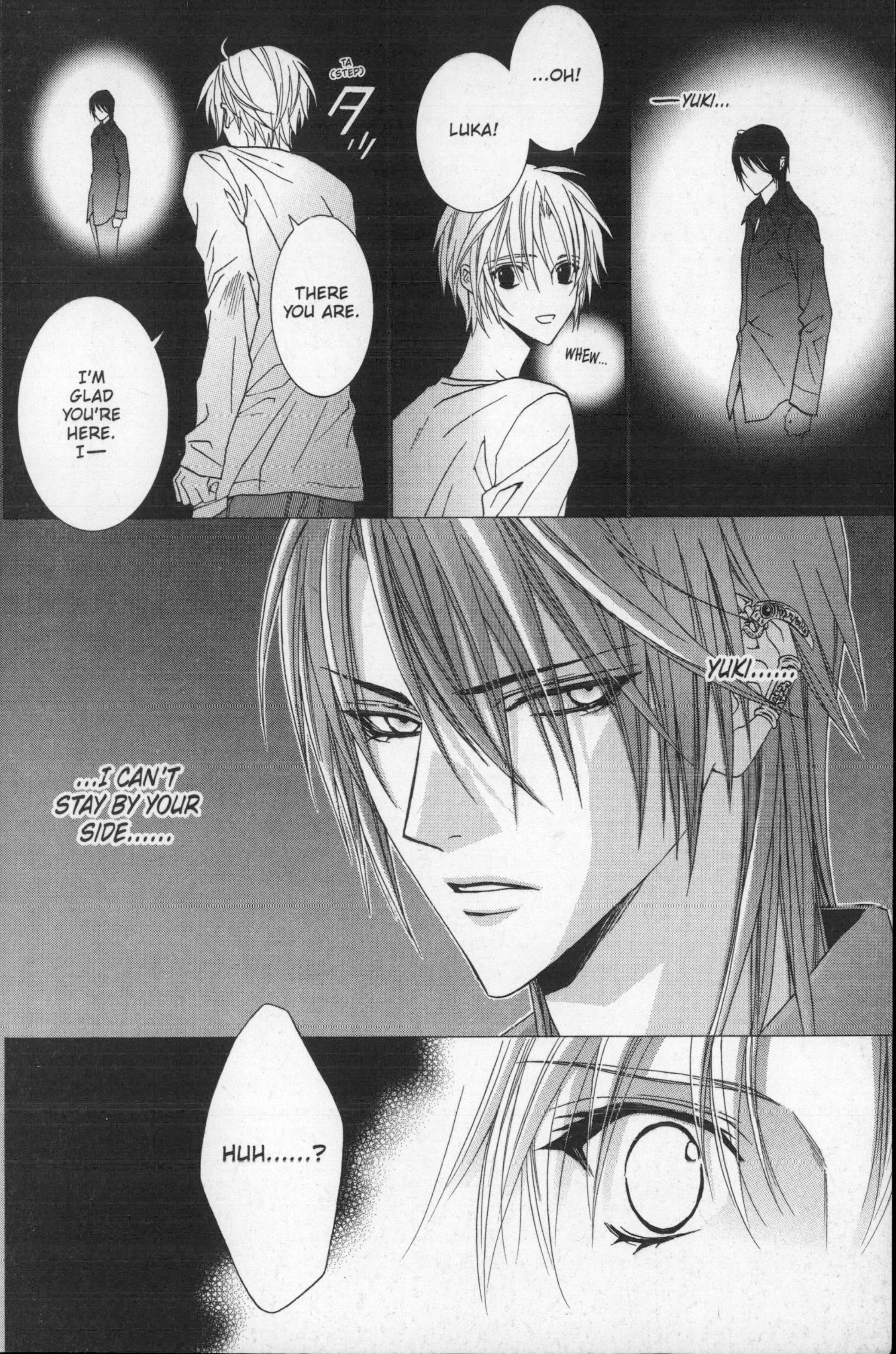
—YUKI...
...OH!
LUKA!
WHEW...
TA (STEP)
THERE YOU ARE.
I'M GLAD YOU'RE HERE. I—
YUKI......
...I CAN'T STAY BY YOUR SIDE......
HUH......?

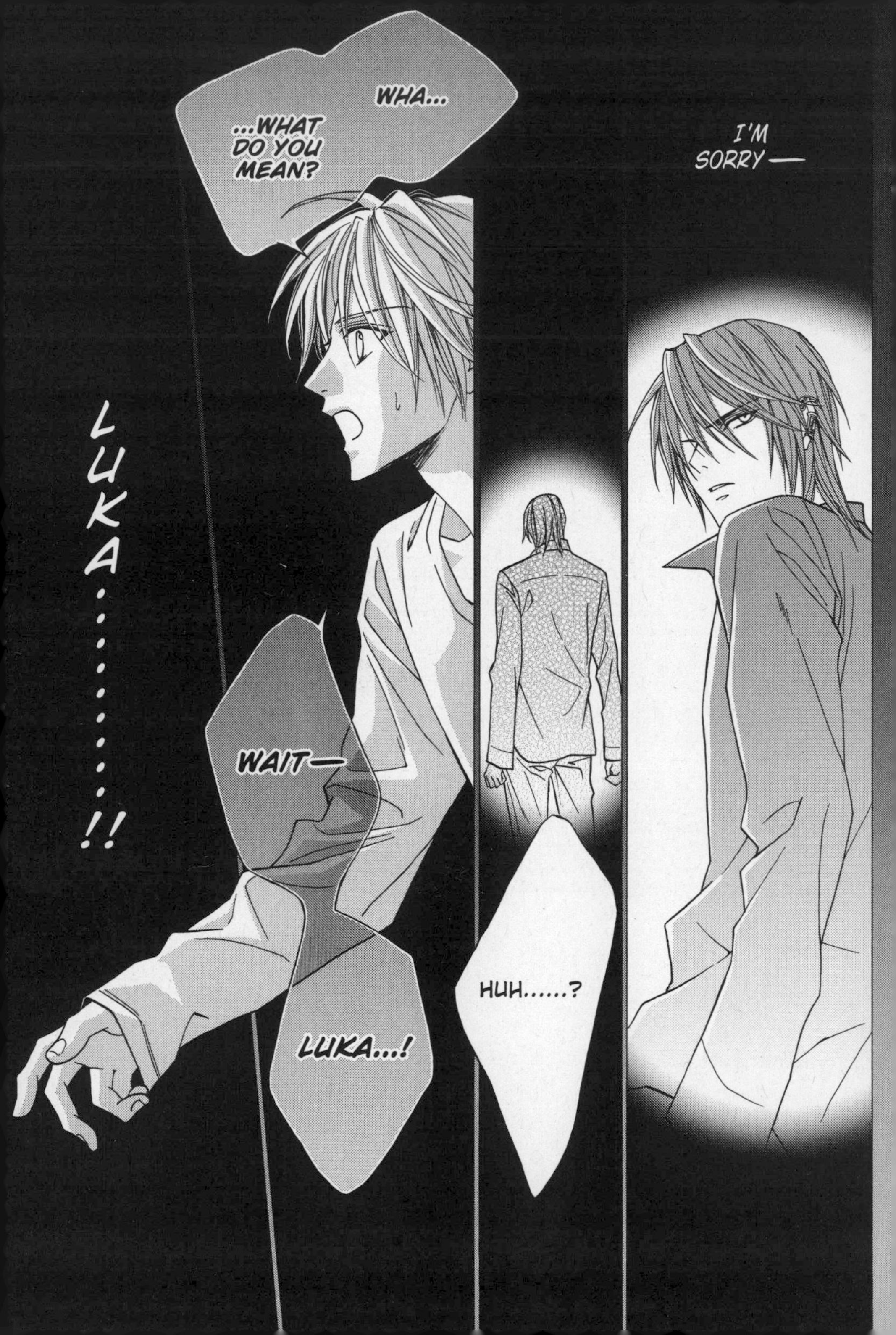

I'M SORRY—
HUH......?
WHA... ...WHAT DO YOU MEAN?
WAIT—
LUKA...!
LUKA.........!!

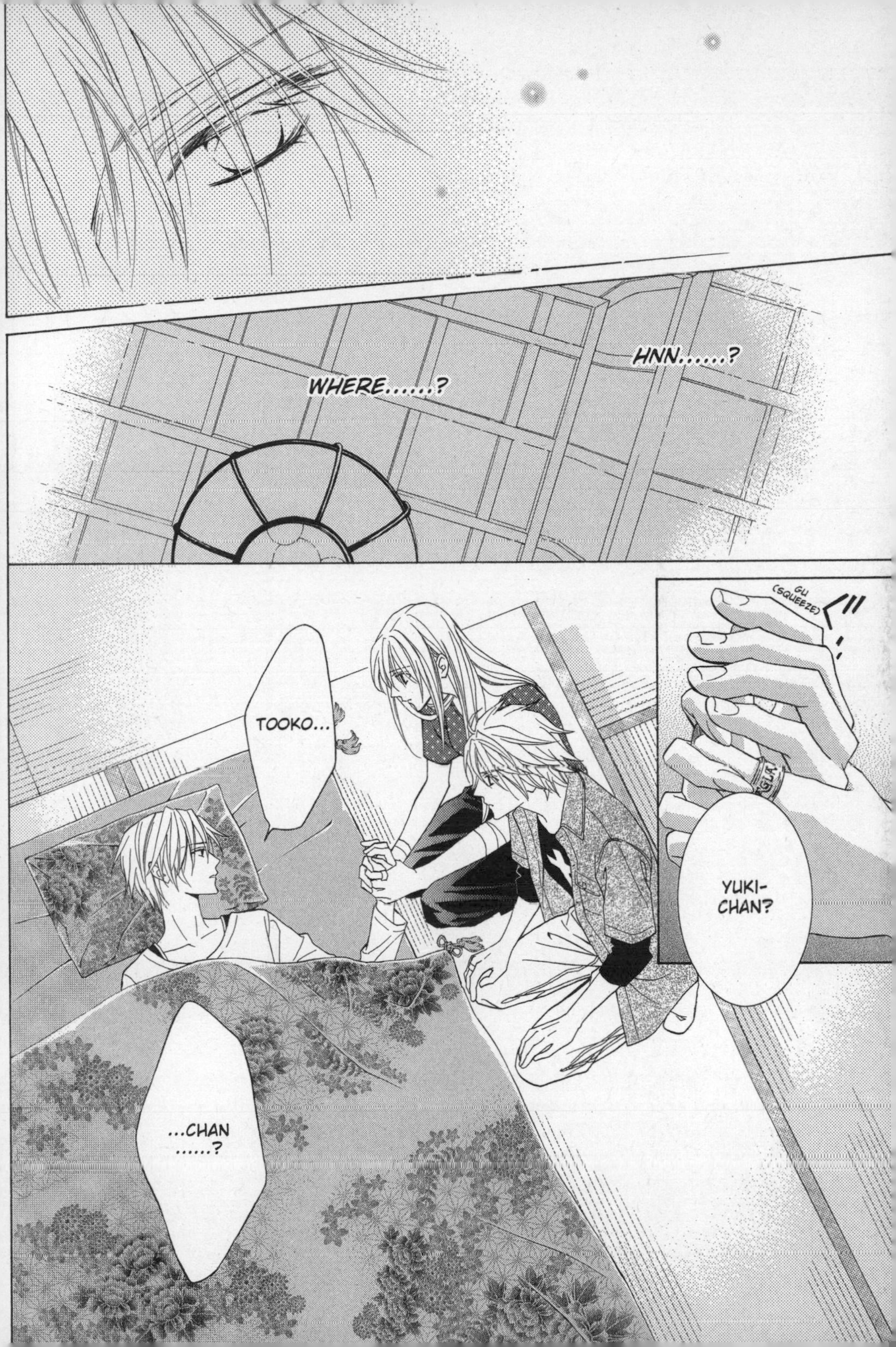
HNN......?
WHERE......?
GU (SQUEEZE)
YUKI-CHAN?
TOOKO...
...CHAN ......?

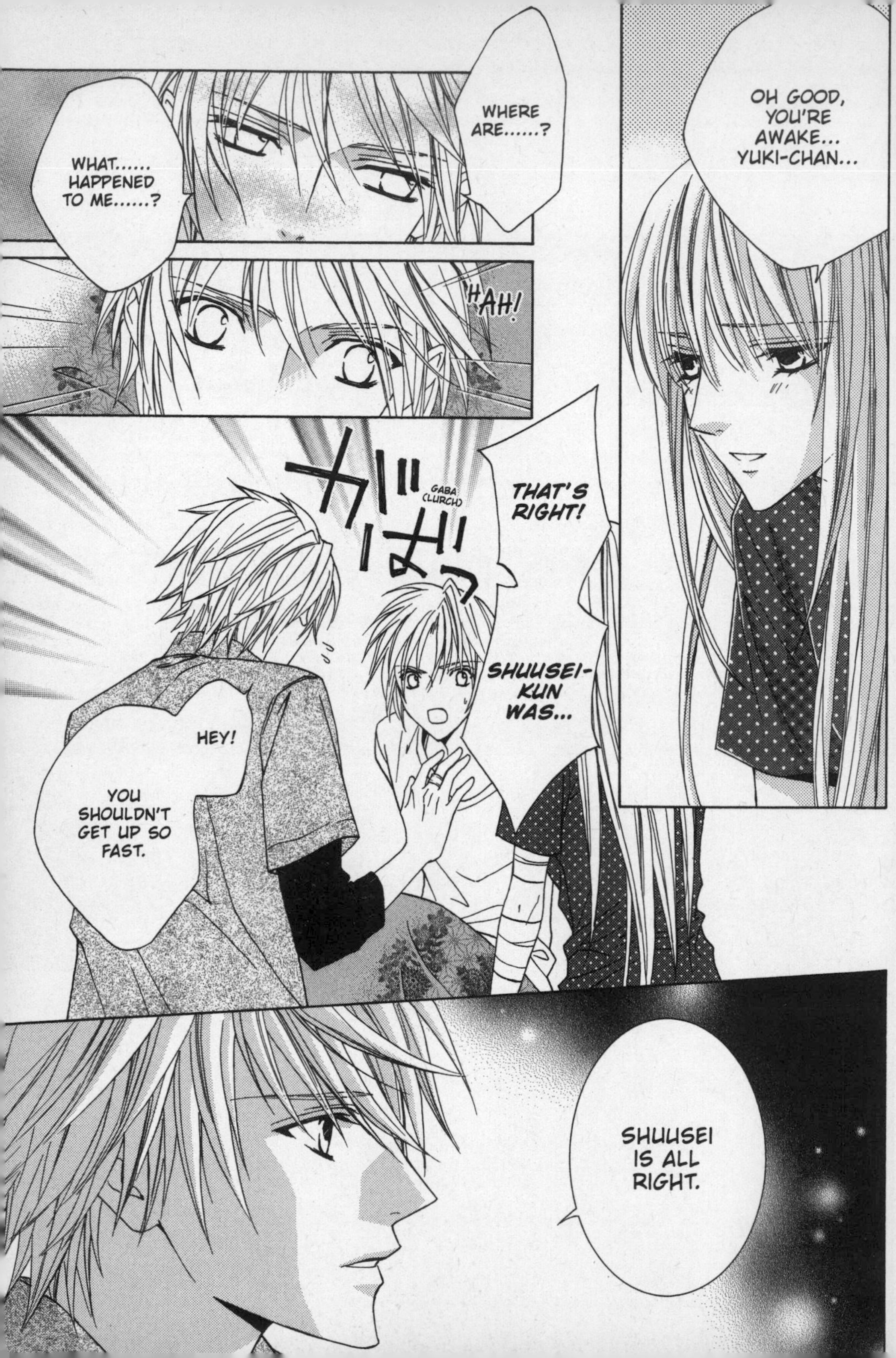
OH GOOD, YOU'RE AWAKE... YUKI-CHAN...
WHERE ARE......?
WHAT...... HAPPENED TO ME......?
HAH!
GABA (LURCH)
THAT'S RIGHT!
SHUUSEI-KUN WAS...
HEY!
YOU SHOULDN'T GET UP SO FAST.
SHUUSEI IS ALL RIGHT.

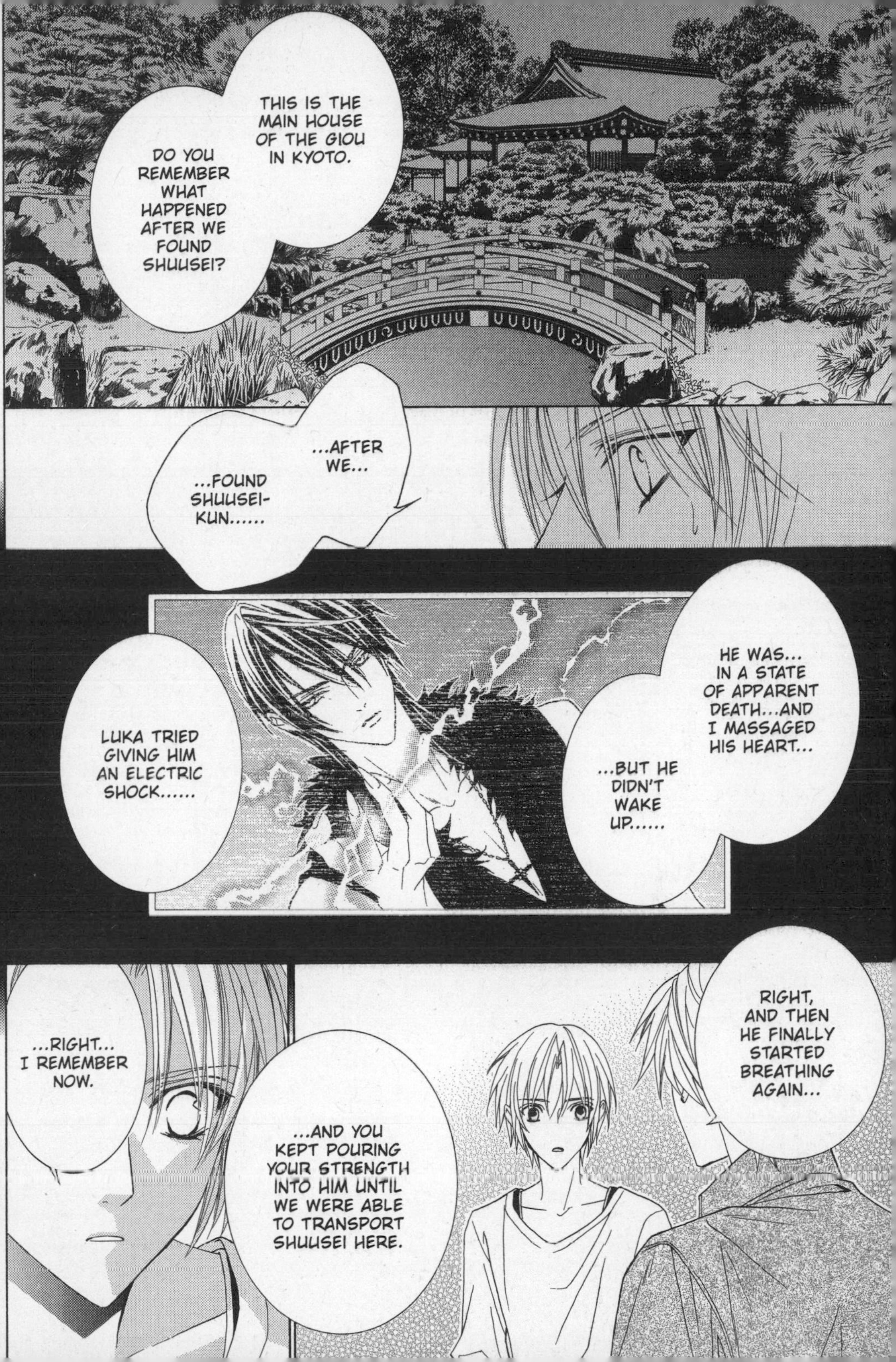
THIS IS THE MAIN HOUSE OF THE GIOU IN KYOTO.
DO YOU REMEMBER WHAT HAPPENED AFTER WE FOUND SHUUSEI?
...AFTER WE...
...FOUND SHUUSEI-KUN......
HE WAS... IN A STATE OF APPARENT DEATH...AND I MASSAGED HIS HEART...
...BUT HE DIDN'T WAKE UP......
LUKA TRIED GIVING HIM AN ELECTRIC SHOCK......
RIGHT, AND THEN HE FINALLY STARTED BREATHING AGAIN...
...AND YOU KEPT POURING YOUR STRENGTH INTO HIM UNTIL WE WERE ABLE TO TRANSPORT SHUUSEI HERE.
...RIGHT... I REMEMBER NOW.

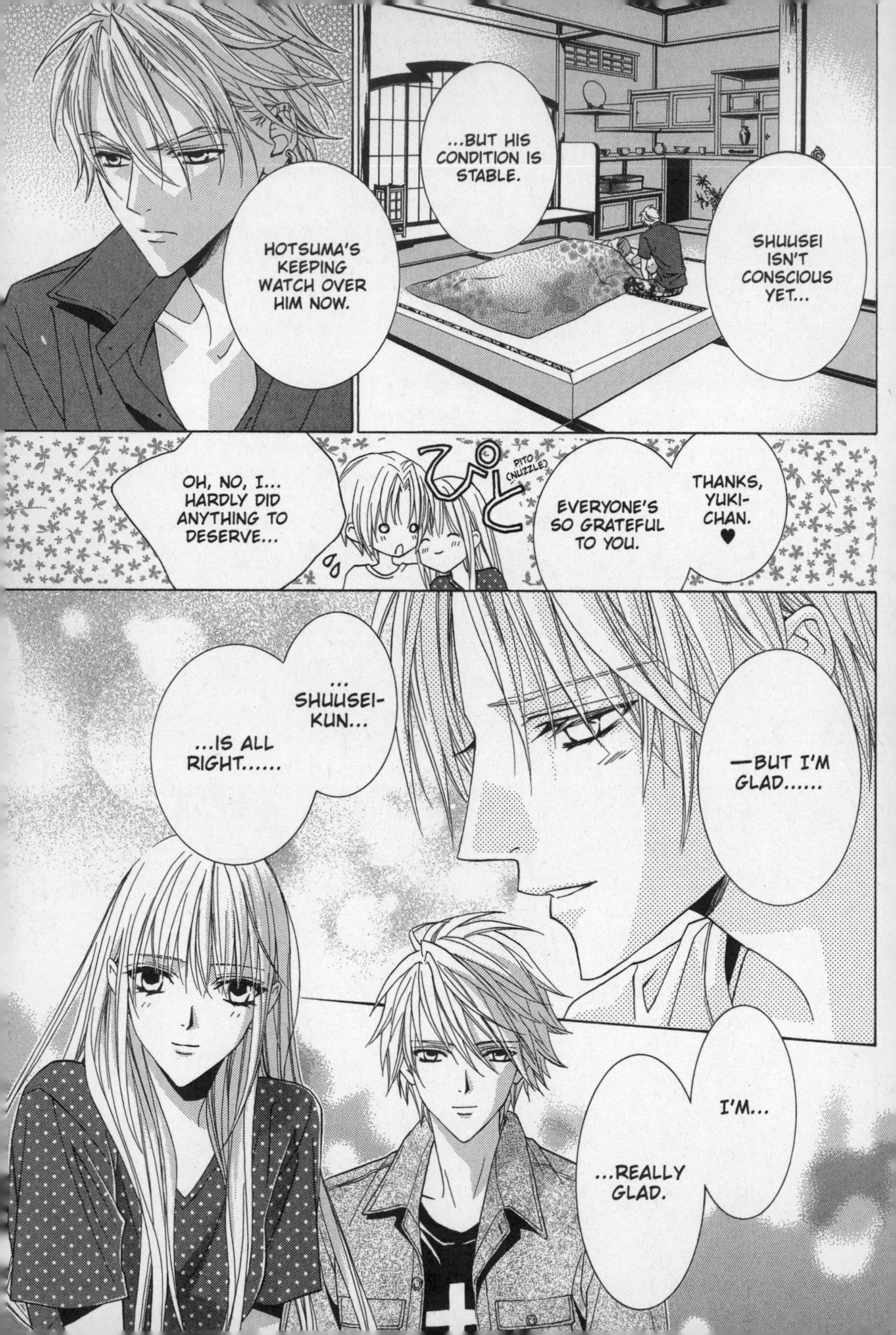
SHUUSEI ISN'T CONSCIOUS YET...
...BUT HIS CONDITION IS STABLE.
HOTSUMA'S KEEPING WATCH OVER HIM NOW.
THANKS, YUKI-CHAN. ♥
EVERYONE'S SO GRATEFUL TO YOU.
ぴと
PITO (NUZZLE)
OH, NO, I... HARDLY DID ANYTHING TO DESERVE...
—BUT I'M GLAD......
... SHUUSEI-KUN...
...IS ALL RIGHT......
I'M...
...REALLY GLAD.

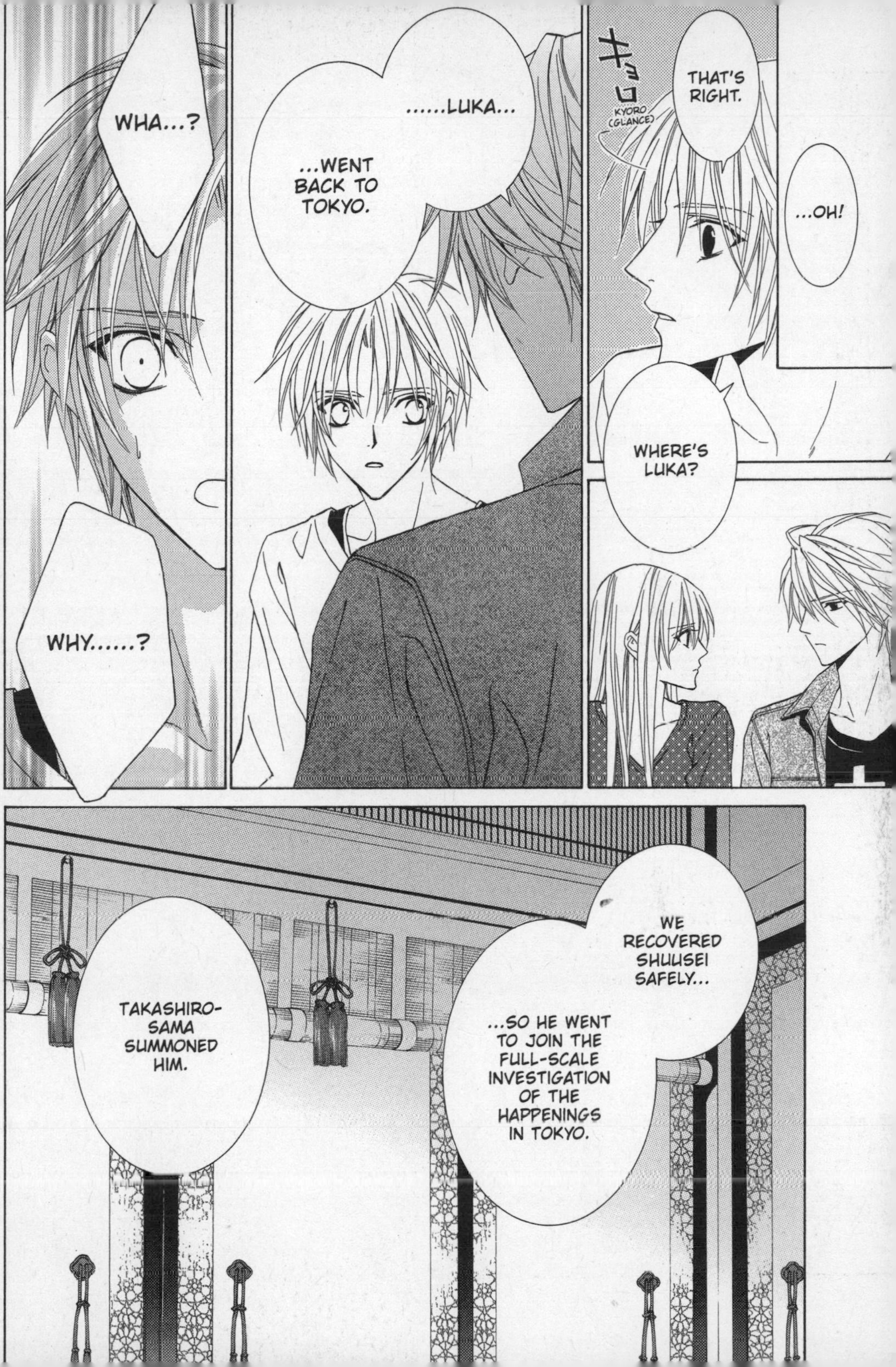
...OH!
キョロ
KYORO (GLANCE)
THAT'S RIGHT.
WHERE'S LUKA?
......LUKA...
...WENT BACK TO TOKYO.
WHA...?
WHY......?
WE RECOVERED SHUUSEI SAFELY...
...SO HE WENT TO JOIN THE FULL-SCALE INVESTIGATION OF THE HAPPENINGS IN TOKYO.
TAKASHIRO-SAMA SUMMONED HIM.

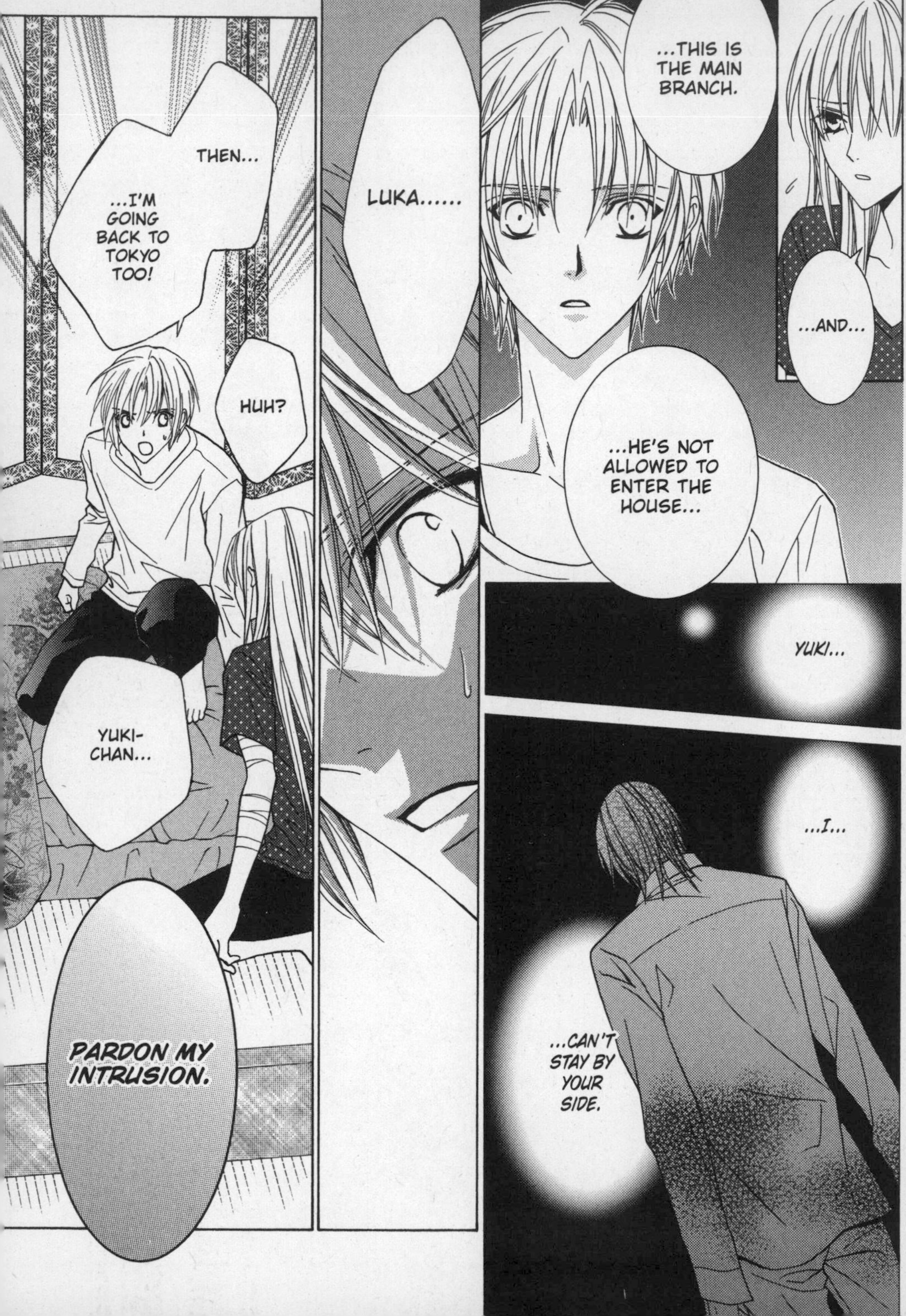
...THIS IS THE MAIN BRANCH.
...AND...
...HE'S NOT ALLOWED TO ENTER THE HOUSE...
YUKI...
...I...
...CAN'T STAY BY YOUR SIDE.
LUKA......
THEN...
...I'M GOING BACK TO TOKYO TOO!
HUH?
YUKI-CHAN...
PARDON MY INTRUSION.

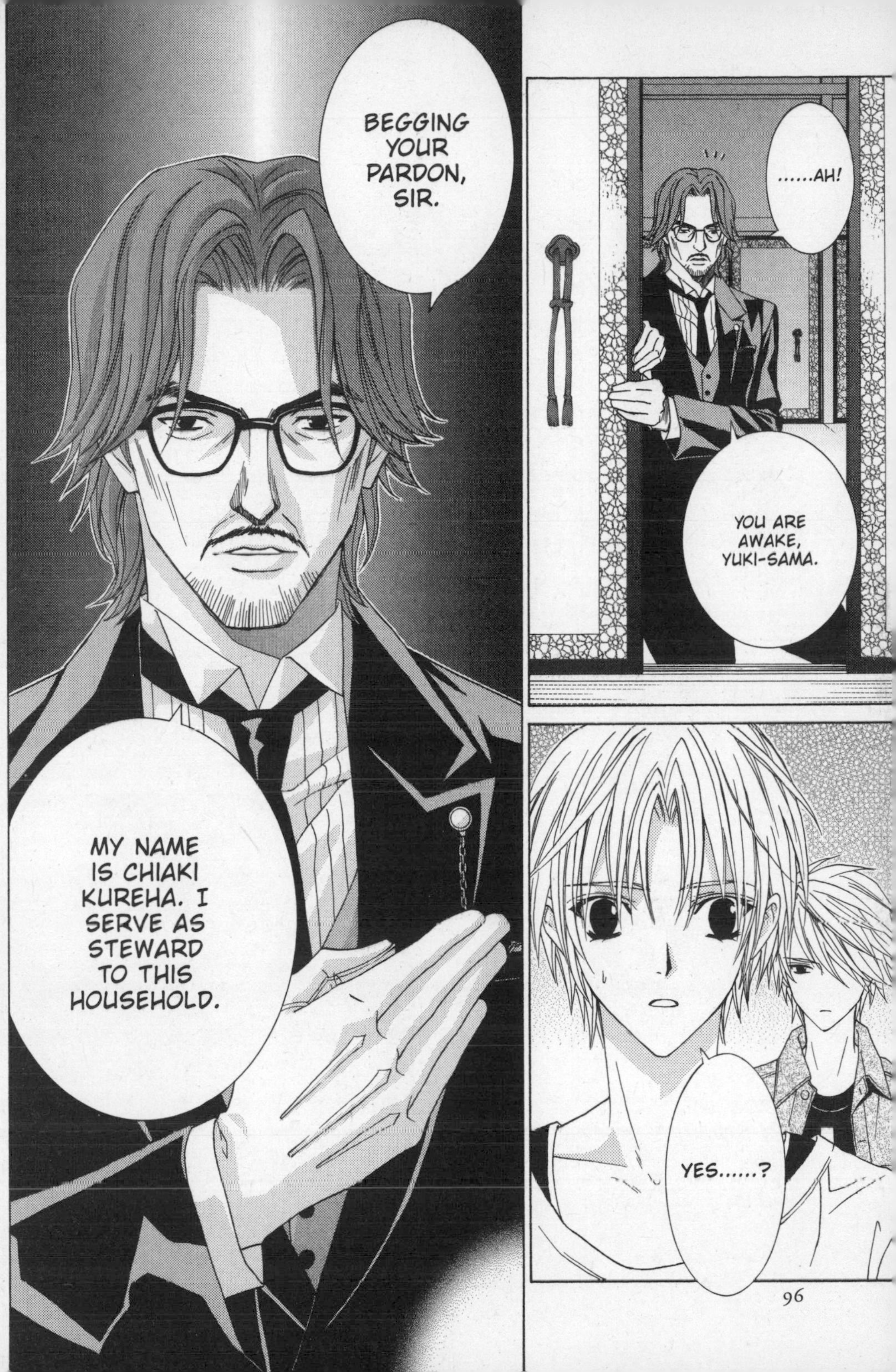
......AH!
YOU ARE AWAKE, YUKI-SAMA.
YES......?
BEGGING YOUR PARDON, SIR.
MY NAME IS CHIAKI KUREHA. I SERVE AS STEWARD TO THIS HOUSEHOLD.

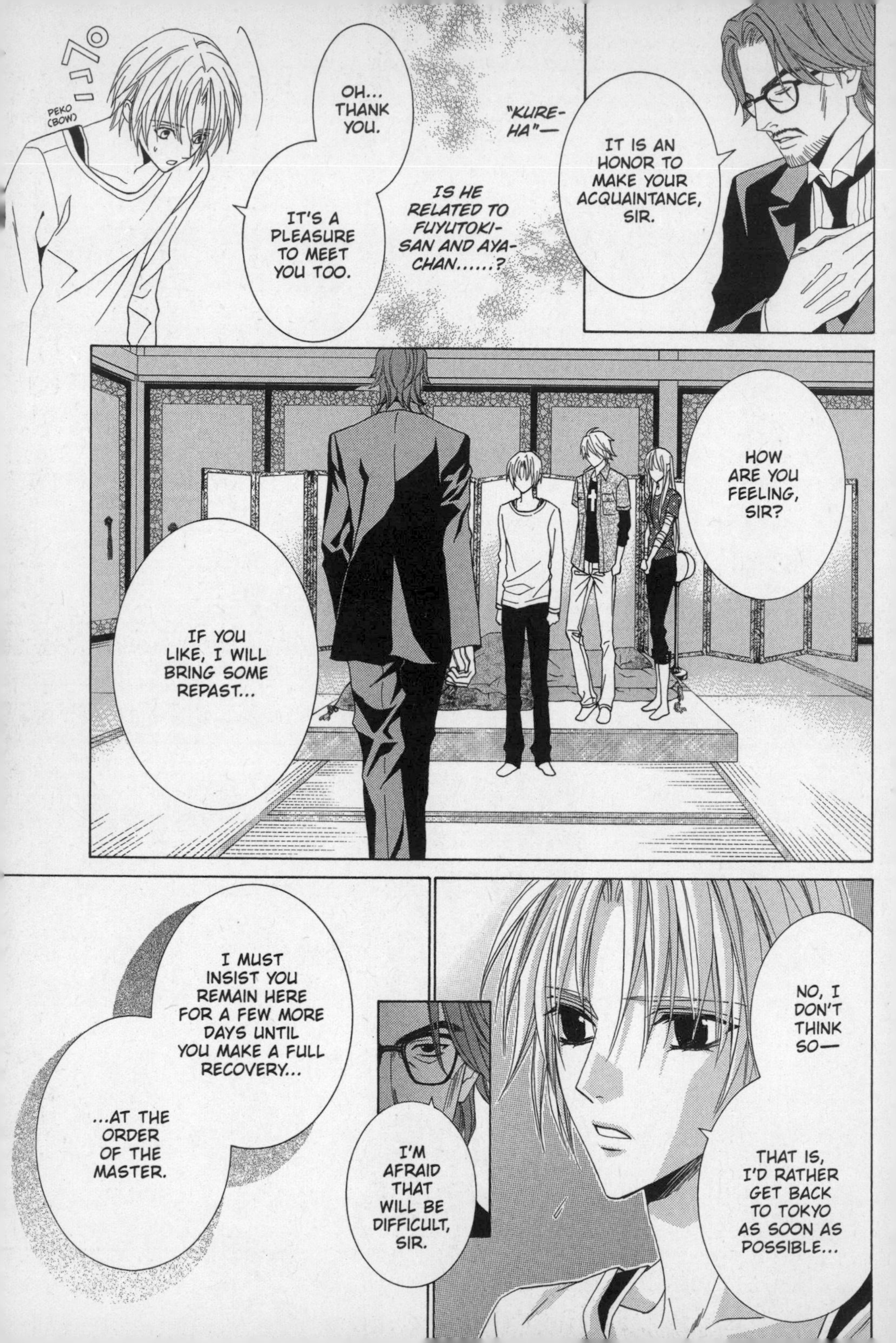
IT IS AN HONOR TO MAKE YOUR ACQUAINTANCE, SIR.
"KUREHA"—
IS HE RELATED TO FUYUTOKI-SAN AND AYA-CHAN......?
OH... THANK YOU.
IT'S A PLEASURE TO MEET YOU TOO.
PEKO (BOW)
HOW ARE YOU FEELING, SIR?
IF YOU LIKE, I WILL BRING SOME REPAST...
NO, I DON'T THINK SO—
THAT IS, I'D RATHER GET BACK TO TOKYO AS SOON AS POSSIBLE...
I'M AFRAID THAT WILL BE DIFFICULT, SIR.
I MUST INSIST YOU REMAIN HERE FOR A FEW MORE DAYS UNTIL YOU MAKE A FULL RECOVERY...
...AT THE ORDER OF THE MASTER.

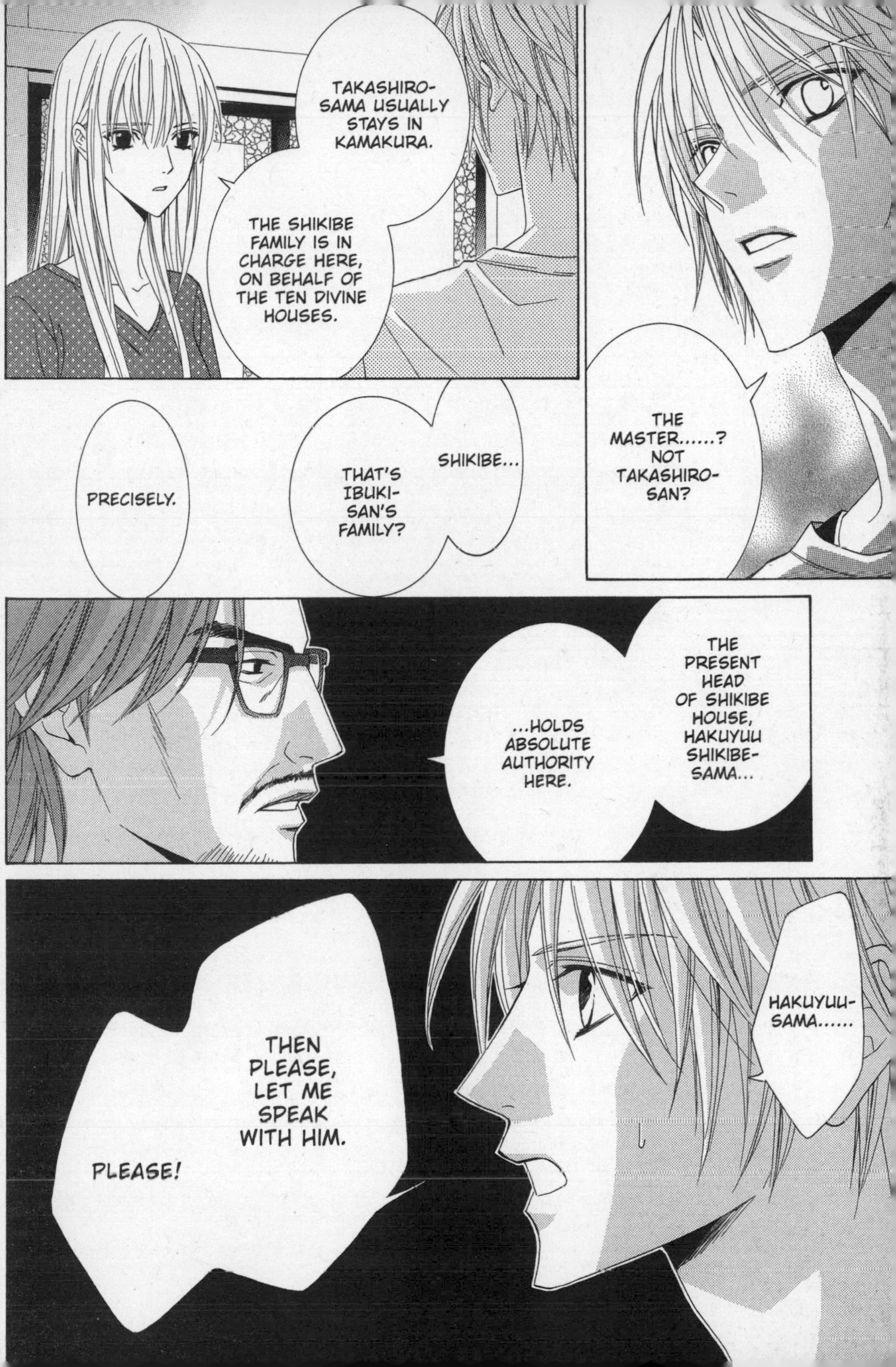
THE MASTER......? NOT TAKASHIRO-SAN?
TAKASHIRO-SAMA USUALLY STAYS IN KAMAKURA.
THE SHIKIBE FAMILY IS IN CHARGE HERE, ON BEHALF OF THE TEN DIVINE HOUSES.
SHIKIBE...
THAT'S IBUKI-SAN'S FAMILY?
PRECISELY.
THE PRESENT HEAD OF SHIKIBE HOUSE, HAKUYUU SHIKIBE-SAMA...
...HOLDS ABSOLUTE AUTHORITY HERE.
HAKUYUU-SAMA......
THEN PLEASE, LET ME SPEAK WITH HIM.
PLEASE!

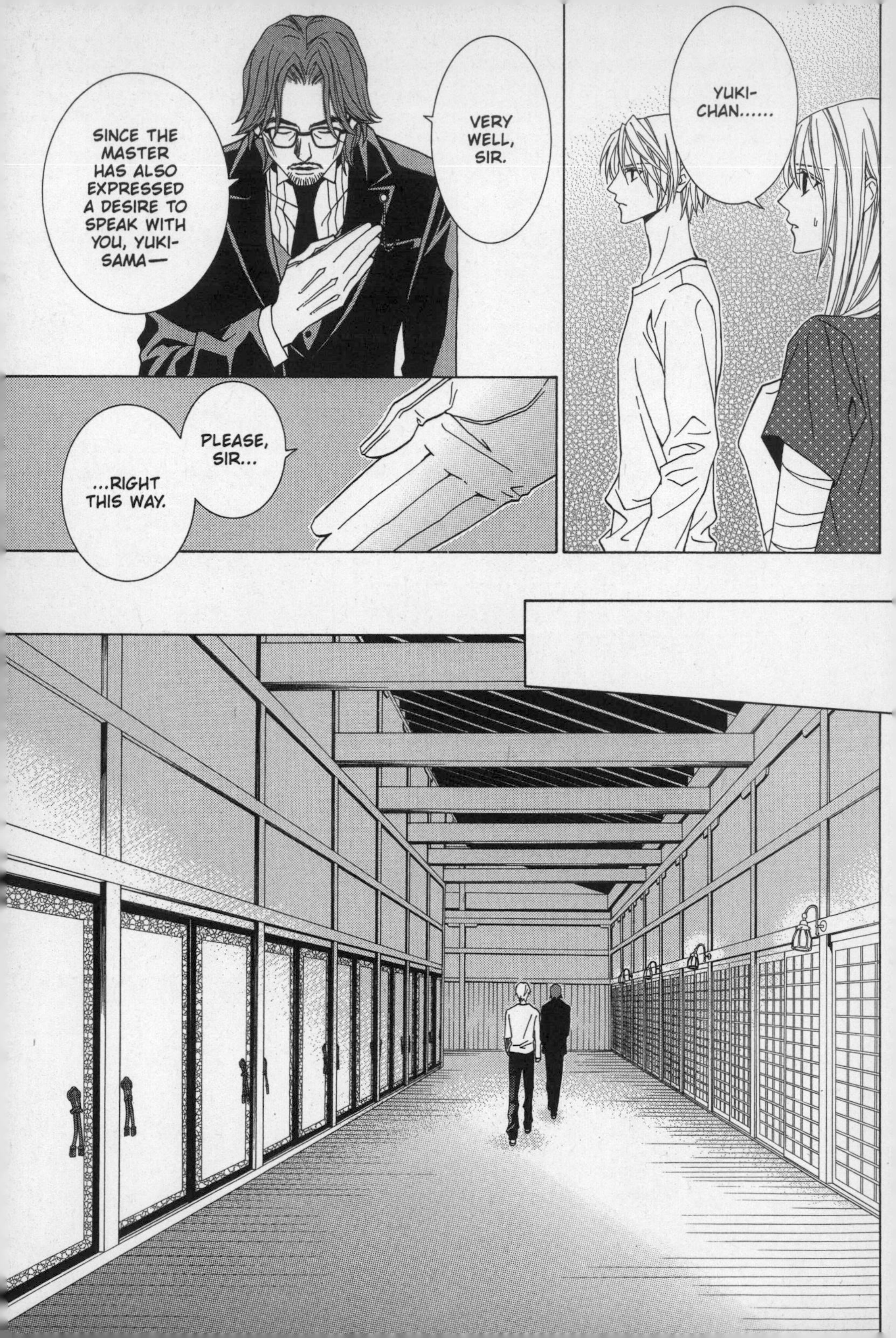
YUKI-CHAN......
VERY WELL, SIR.
SINCE THE MASTER HAS ALSO EXPRESSED A DESIRE TO SPEAK WITH YOU, YUKI-SAMA—
PLEASE, SIR...
...RIGHT THIS WAY.

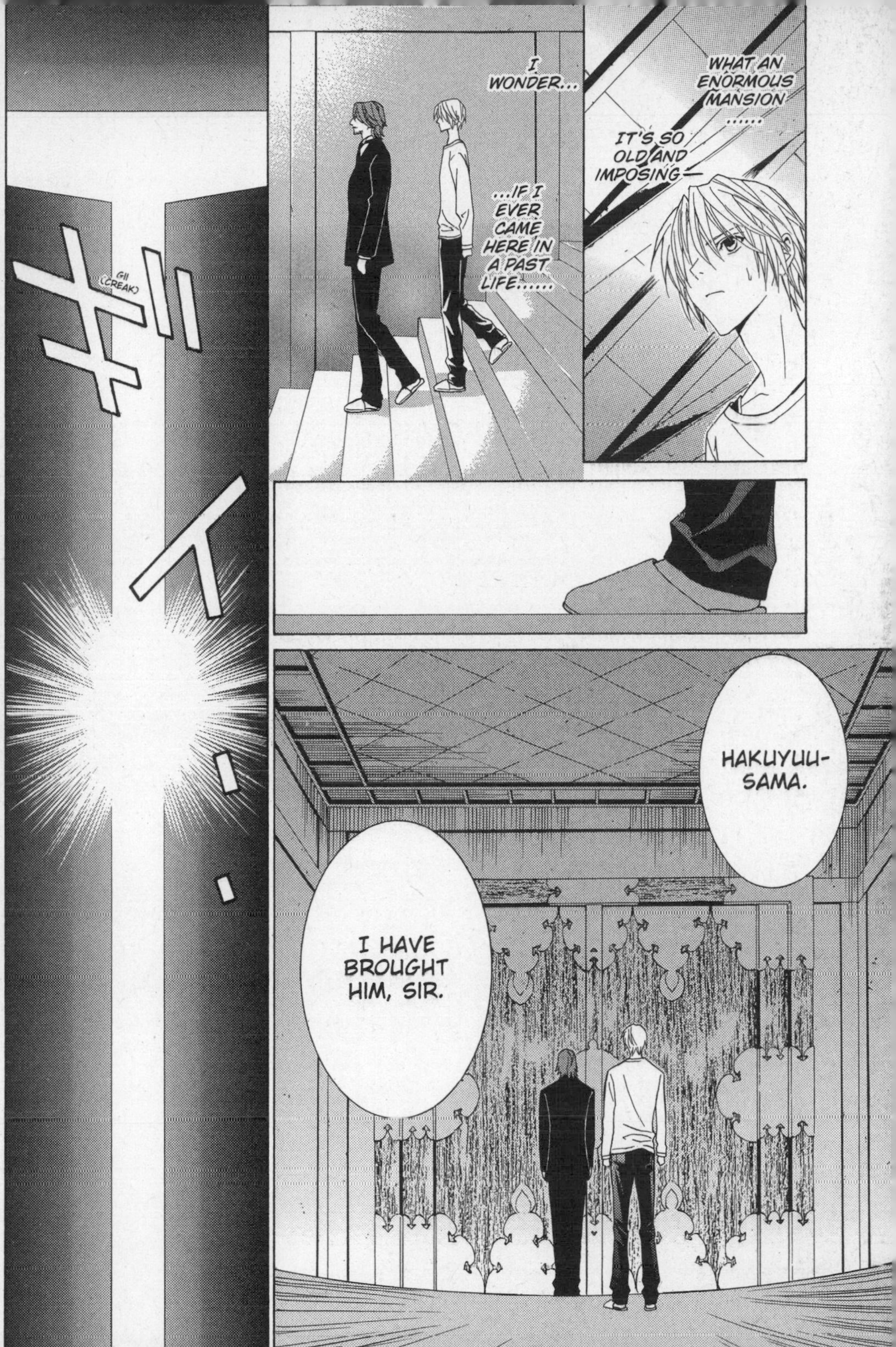
WHAT AN ENORMOUS MANSION ......
IT'S SO OLD AND IMPOSING—
I WONDER...
...IF I EVER CAME HERE IN A PAST LIFE......
HAKUYUU-SAMA.
I HAVE BROUGHT HIM, SIR.
GII (CREAK)

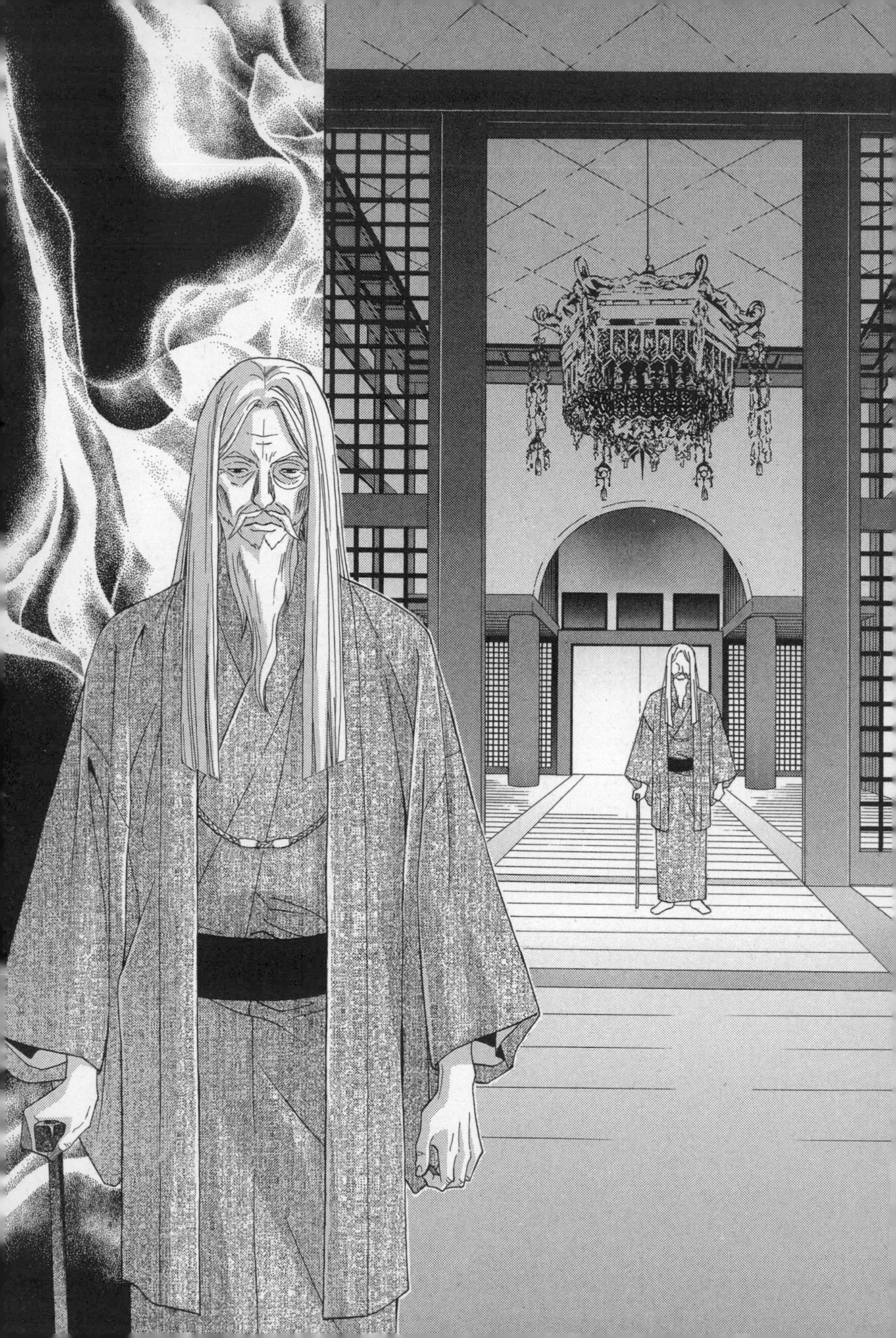

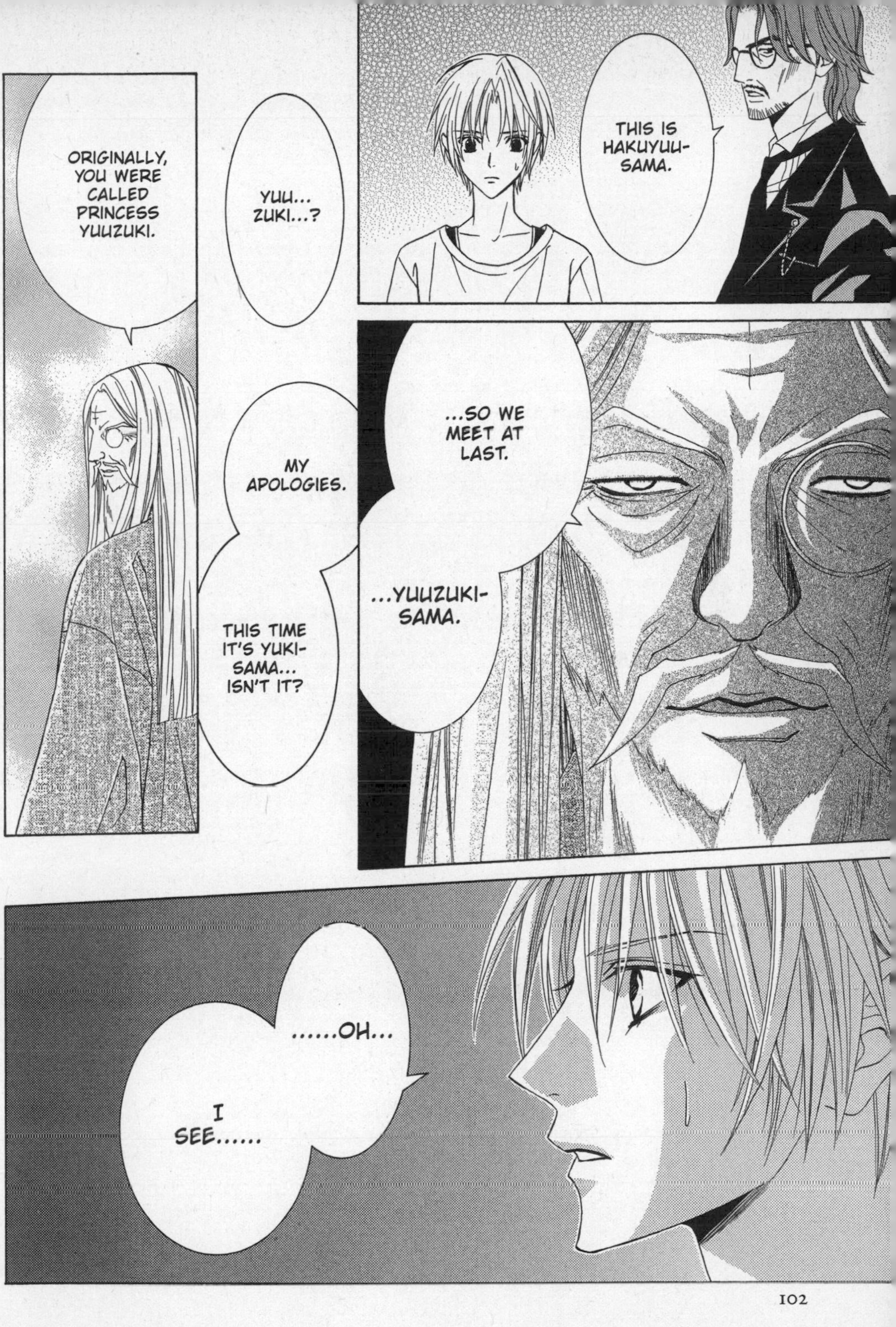
THIS IS HAKUYUU-SAMA.
...SO WE MEET AT LAST.
...YUUZUKI-SAMA.
YUU... ZUKI...?
ORIGINALLY, YOU WERE CALLED PRINCESS YUUZUKI.
MY APOLOGIES.
THIS TIME IT'S YUKI-SAMA... ISN'T IT?
......OH...
I SEE......

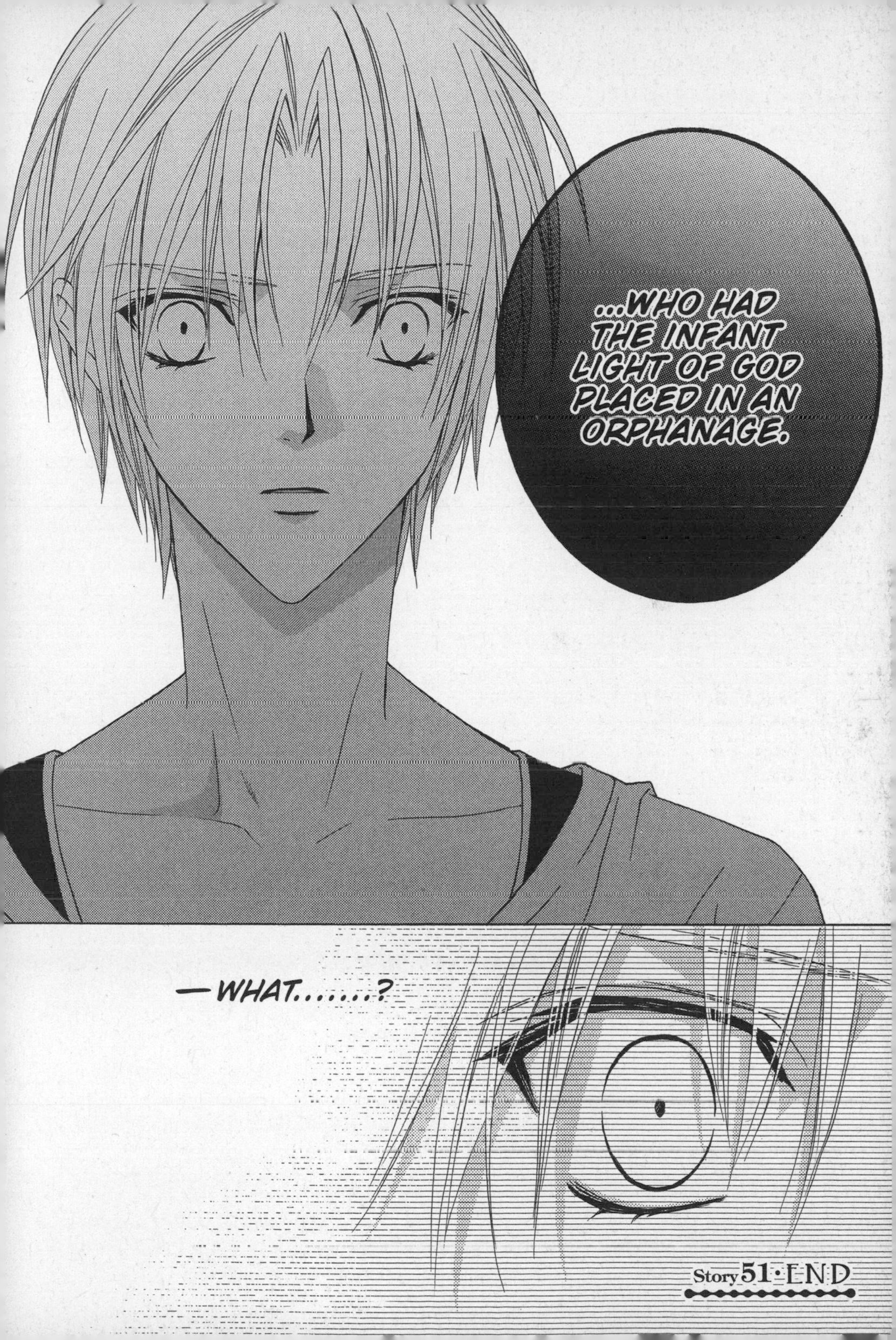
...WHO HAD THE INFANT LIGHT OF GOD PLACED IN AN ORPHANAGE.
—WHAT......?
Story 51 • END

THE
BETRAYAL
kNOWS MY NAME

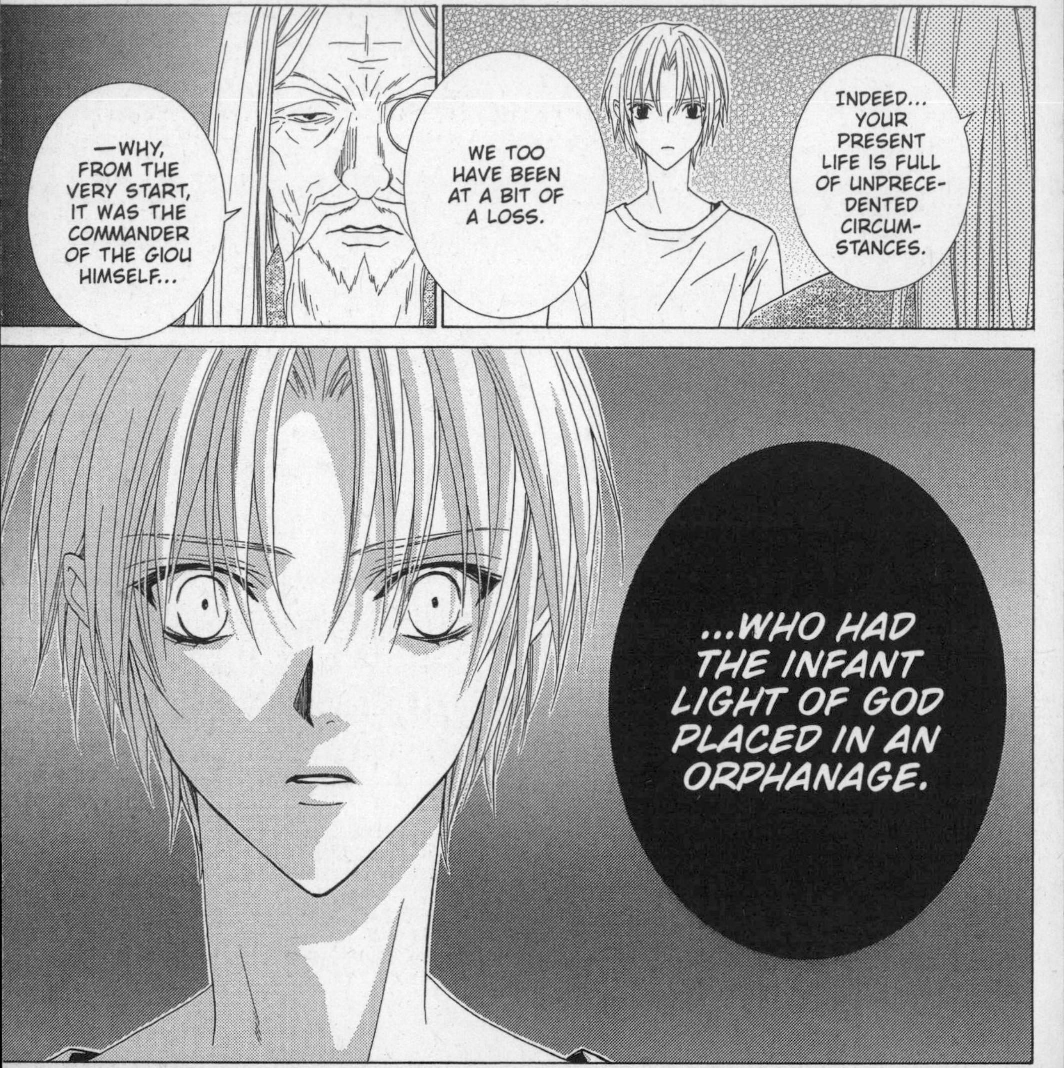
INDEED... YOUR PRESENT LIFE IS FULL OF UNPRECE-DENTED CIRCUM-STANCES.
WE TOO HAVE BEEN AT A BIT OF A LOSS.
—WHY, FROM THE VERY START, IT WAS THE COMMANDER OF THE GIOU HIMSELF...
...WHO HAD THE INFANT LIGHT OF GOD PLACED IN AN ORPHANAGE.

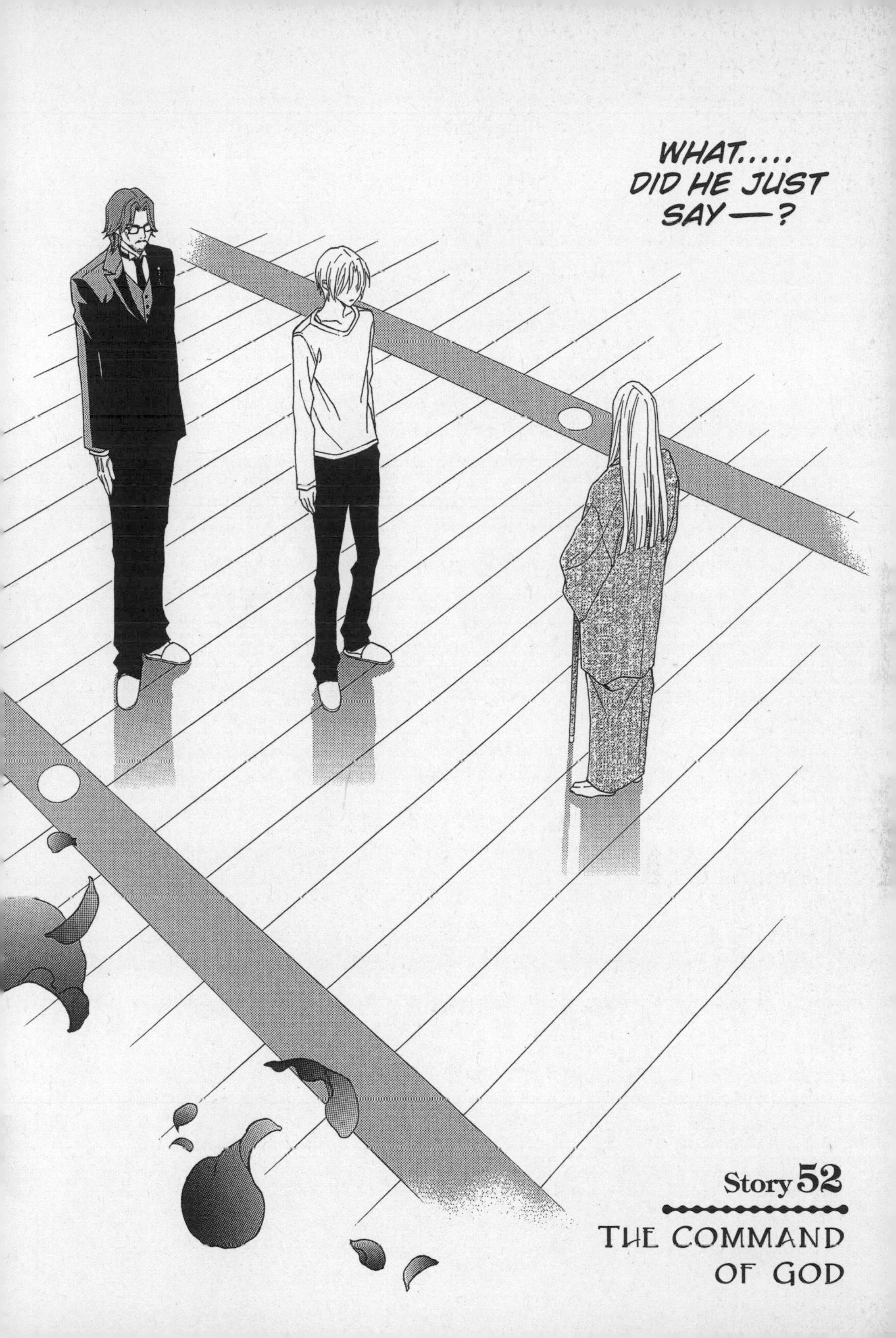
WHAT..... DID HE JUST SAY—?
Story 52
THE COMMAND OF GOD

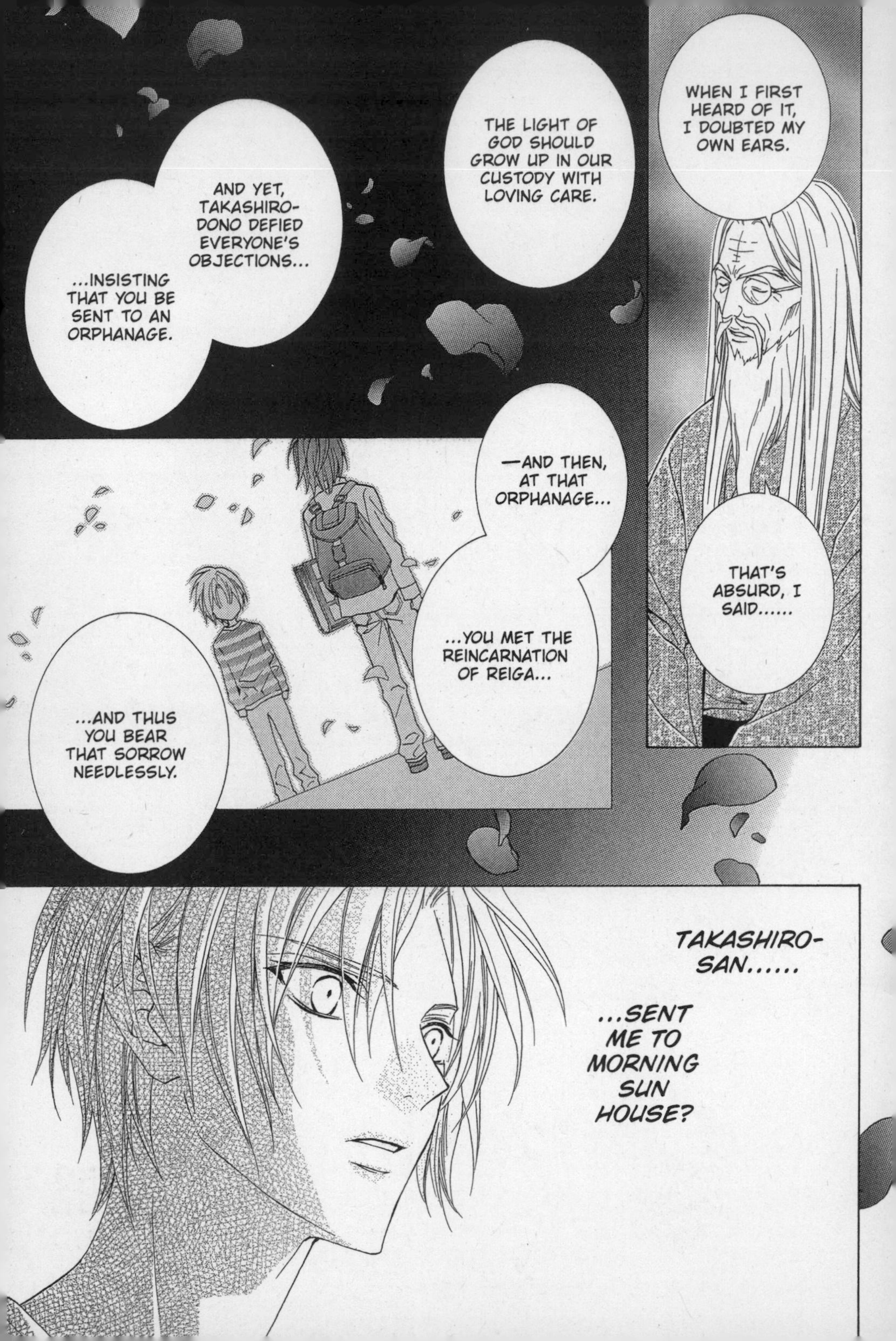
WHEN I FIRST HEARD OF IT, I DOUBTED MY OWN EARS.
THAT'S ABSURD, I SAID......
THE LIGHT OF GOD SHOULD GROW UP IN OUR CUSTODY WITH LOVING CARE.
AND YET, TAKASHIRO-DONO DEFIED EVERYONE'S OBJECTIONS...
...INSISTING THAT YOU BE SENT TO AN ORPHANAGE.
—AND THEN, AT THAT ORPHANAGE...
...YOU MET THE REINCARNATION OF REIGA...
...AND THUS YOU BEAR THAT SORROW NEEDLESSLY.
TAKASHIRO-SAN......
...SENT ME TO MORNING SUN HOUSE?

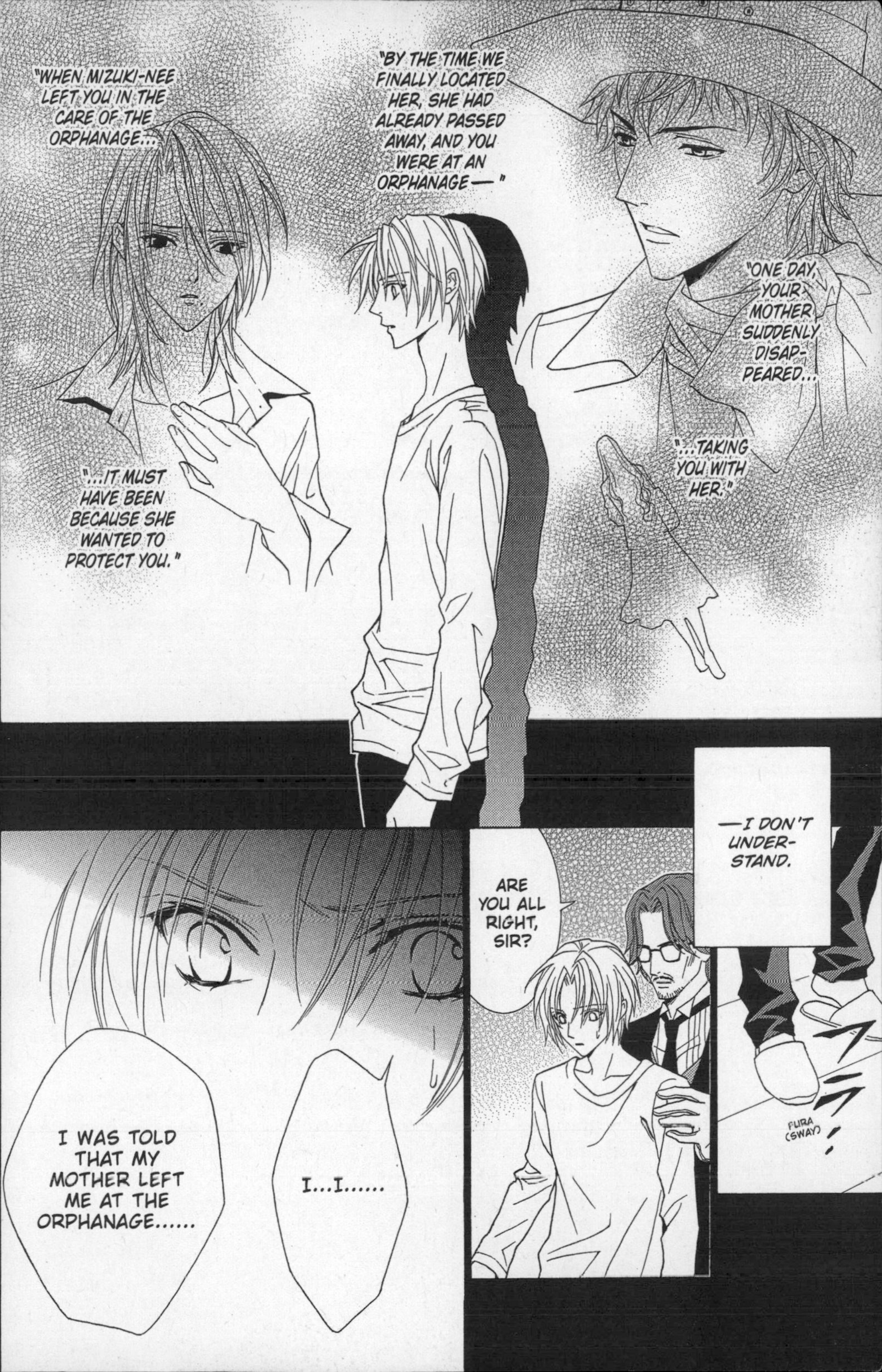
"ONE DAY, YOUR MOTHER SUDDENLY DISAP-PEARED...
"...TAKING YOU WITH HER."
"BY THE TIME WE FINALLY LOCATED HER, SHE HAD ALREADY PASSED AWAY, AND YOU WERE AT AN ORPHANAGE— "
"WHEN MIZUKI-NEE LEFT YOU IN THE CARE OF THE ORPHANAGE...
"...IT MUST HAVE BEEN BECAUSE SHE WANTED TO PROTECT YOU."
—I DON'T UNDER-STAND.
FURA (SWAY)
ARE YOU ALL RIGHT, SIR?
I...I......
I WAS TOLD THAT MY MOTHER LEFT ME AT THE ORPHANAGE......

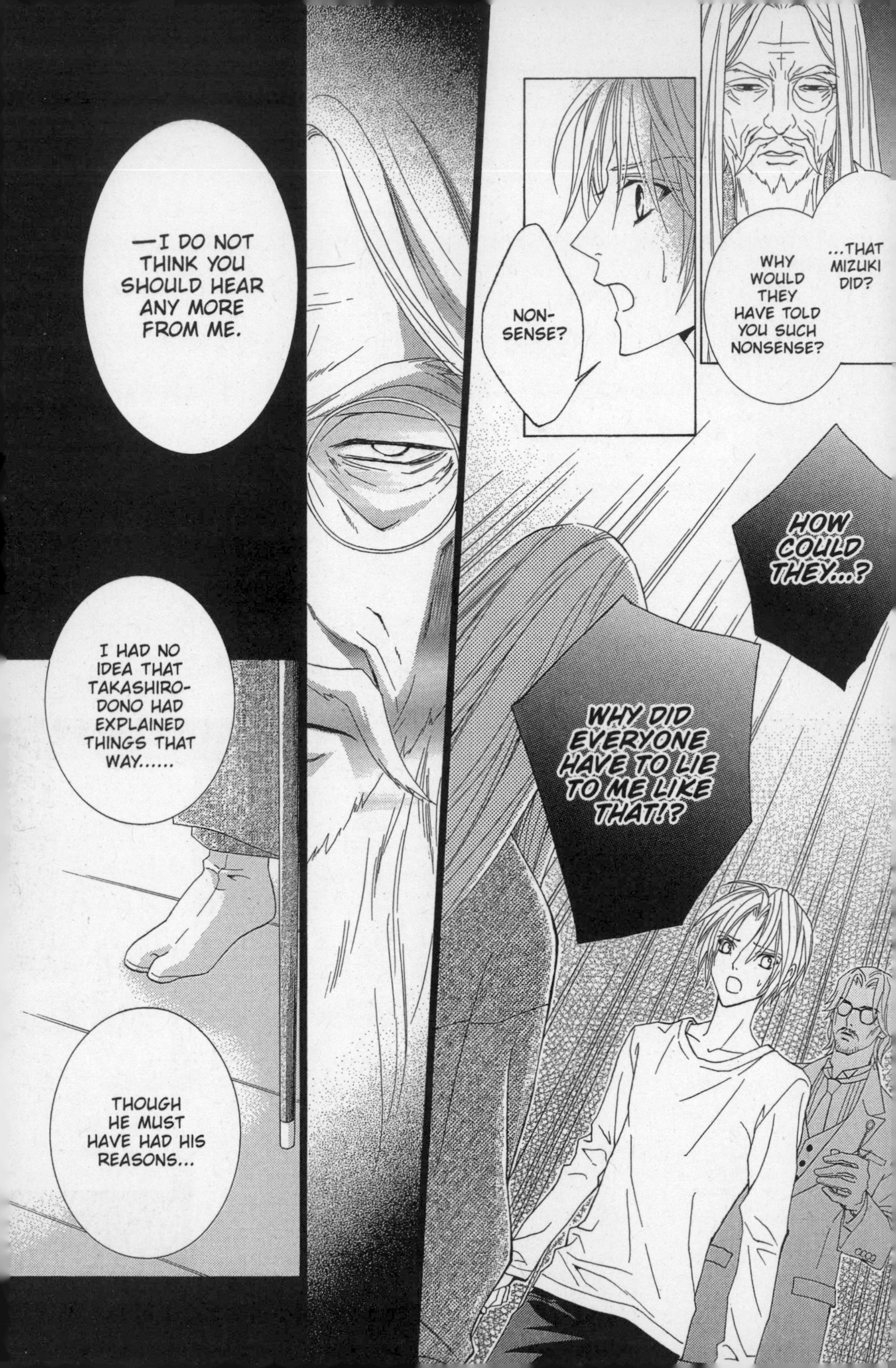
...THAT MIZUKI DID?
WHY WOULD THEY HAVE TOLD YOU SUCH NONSENSE?
NON-SENSE?
HOW COULD THEY...?
WHY DID EVERYONE HAVE TO LIE TO ME LIKE THAT!?
—I DO NOT THINK YOU SHOULD HEAR ANY MORE FROM ME.
I HAD NO IDEA THAT TAKASHIRO-DONO HAD EXPLAINED THINGS THAT WAY......
THOUGH HE MUST HAVE HAD HIS REASONS...

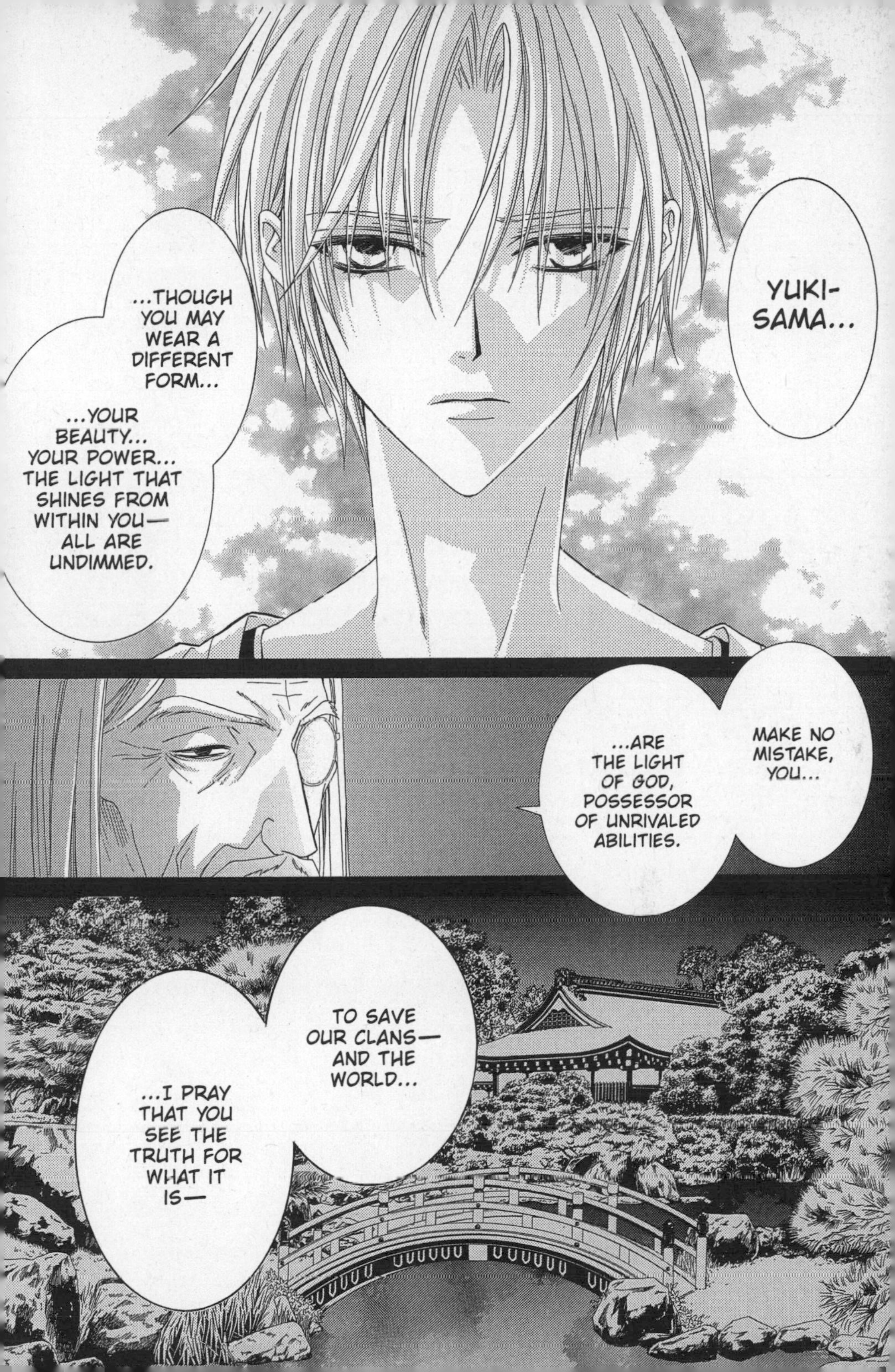
YUKI-SAMA...
...THOUGH YOU MAY WEAR A DIFFERENT FORM... ...YOUR BEAUTY... YOUR POWER... THE LIGHT THAT SHINES FROM WITHIN YOU— ALL ARE UNDIMMED.
MAKE NO MISTAKE, YOU...
...ARE THE LIGHT OF GOD, POSSESSOR OF UNRIVALED ABILITIES.
TO SAVE OUR CLANS— AND THE WORLD...
...I PRAY THAT YOU SEE THE TRUTH FOR WHAT IT IS—

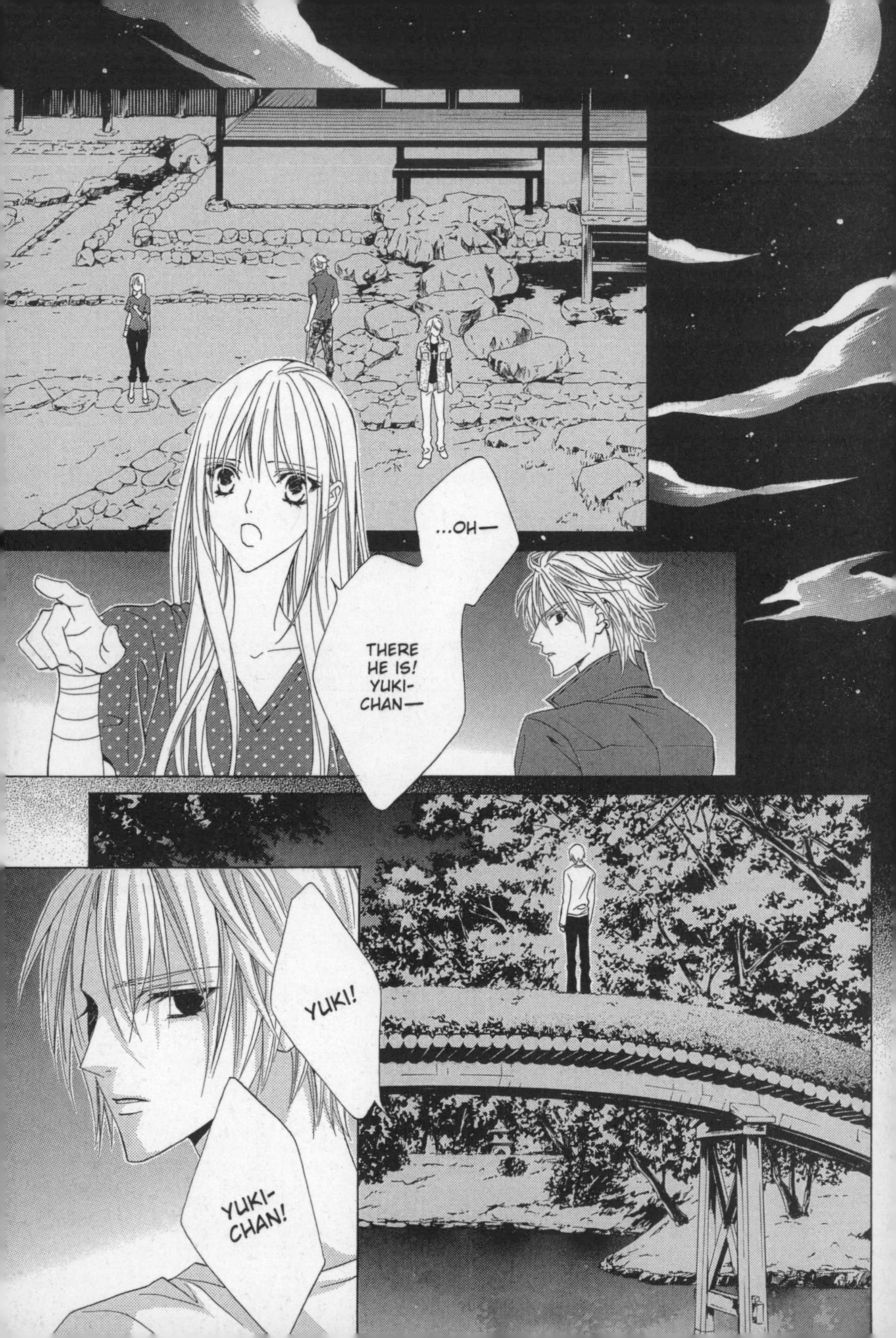
...OH—
THERE HE IS! YUKI-CHAN—
YUKI!
YUKI-CHAN!

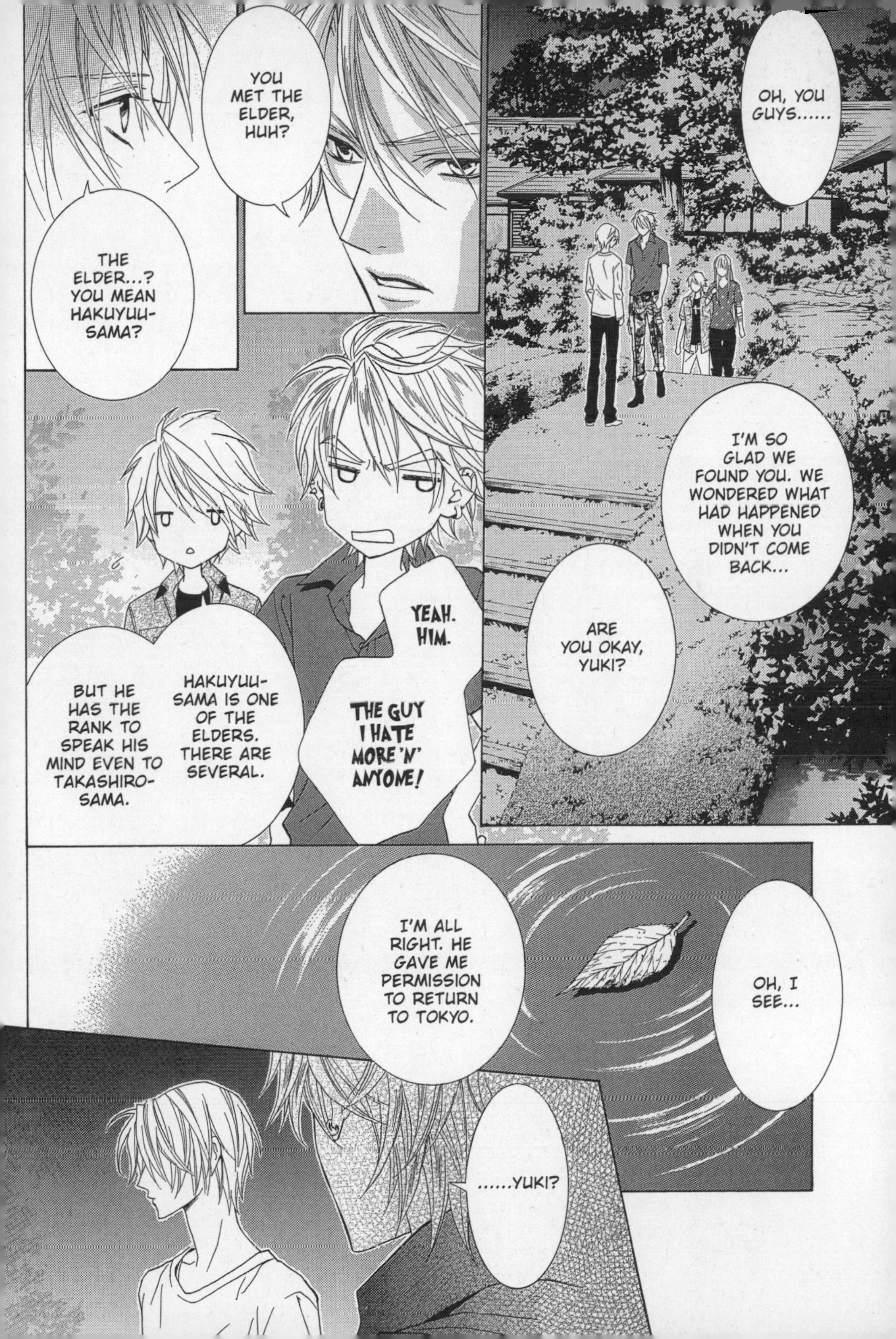
OH, YOU GUYS......
I'M SO GLAD WE FOUND YOU. WE WONDERED WHAT HAD HAPPENED WHEN YOU DIDN'T COME BACK...
ARE YOU OKAY, YUKI?
YOU MET THE ELDER, HUH?
THE ELDER...? YOU MEAN HAKUYUU-SAMA?
YEAH. HIM.
THE GUY I HATE MORE 'N' ANYONE!
HAKUYUU-SAMA IS ONE OF THE ELDERS. THERE ARE SEVERAL.
BUT HE HAS THE RANK TO SPEAK HIS MIND EVEN TO TAKASHIRO-SAMA.
OH, I SEE...
I'M ALL RIGHT. HE GAVE ME PERMISSION TO RETURN TO TOKYO.
......YUKI?

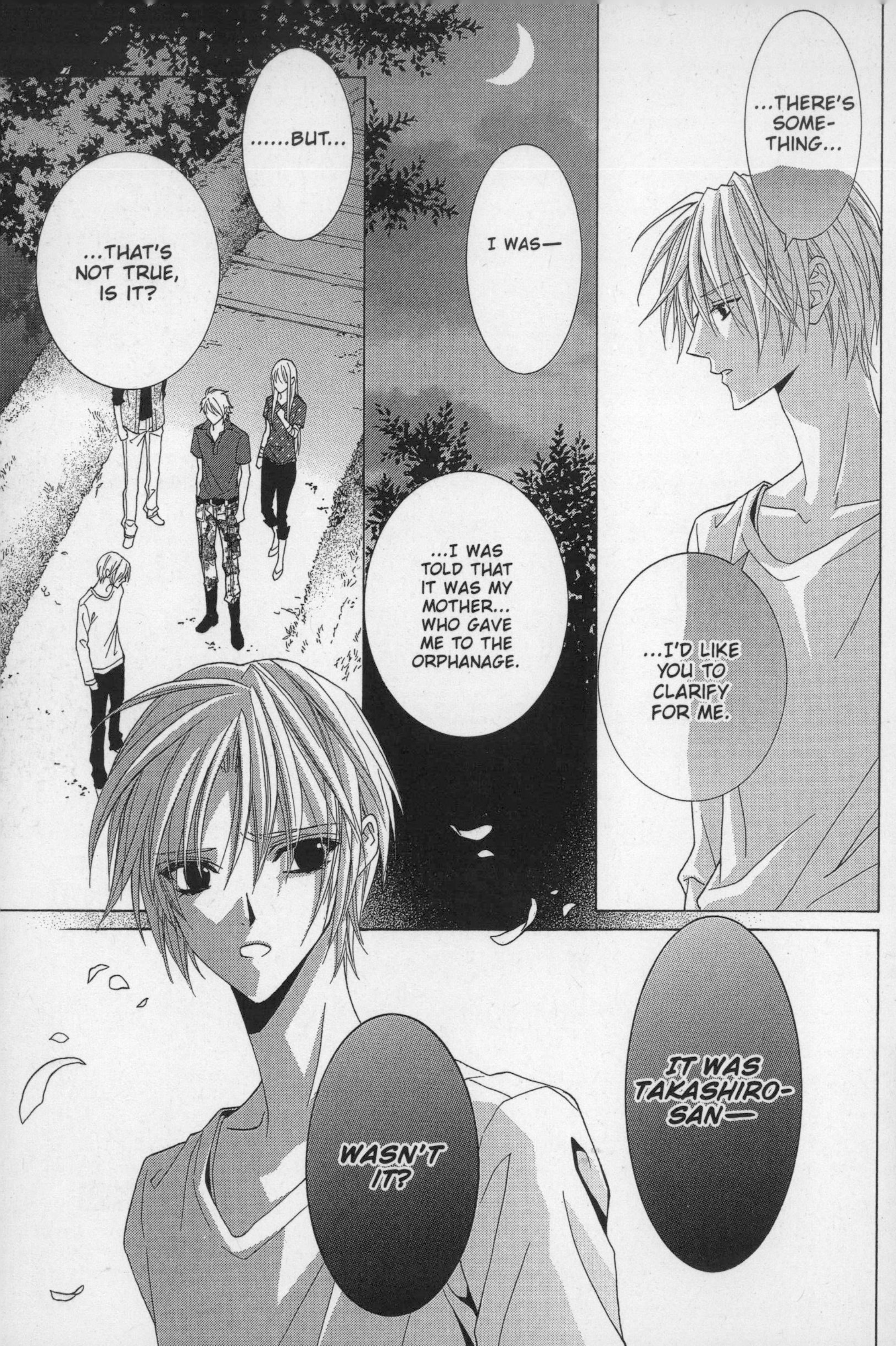
...THERE'S SOME-THING...
...I'D LIKE YOU TO CLARIFY FOR ME.
I WAS—
...I WAS TOLD THAT IT WAS MY MOTHER... WHO GAVE ME TO THE ORPHANAGE.
......BUT...
...THAT'S NOT TRUE, IS IT?
IT WAS TAKASHIRO-SAN—
WASN'T IT?

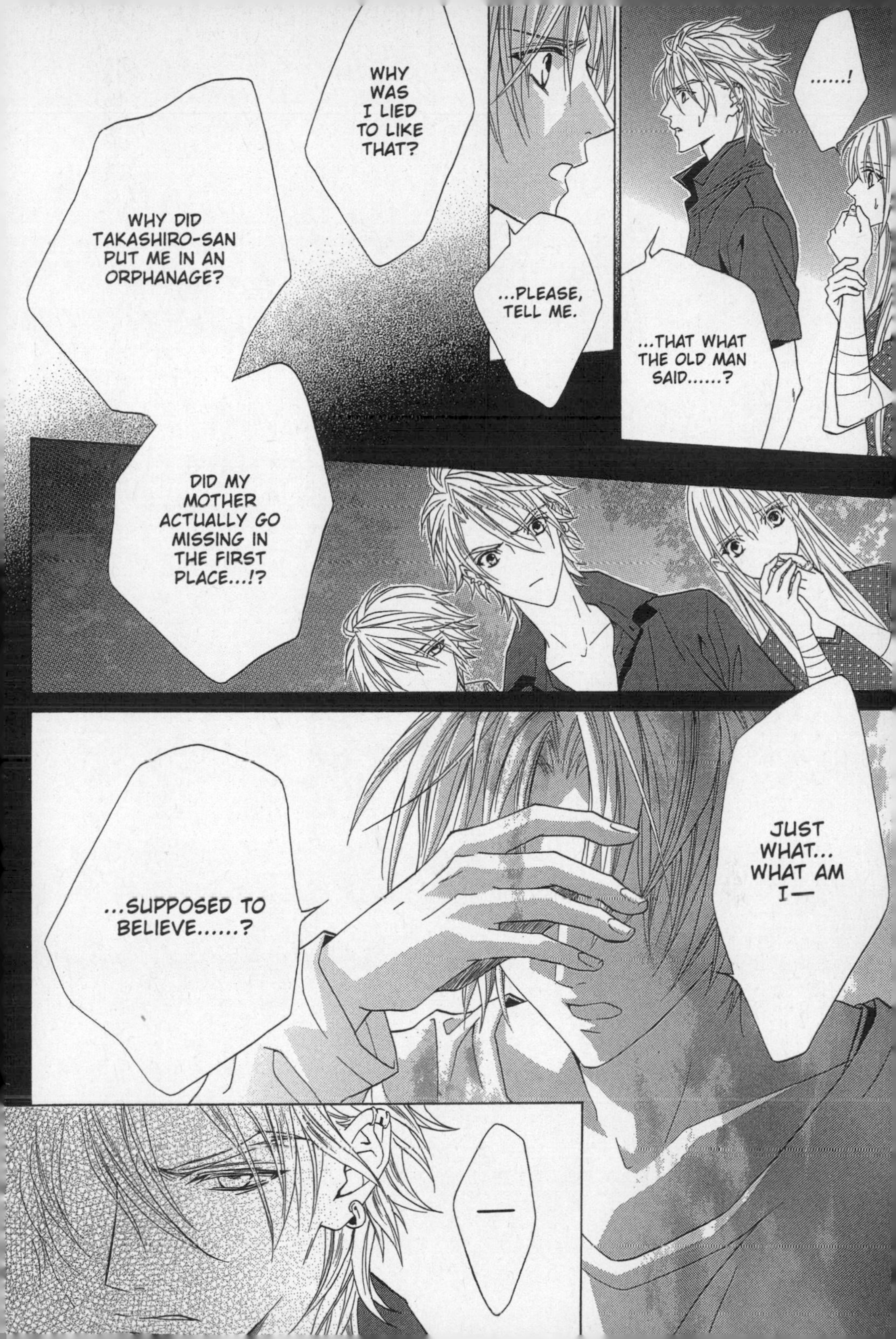
......!
...THAT WHAT THE OLD MAN SAID......?
WHY WAS I LIED TO LIKE THAT?
...PLEASE, TELL ME.
WHY DID TAKASHIRO-SAN PUT ME IN AN ORPHANAGE?
DID MY MOTHER ACTUALLY GO MISSING IN THE FIRST PLACE...!?
JUST WHAT... WHAT AM I—
...SUPPOSED TO BELIEVE......?
—

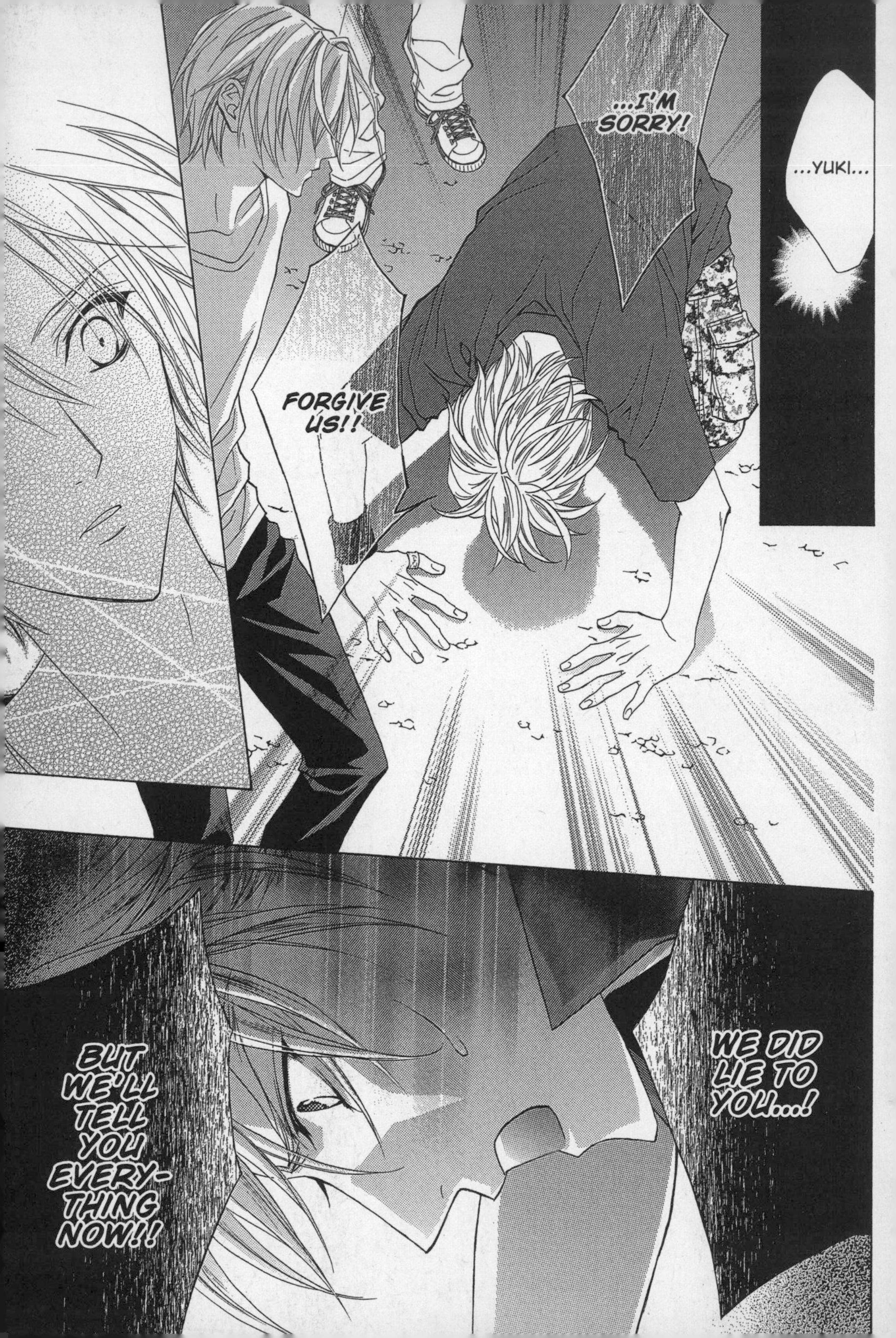
...YUKI...
...I'M SORRY!
FORGIVE US!!
WE DID LIE TO YOU...!
BUT WE'LL TELL YOU EVERY-THING NOW!!

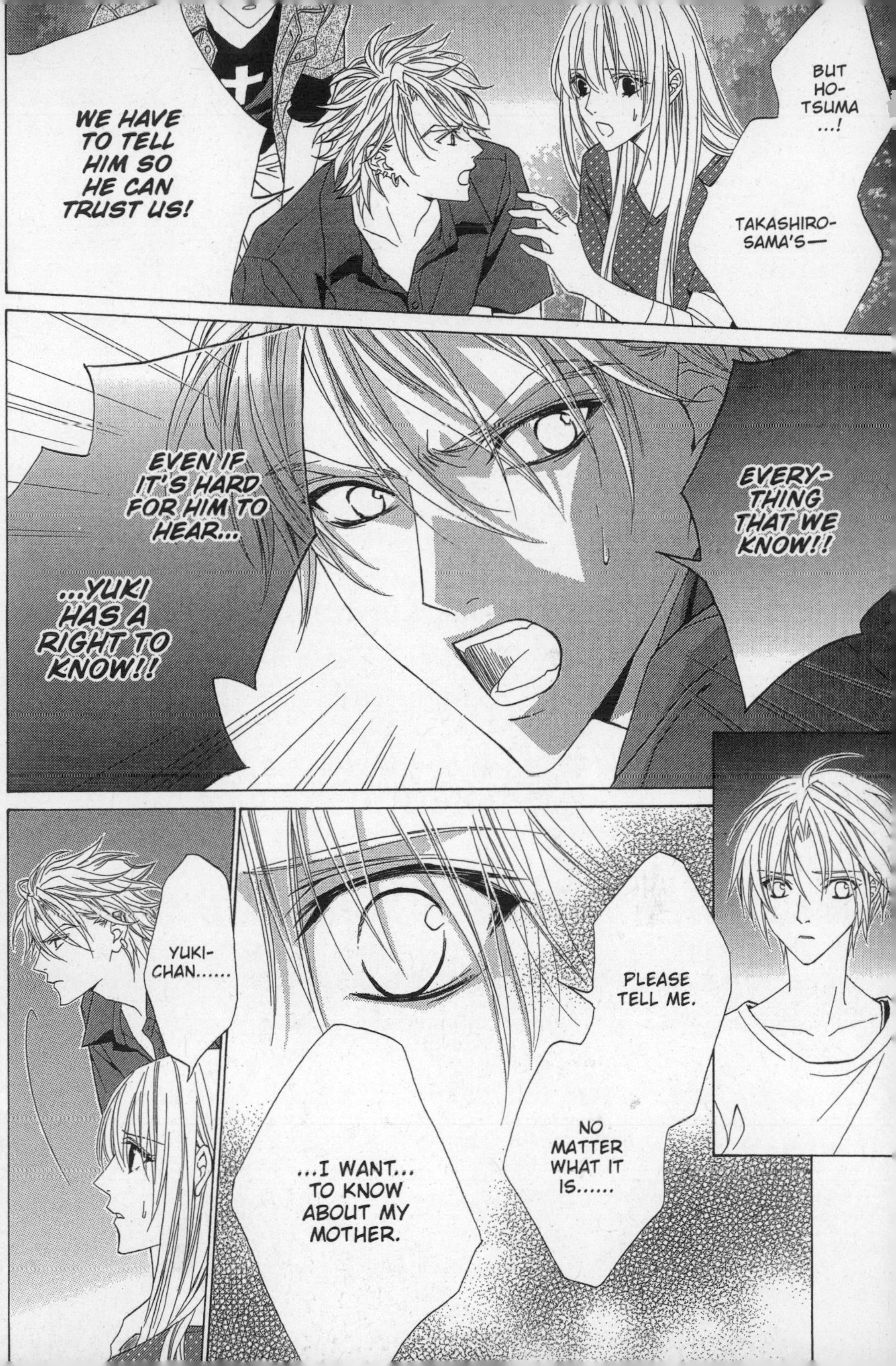
BUT HO-TSUMA ...!
TAKASHIRO-SAMA'S—
WE HAVE TO TELL HIM SO HE CAN TRUST US!
EVERY-THING THAT WE KNOW!!
EVEN IF IT'S HARD FOR HIM TO HEAR...
...YUKI HAS A RIGHT TO KNOW!!
PLEASE TELL ME.
NO MATTER WHAT IT IS......
...I WANT... TO KNOW ABOUT MY MOTHER.
YUKI-CHAN......

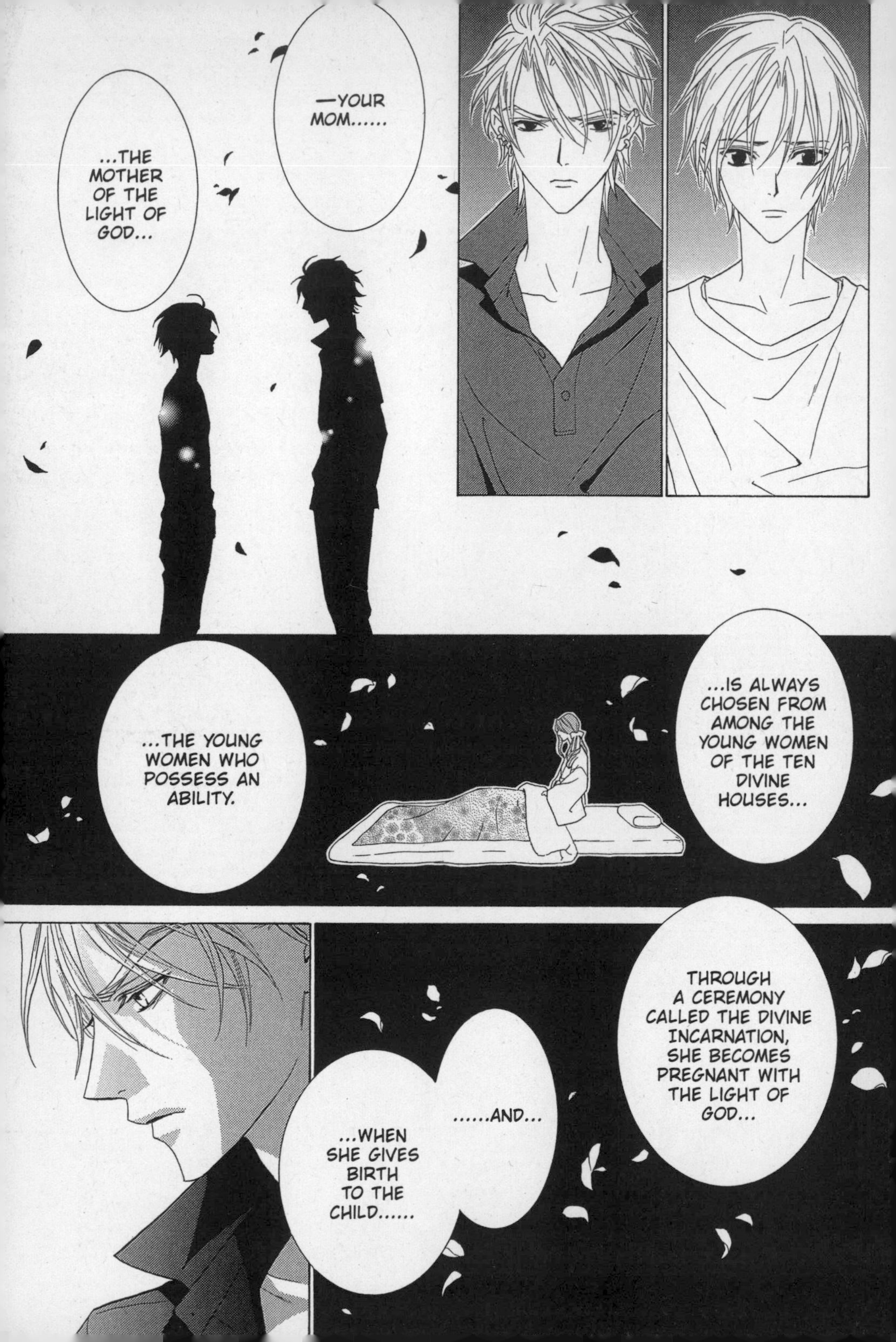
—YOUR MOM......
...THE MOTHER OF THE LIGHT OF GOD...
...IS ALWAYS CHOSEN FROM AMONG THE YOUNG WOMEN OF THE TEN DIVINE HOUSES...
...THE YOUNG WOMEN WHO POSSESS AN ABILITY.
THROUGH A CEREMONY CALLED THE DIVINE INCARNATION, SHE BECOMES PREGNANT WITH THE LIGHT OF GOD...
......AND...
...WHEN SHE GIVES BIRTH TO THE CHILD......

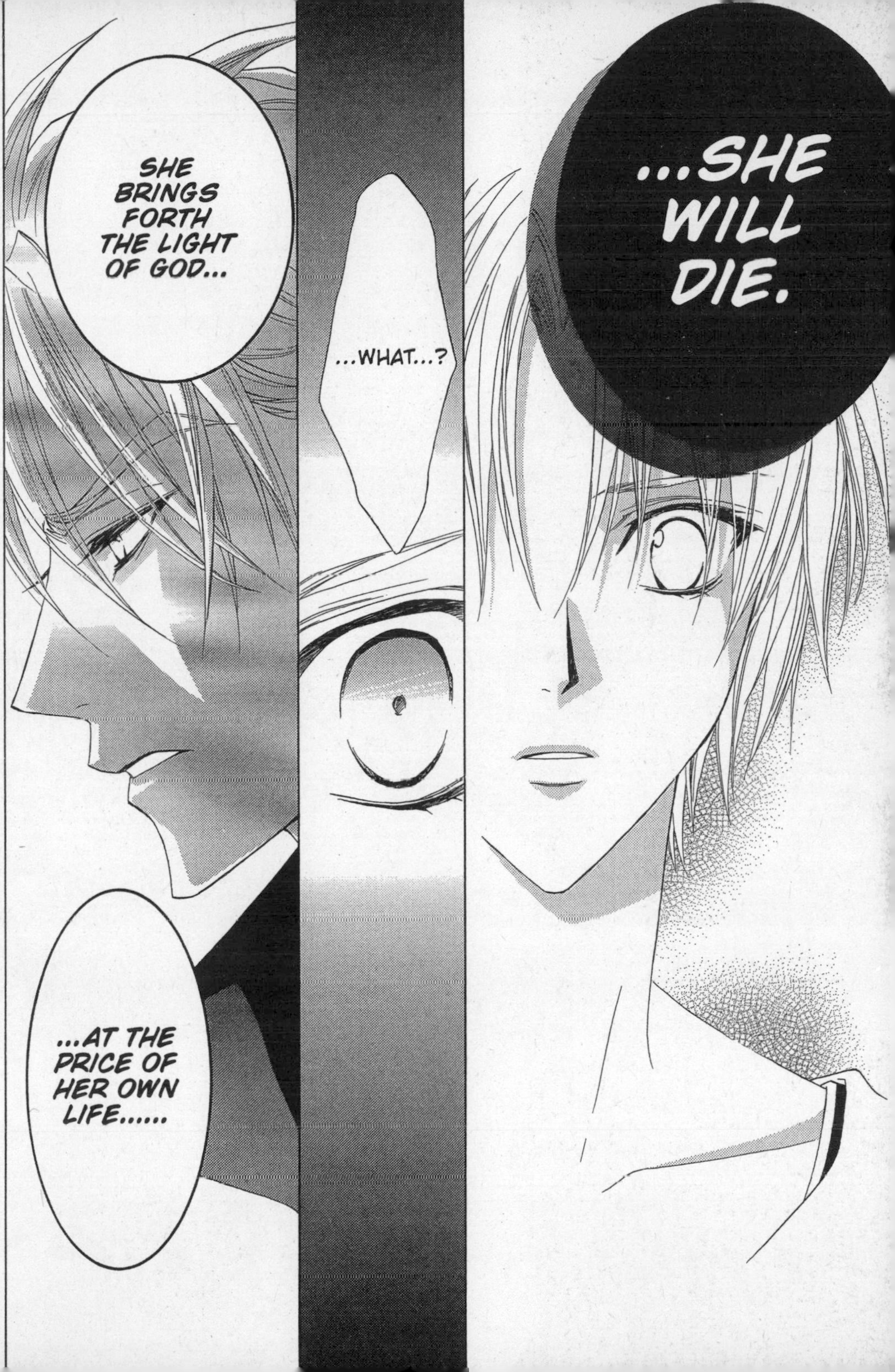
...SHE WILL DIE.
...WHAT...?
SHE BRINGS FORTH THE LIGHT OF GOD...
...AT THE PRICE OF HER OWN LIFE......

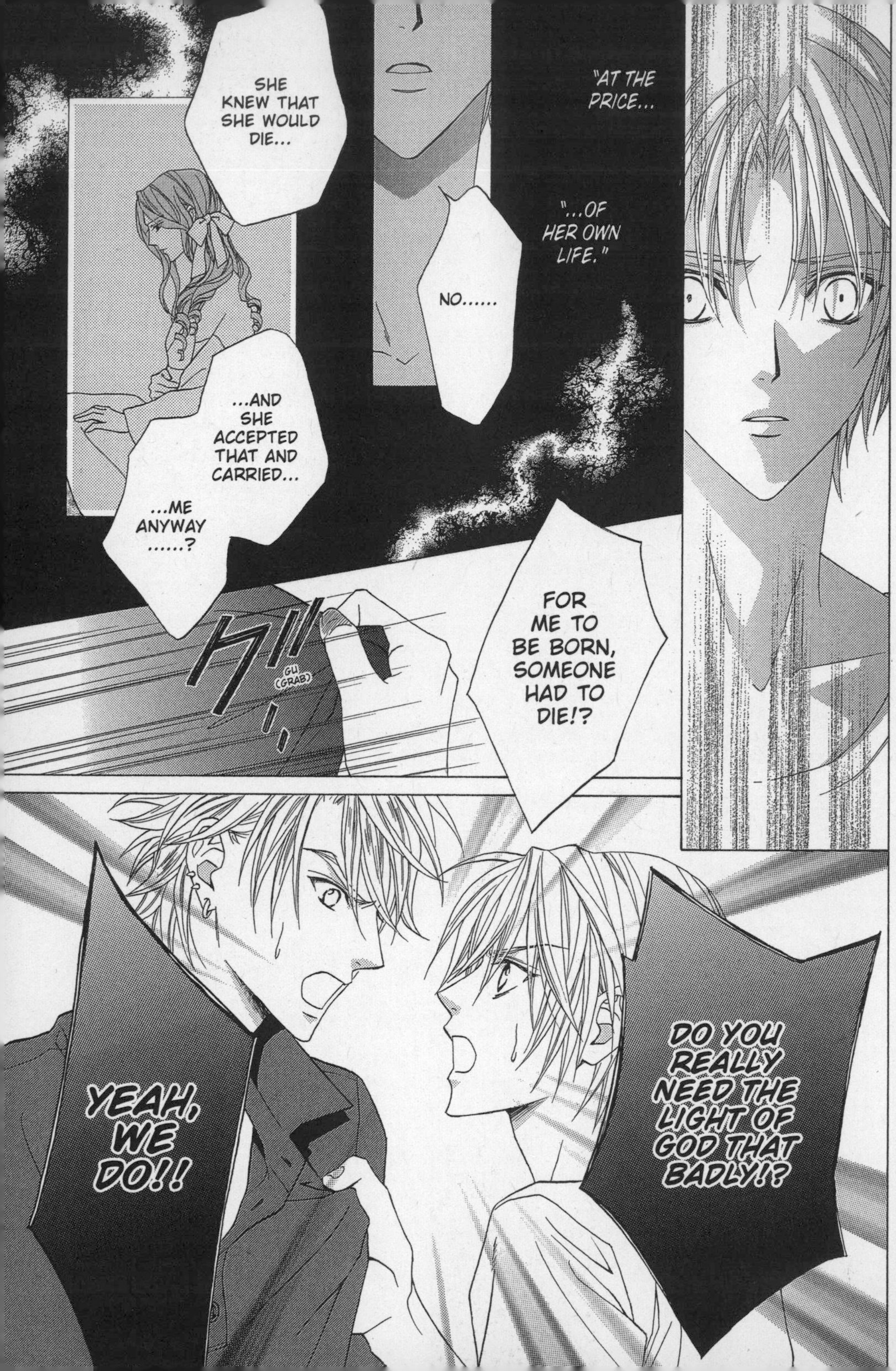
"AT THE PRICE...
"...OF HER OWN LIFE."
NO......
SHE KNEW THAT SHE WOULD DIE...
...AND SHE ACCEPTED THAT AND CARRIED...
...ME ANYWAY ......?
FOR ME TO BE BORN, SOMEONE HAD TO DIE!?
GU (GRAB)
DO YOU REALLY NEED THE LIGHT OF GOD THAT BADLY!?
YEAH, WE DO!!

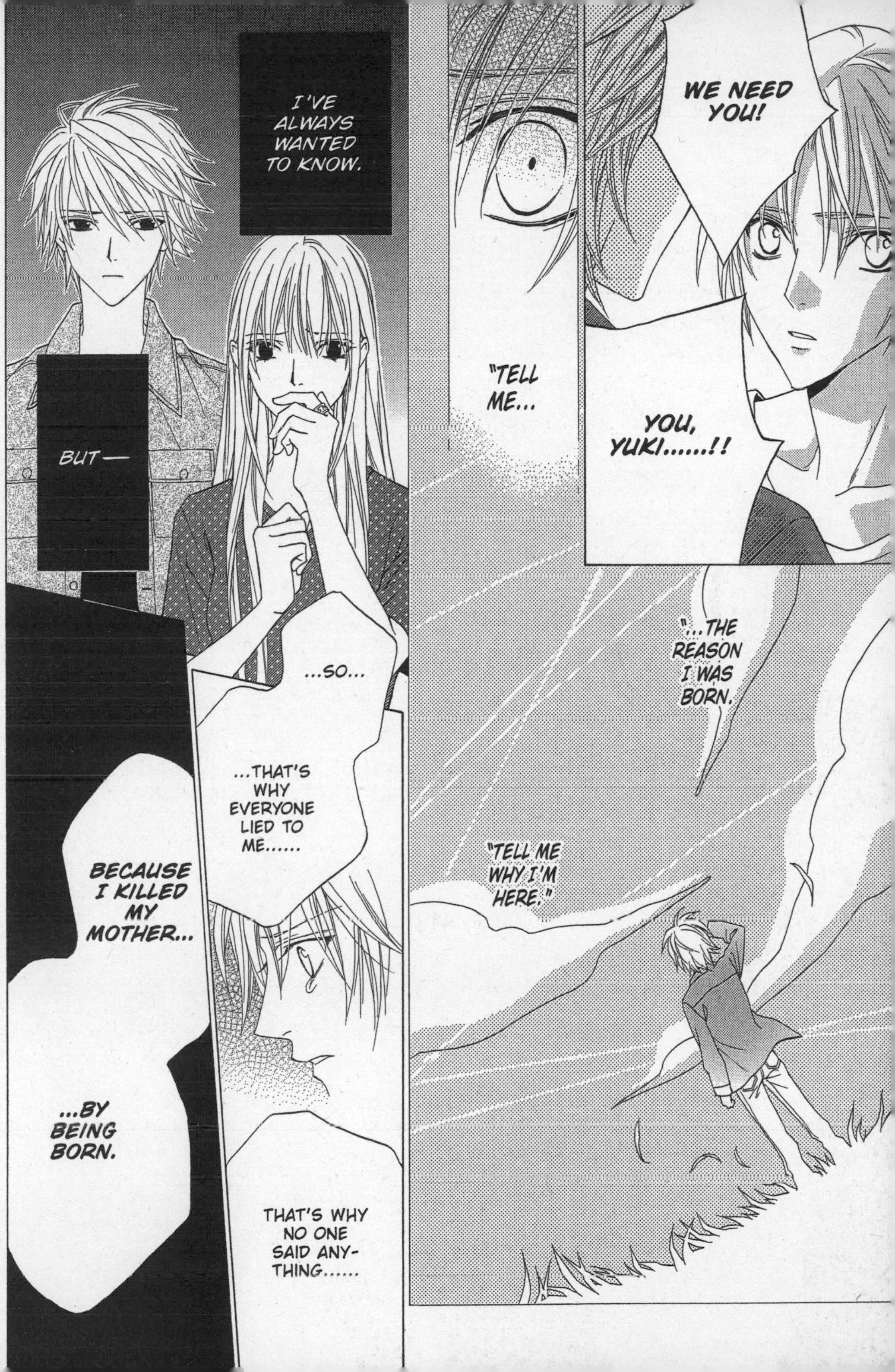

WE NEED YOU!
YOU, YUKI......!!
"TELL ME...
"...THE REASON I WAS BORN.
"TELL ME WHY I'M HERE."
I'VE ALWAYS WANTED TO KNOW.
BUT—
...SO...
...THAT'S WHY EVERYONE LIED TO ME......
BECAUSE I KILLED MY MOTHER...
...BY BEING BORN.
THAT'S WHY NO ONE SAID ANY-THING......

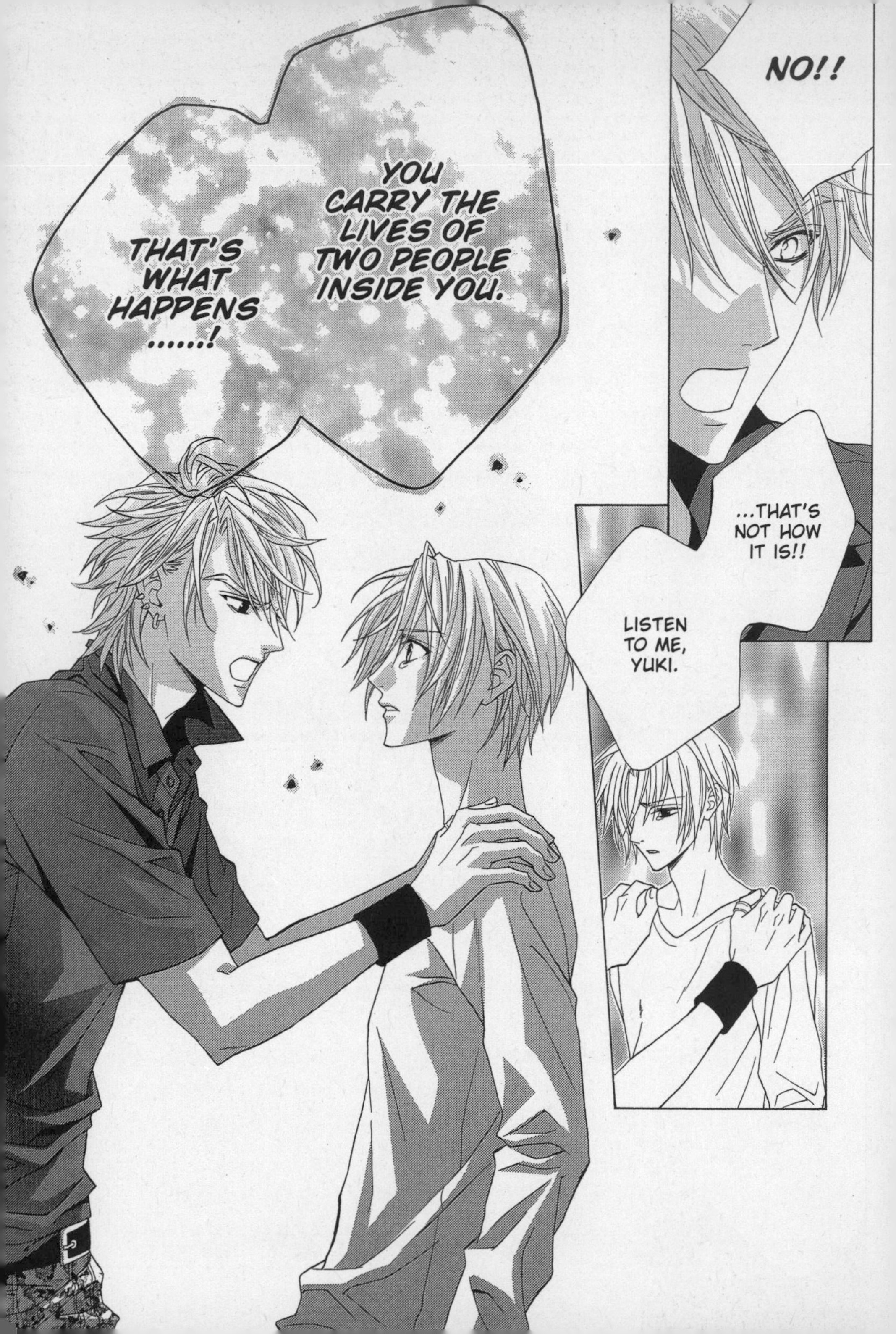
NO!!
...THAT'S NOT HOW IT IS!!
LISTEN TO ME, YUKI.
YOU CARRY THE LIVES OF TWO PEOPLE INSIDE YOU.
THAT'S WHAT HAPPENS......!

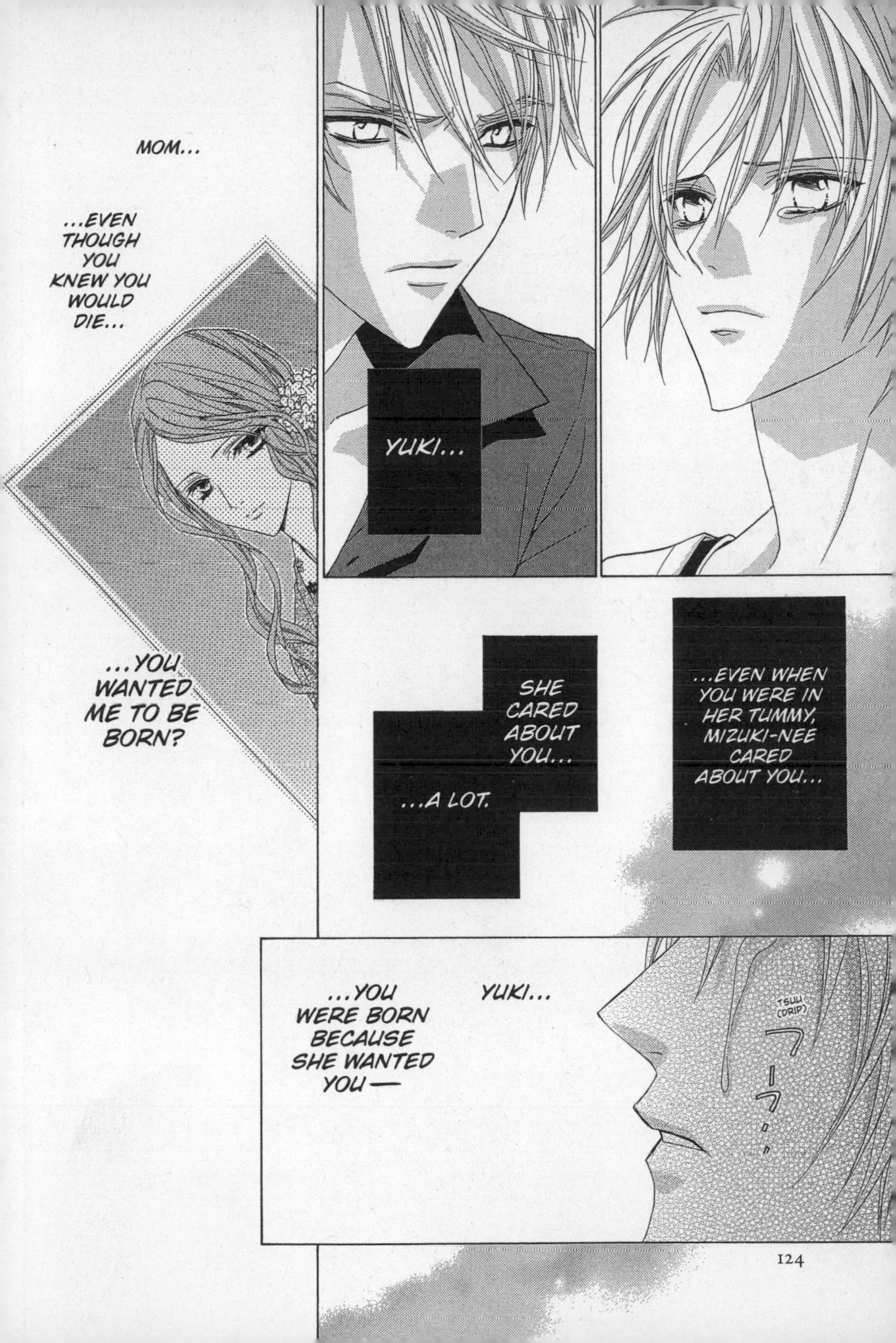
YUKI...
...EVEN WHEN YOU WERE IN HER TUMMY, MIZUKI-NEE CARED ABOUT YOU...
SHE CARED ABOUT YOU...
...A LOT.
MOM...
...EVEN THOUGH YOU KNEW YOU WOULD DIE...
...YOU WANTED ME TO BE BORN?
TSUU (DRIP)
YUKI...
...YOU WERE BORN BECAUSE SHE WANTED YOU—

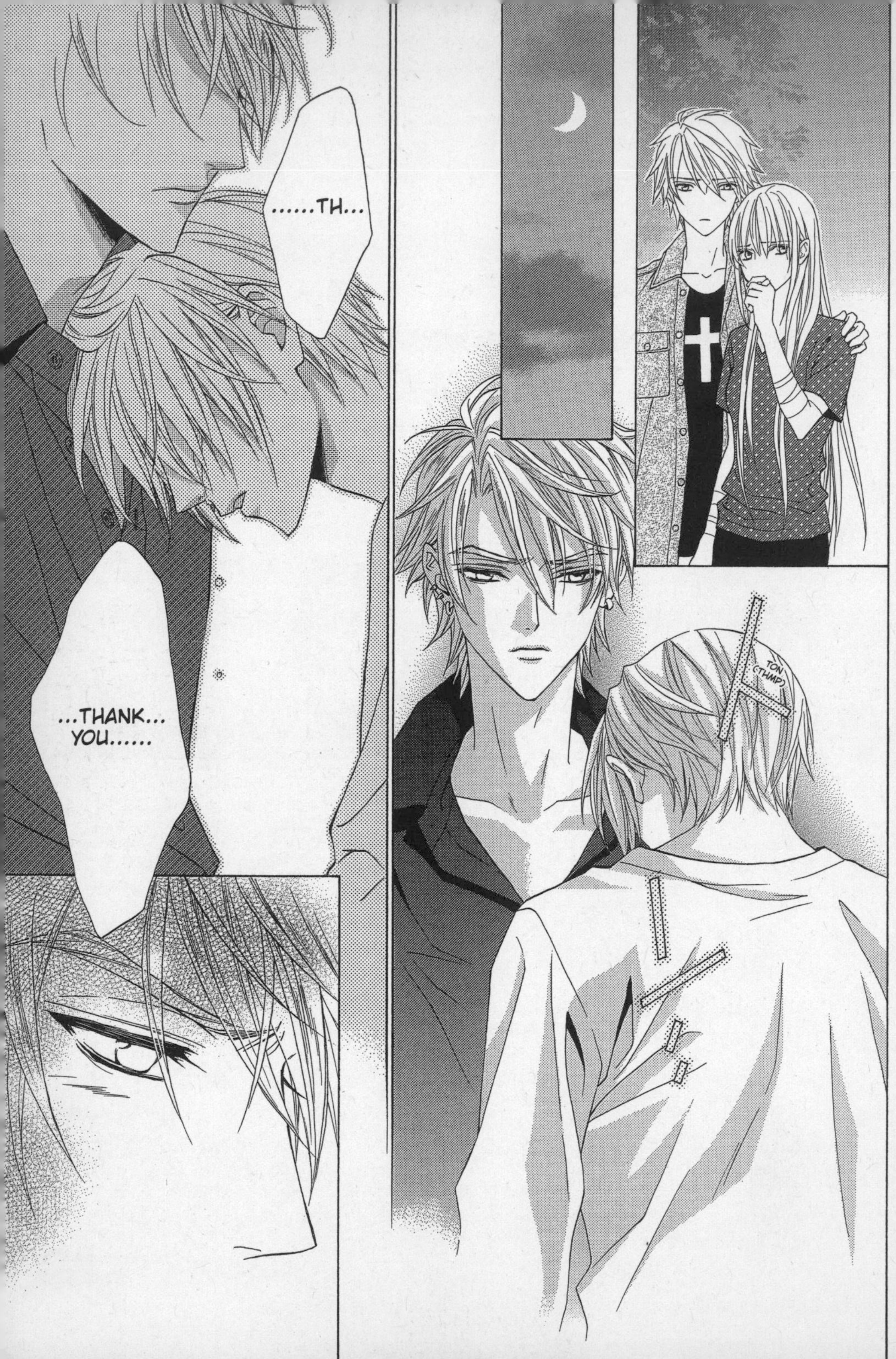
TON (THMP)
......TH...
...THANK... YOU......

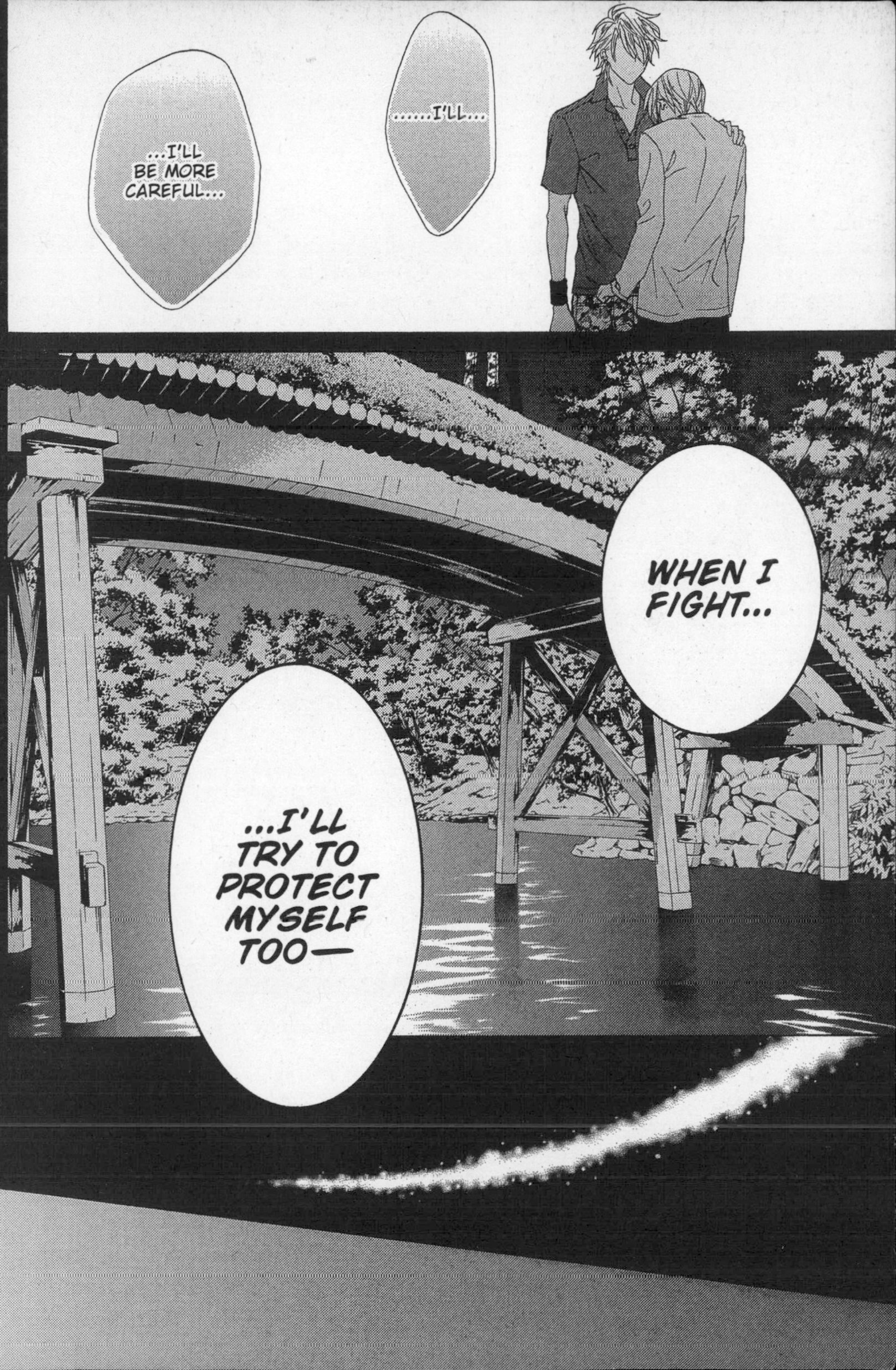
......I'LL...
...I'LL BE MORE CAREFUL...
WHEN I FIGHT...
...I'LL TRY TO PROTECT MYSELF TOO—

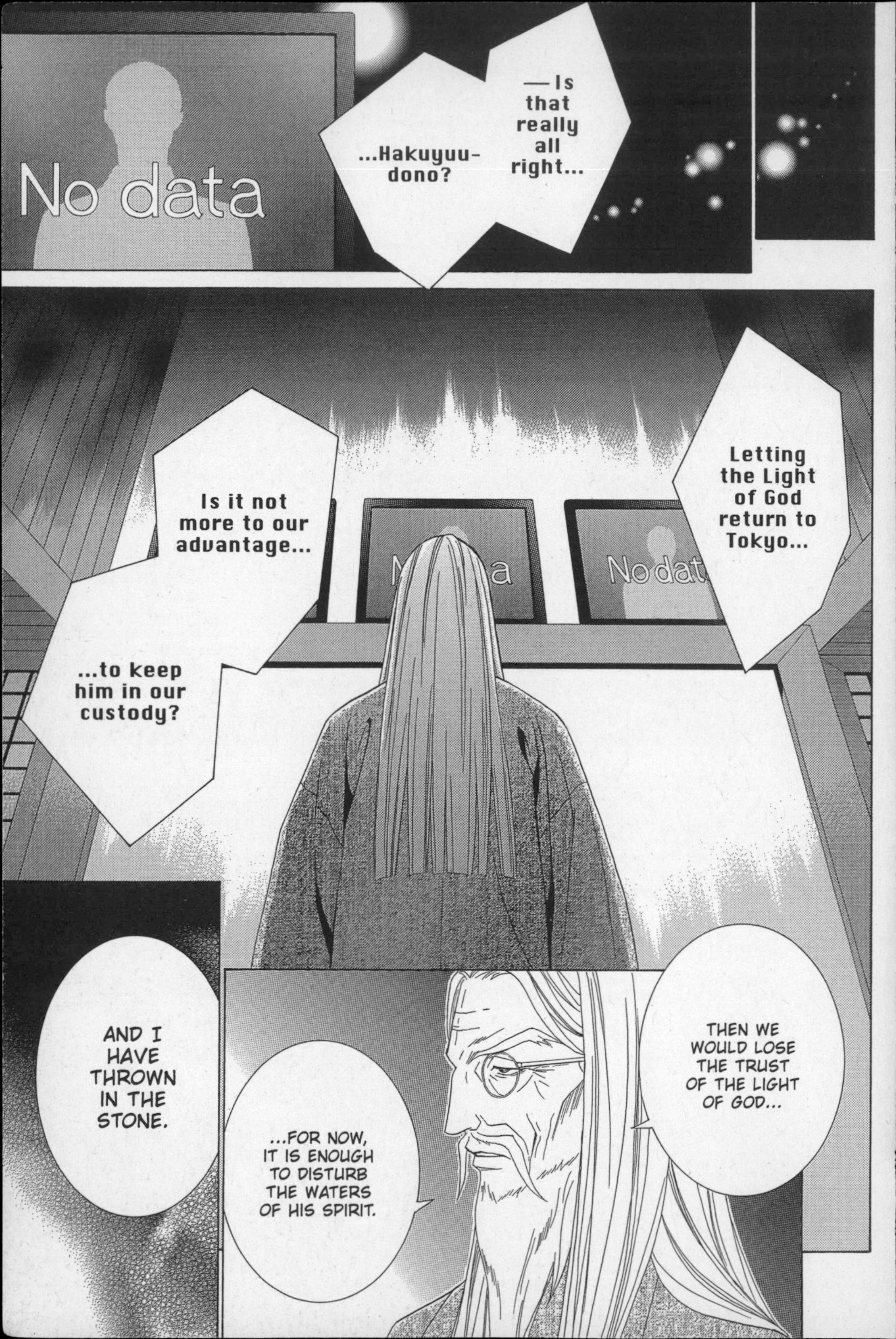
—Is that really all right...
...Hakuyuu-dono?
No data
Letting the Light of God return to Tokyo...
Is it not more to our advantage...
...to keep him in our custody?
No data
THEN WE WOULD LOSE THE TRUST OF THE LIGHT OF GOD...
...FOR NOW, IT IS ENOUGH TO DISTURB THE WATERS OF HIS SPIRIT.
AND I HAVE THROWN IN THE STONE.

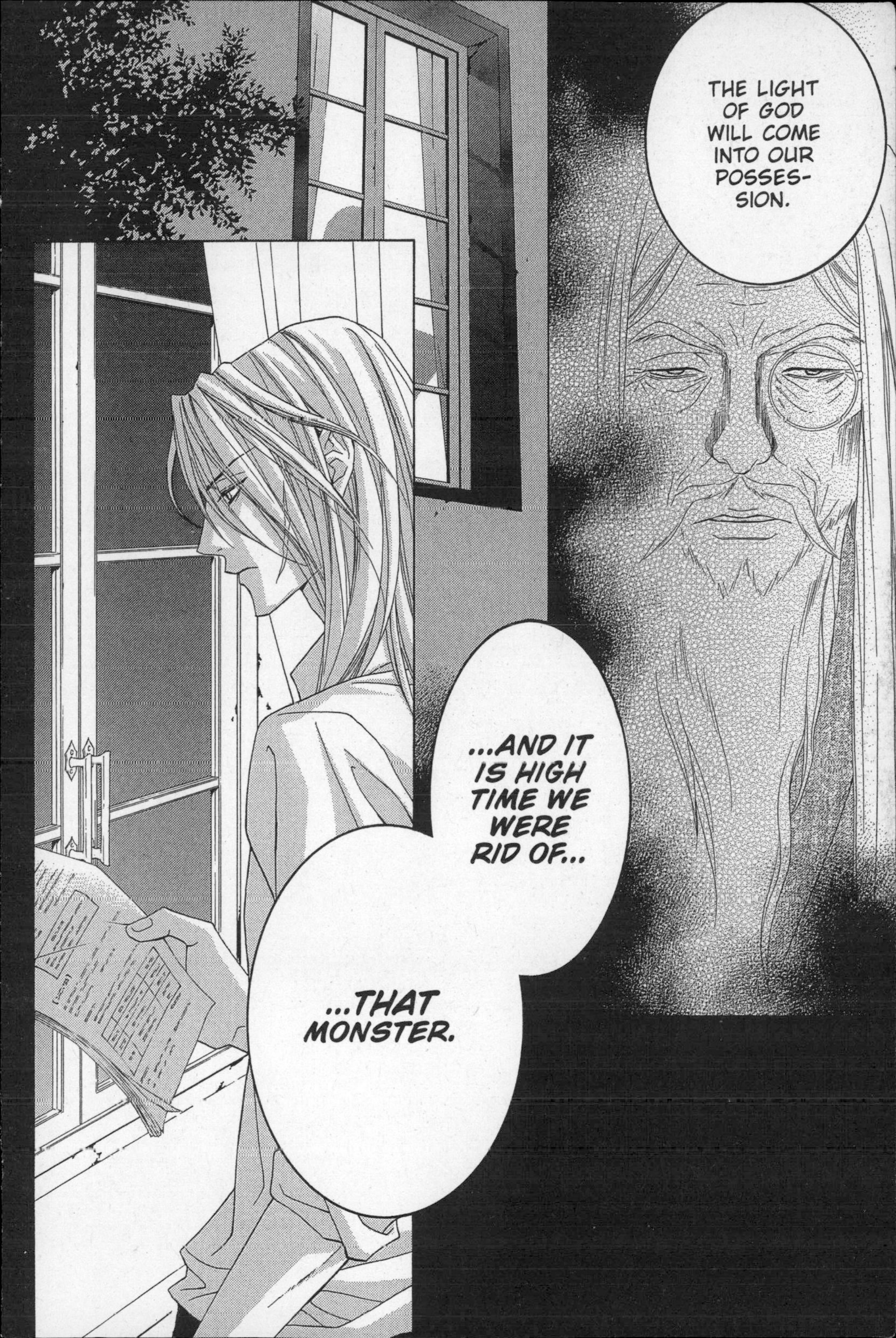
THE LIGHT OF GOD WILL COME INTO OUR POSSES-SION.
...AND IT IS HIGH TIME WE WERE RID OF...
...THAT MONSTER.

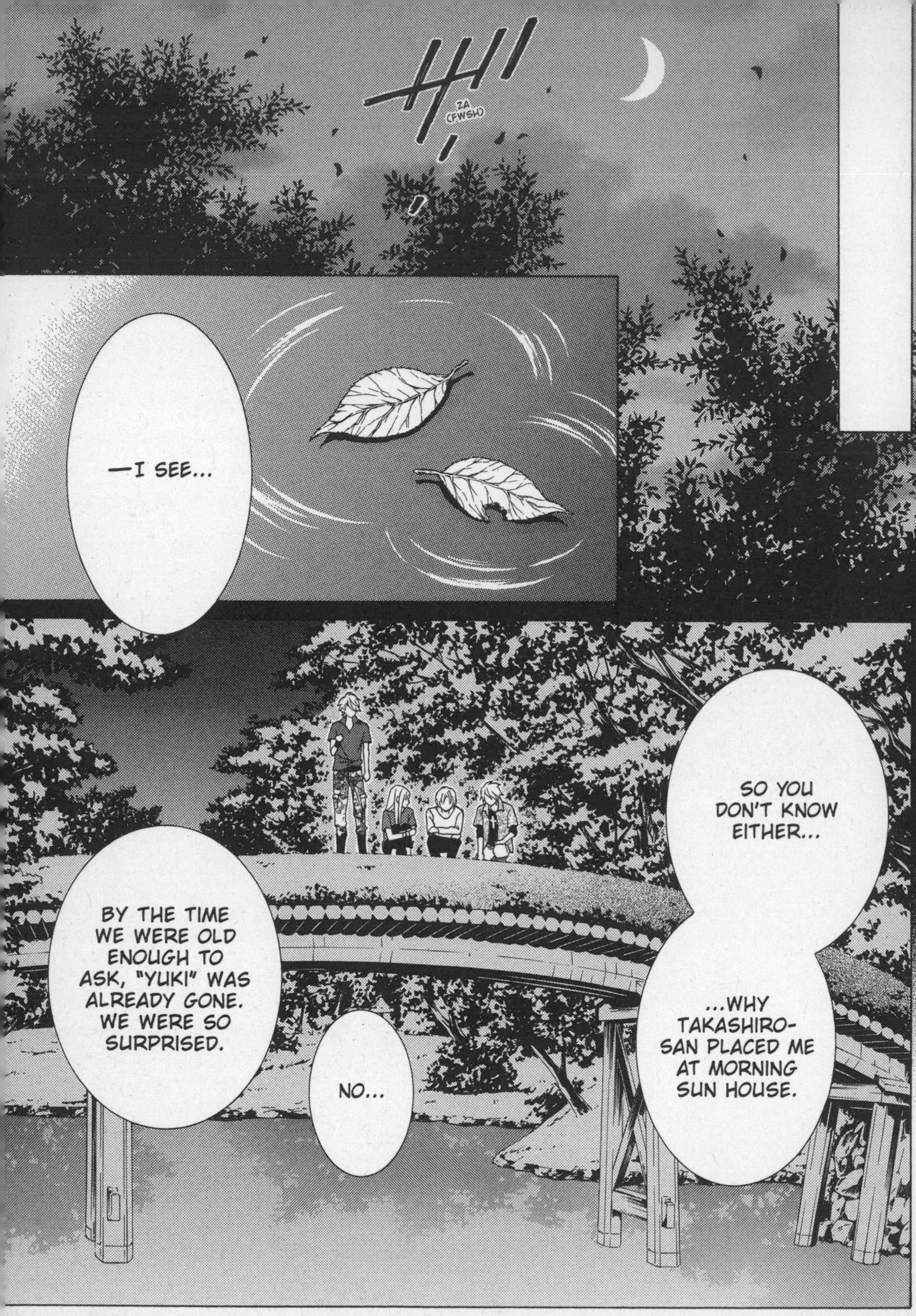
ZA (FWSH)
—I SEE...
SO YOU DON'T KNOW EITHER...
...WHY TAKASHIRO-SAN PLACED ME AT MORNING SUN HOUSE.
NO...
BY THE TIME WE WERE OLD ENOUGH TO ASK, "YUKI" WAS ALREADY GONE. WE WERE SO SURPRISED.

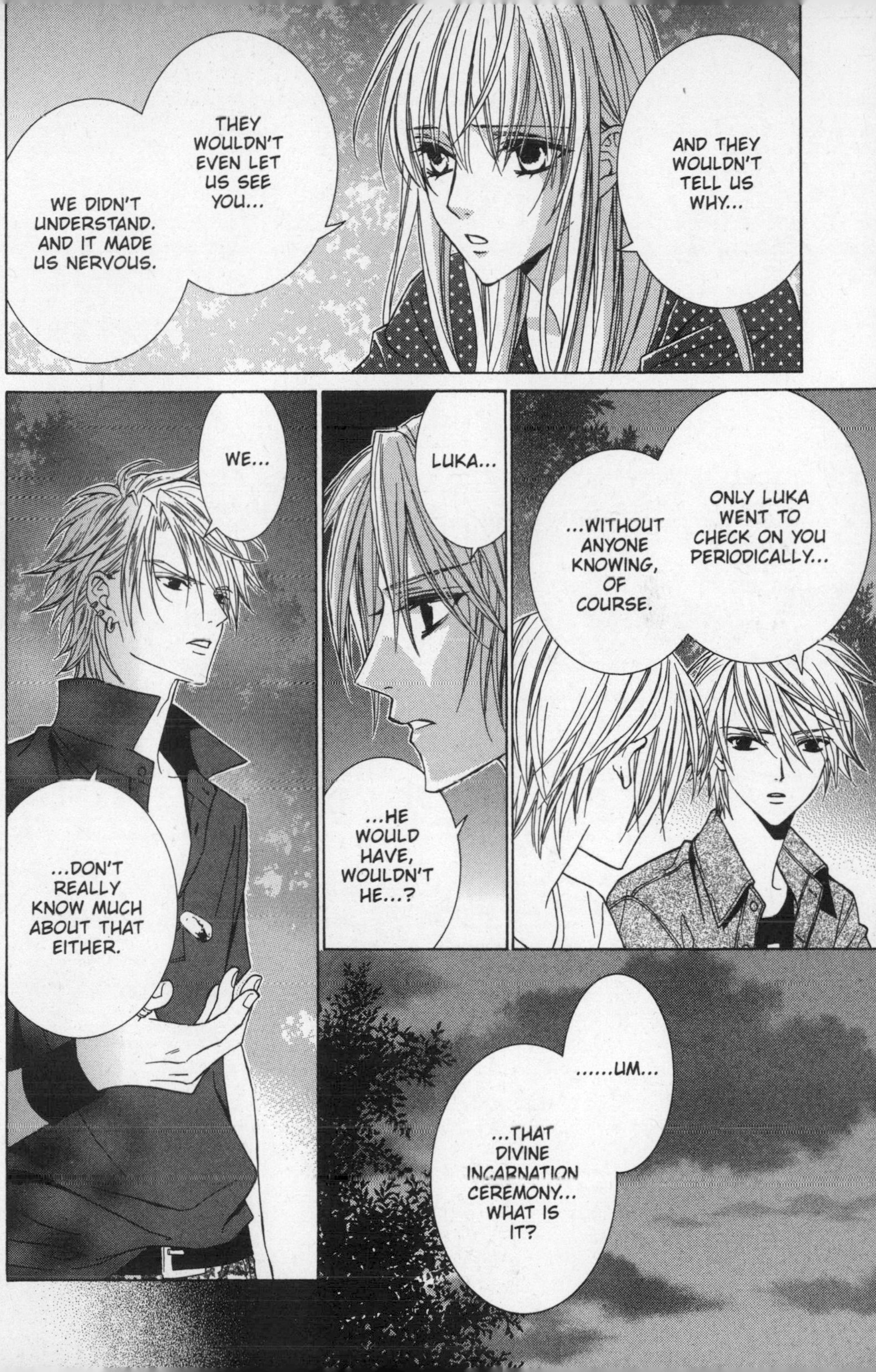
AND THEY WOULDN'T TELL US WHY...
THEY WOULDN'T EVEN LET US SEE YOU...
WE DIDN'T UNDERSTAND. AND IT MADE US NERVOUS.
ONLY LUKA WENT TO CHECK ON YOU PERIODICALLY...
...WITHOUT ANYONE KNOWING, OF COURSE.
LUKA...
...HE WOULD HAVE, WOULDN'T HE...?
......UM...
...THAT DIVINE INCARNATION CEREMONY... WHAT IS IT?
WE...
...DON'T REALLY KNOW MUCH ABOUT THAT EITHER.

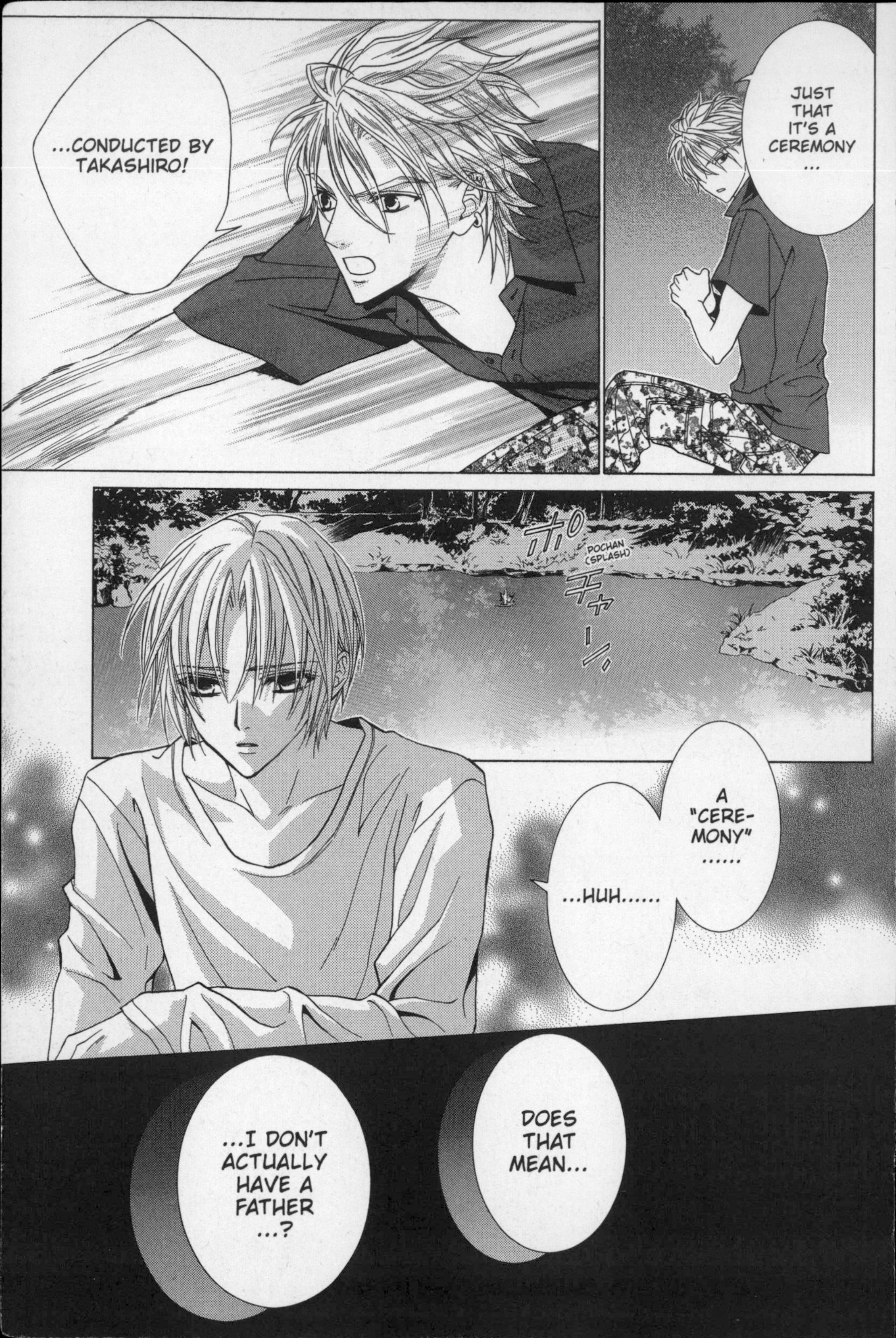
JUST THAT IT'S A CEREMONY ...
...CONDUCTED BY TAKASHIRO!
ポチャーン!
POCHAN (SPLASH)
A "CERE-MONY" ......
...HUH......
DOES THAT MEAN...
...I DON'T ACTUALLY HAVE A FATHER ...?

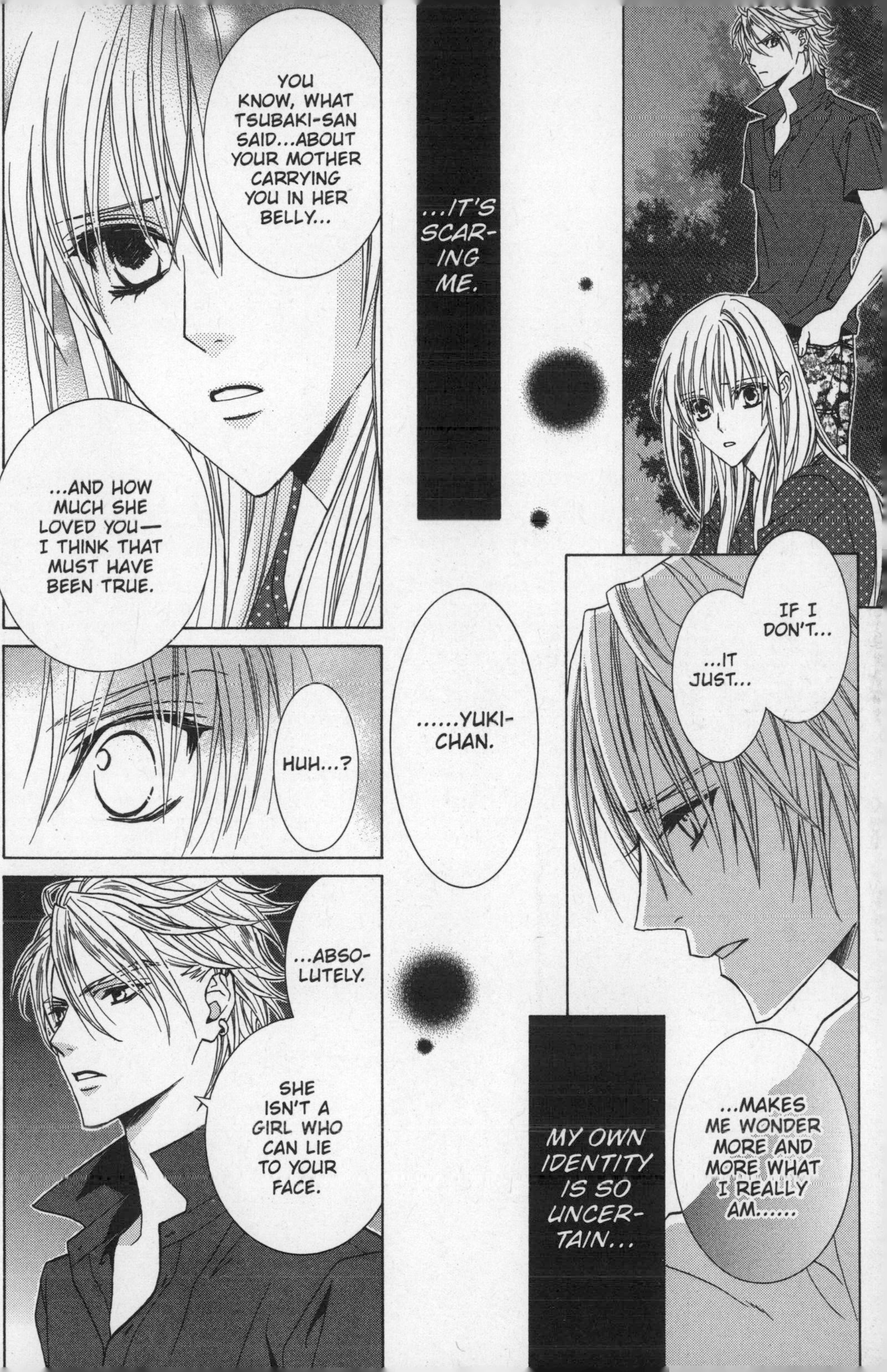
...IT'S SCARING ME.
YOU KNOW, WHAT TSUBAKI-SAN SAID...ABOUT YOUR MOTHER CARRYING YOU IN HER BELLY...
...AND HOW MUCH SHE LOVED YOU—I THINK THAT MUST HAVE BEEN TRUE.
HUH...?
......YUKI-CHAN.
...ABSOLUTELY.
SHE ISN'T A GIRL WHO CAN LIE TO YOUR FACE.
IF I DON'T...
...IT JUST...
MY OWN IDENTITY IS SO UNCERTAIN...
...MAKES ME WONDER MORE AND MORE WHAT I REALLY AM......

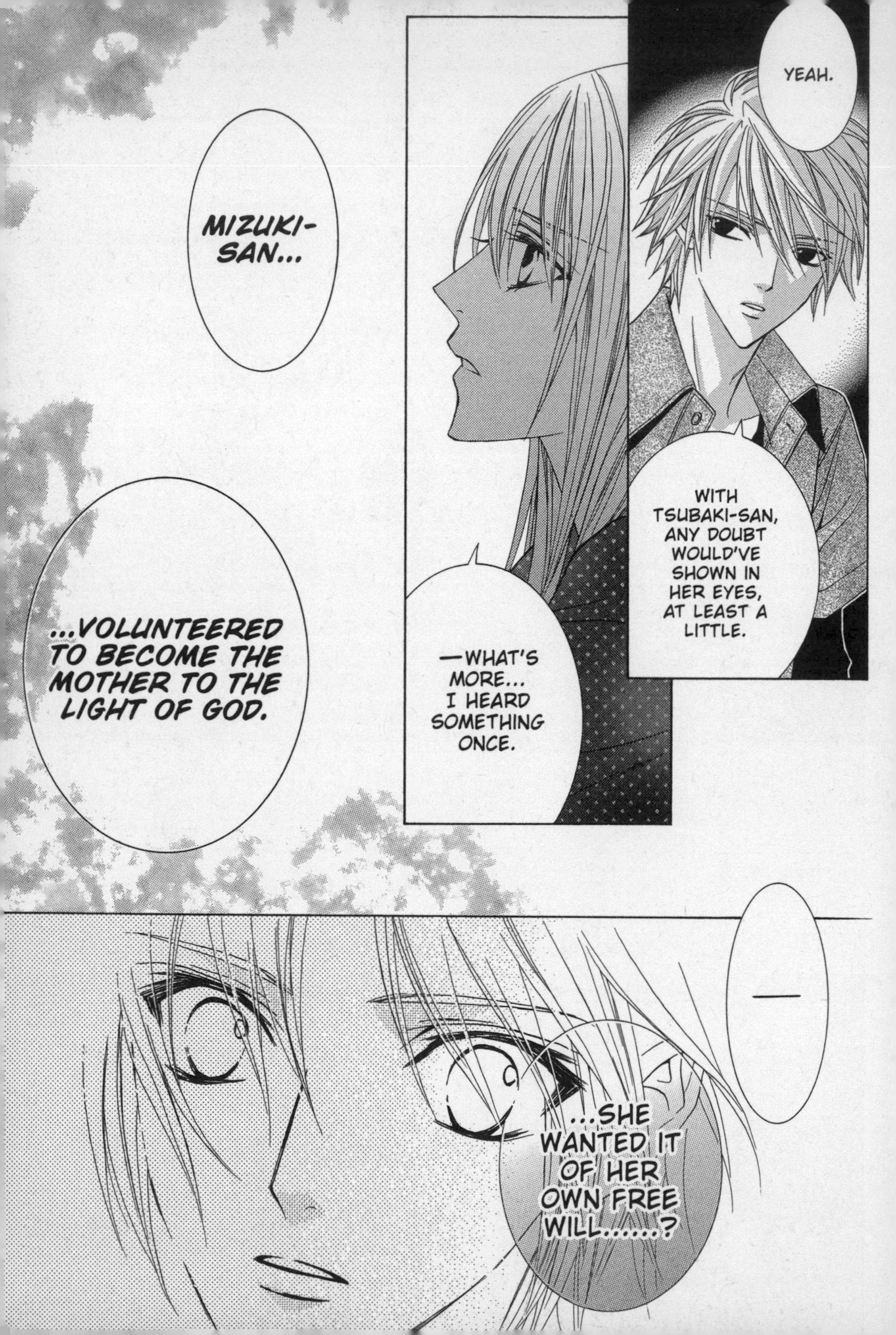
YEAH.
WITH TSUBAKI-SAN, ANY DOUBT WOULD'VE SHOWN IN HER EYES, AT LEAST A LITTLE.
—WHAT'S MORE... I HEARD SOMETHING ONCE.
MIZUKI-SAN...
...VOLUNTEERED TO BECOME THE MOTHER TO THE LIGHT OF GOD.
—
...SHE WANTED IT OF HER OWN FREE WILL......?

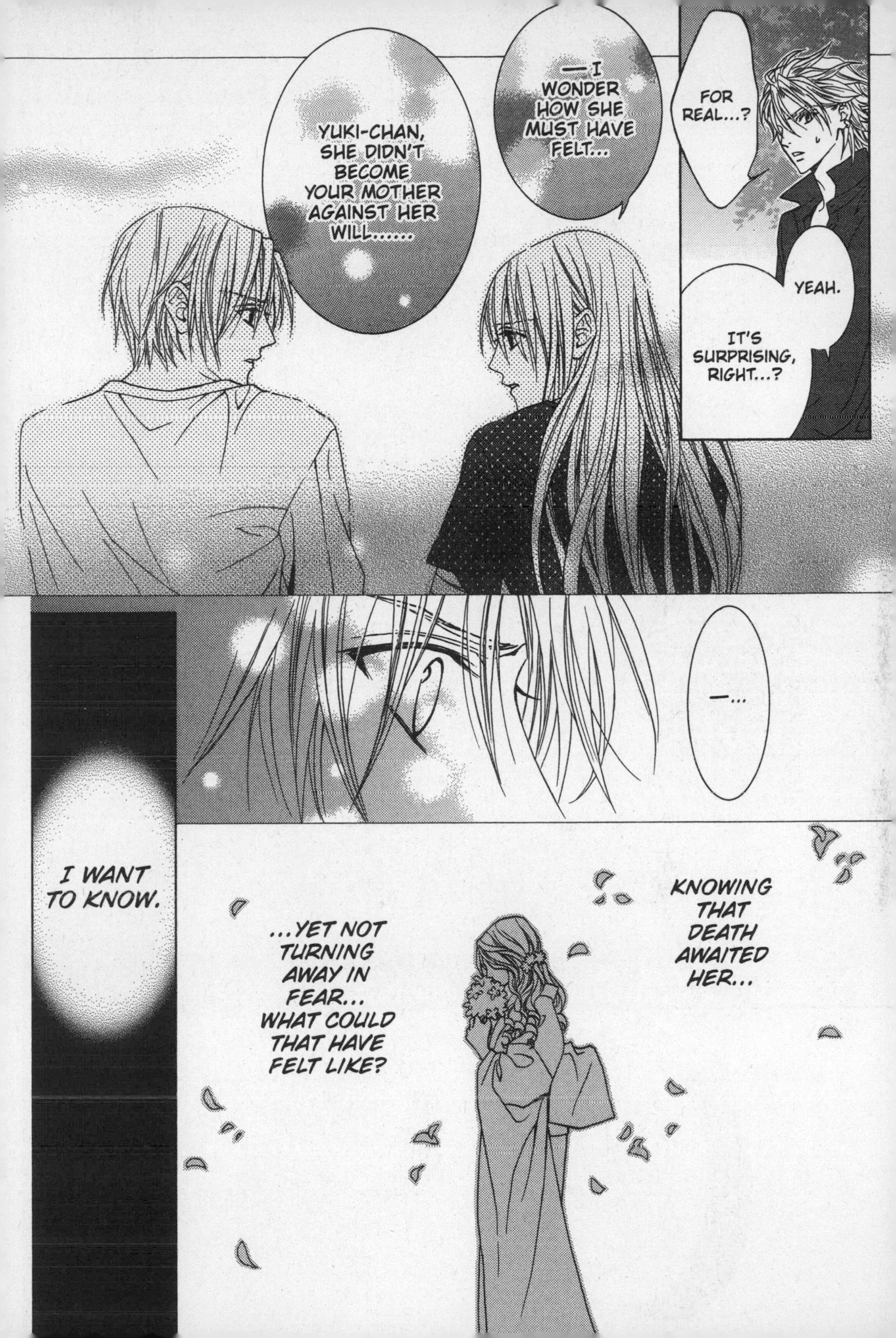
FOR REAL...?
YEAH.
IT'S SURPRISING, RIGHT...?
—I WONDER HOW SHE MUST HAVE FELT...
YUKI-CHAN, SHE DIDN'T BECOME YOUR MOTHER AGAINST HER WILL......
—...
KNOWING THAT DEATH AWAITED HER...
...YET NOT TURNING AWAY IN FEAR... WHAT COULD THAT HAVE FELT LIKE?
I WANT TO KNOW.

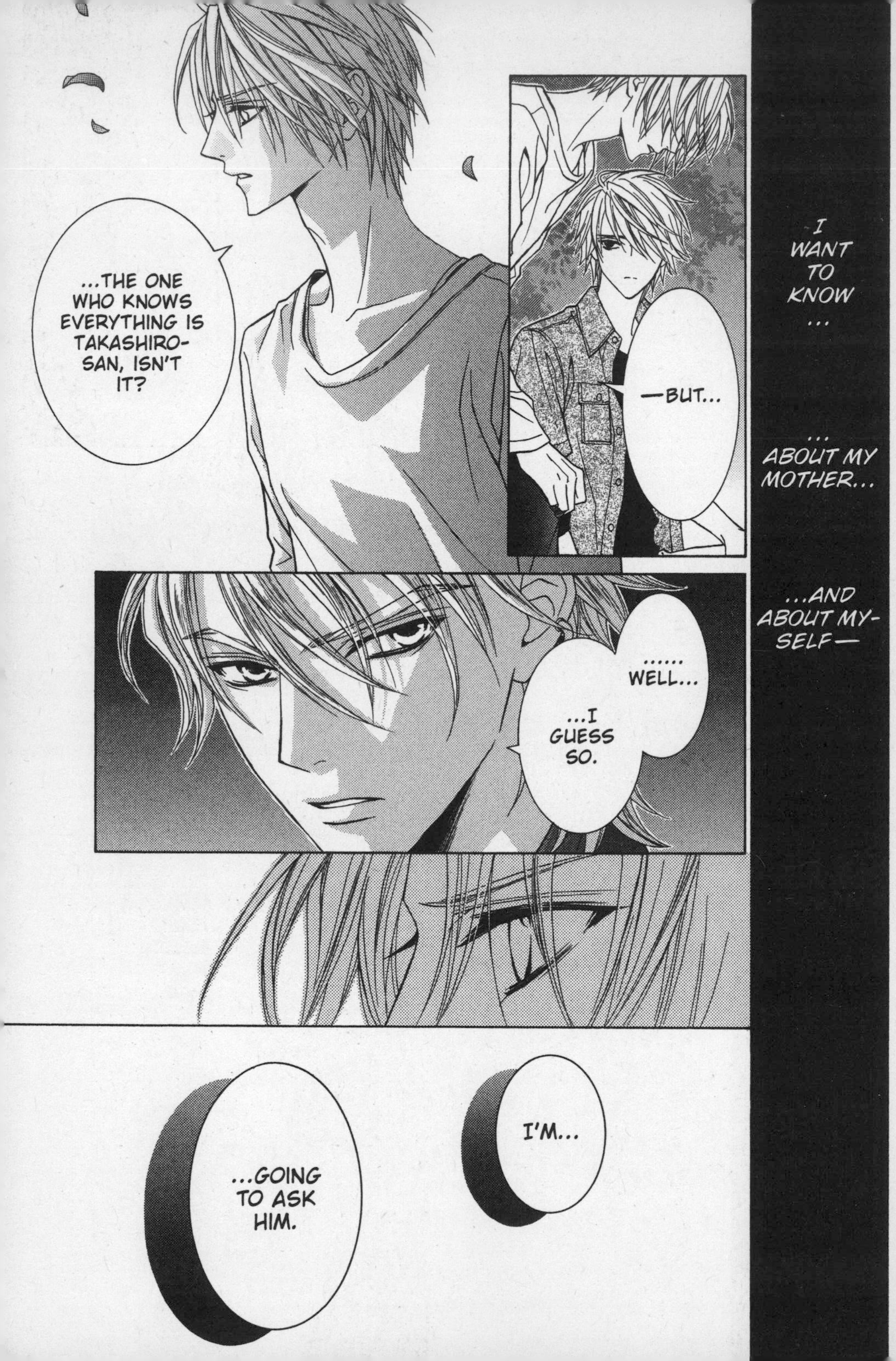
I WANT TO KNOW...
...ABOUT MY MOTHER...
...AND ABOUT MYSELF—
...THE ONE WHO KNOWS EVERYTHING IS TAKASHIRO-SAN, ISN'T IT?
—BUT...
...... WELL...
...I GUESS SO.
I'M...
...GOING TO ASK HIM.

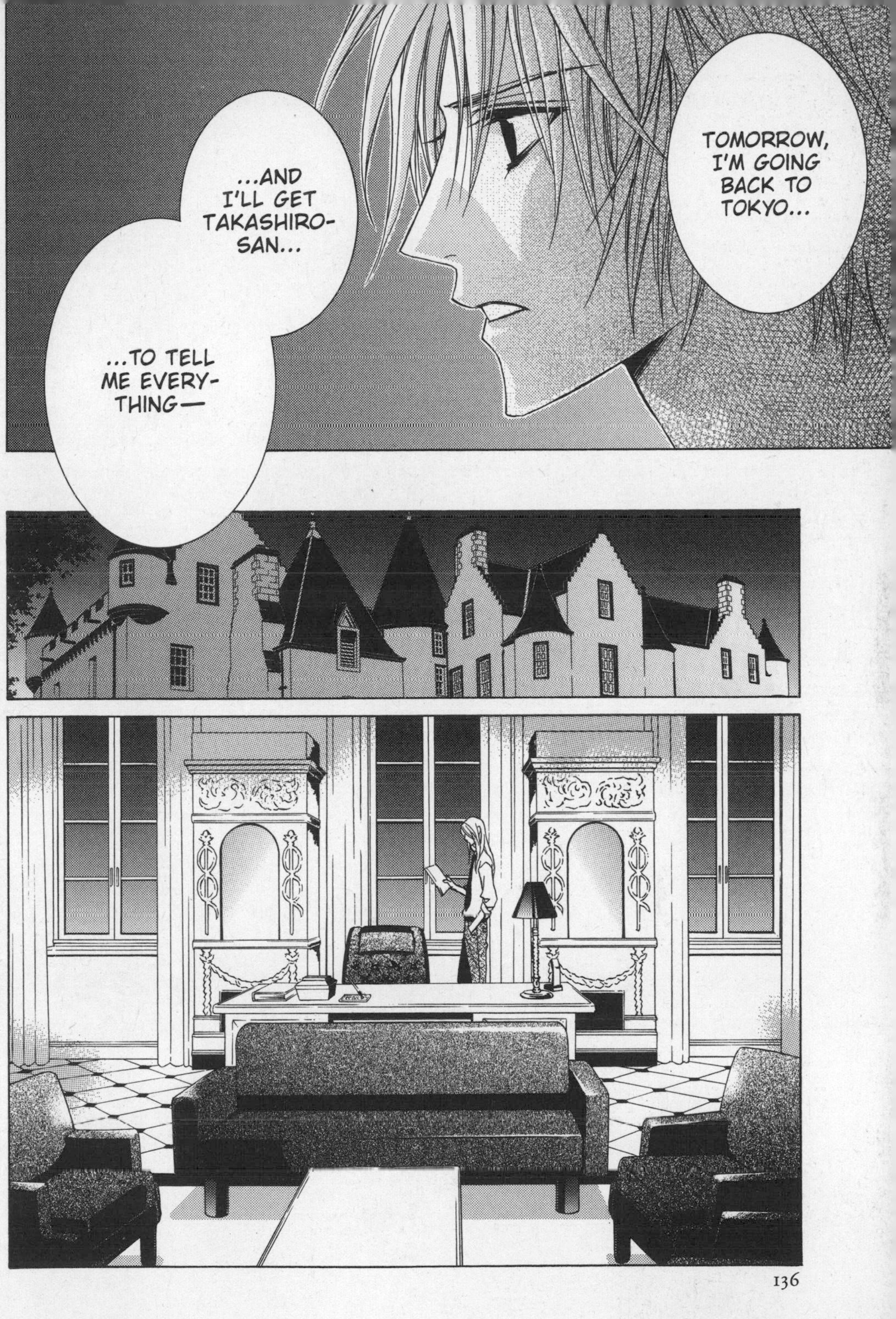
TOMORROW, I'M GOING BACK TO TOKYO...
...AND I'LL GET TAKASHIRO-SAN...
...TO TELL ME EVERY-THING—

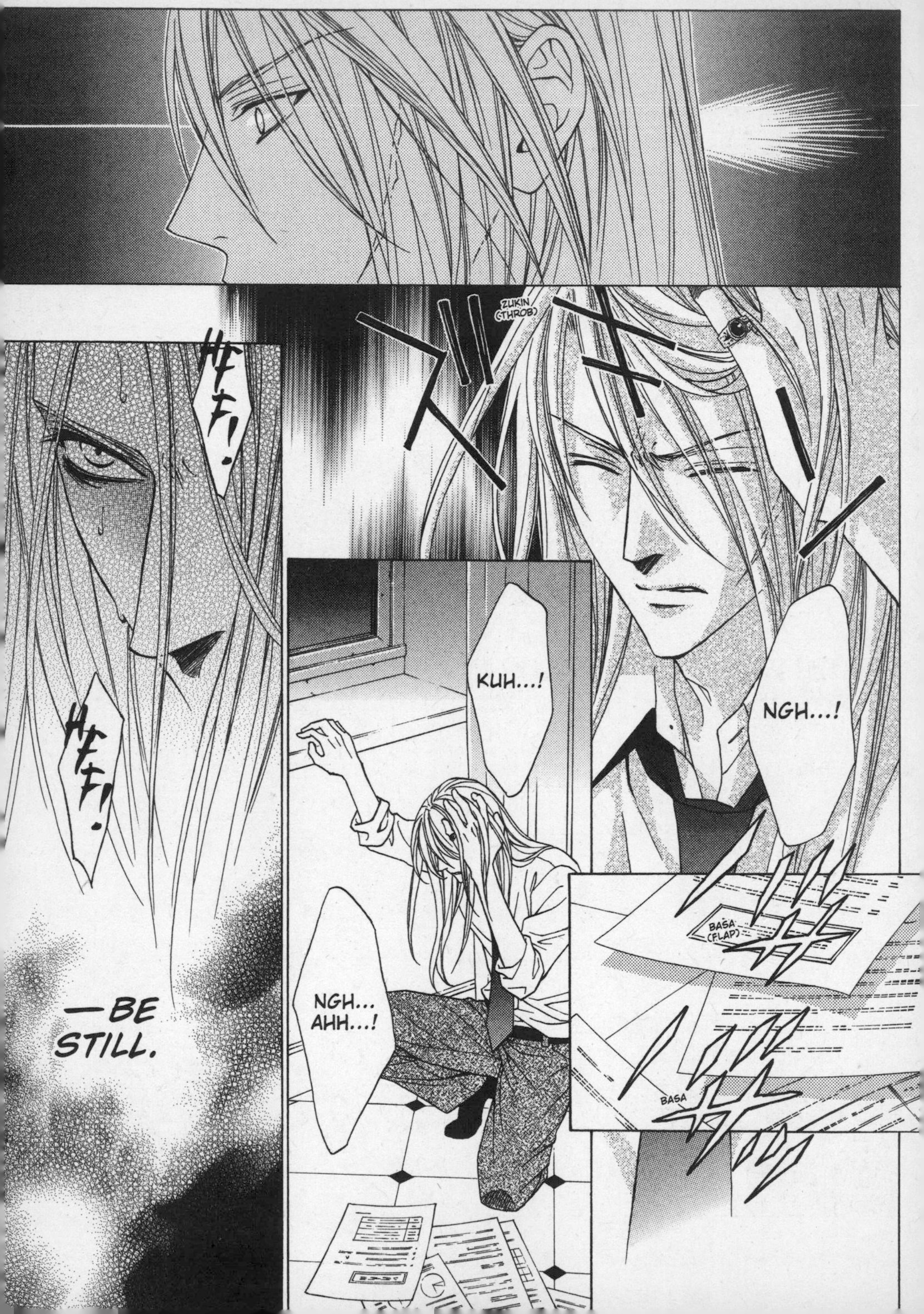
ZUKIN (THROB)
NGH...!
BASA (FLAP)
BASA
KUH...!
NGH... AHH...!
HFF!
HFF!
—BE STILL.

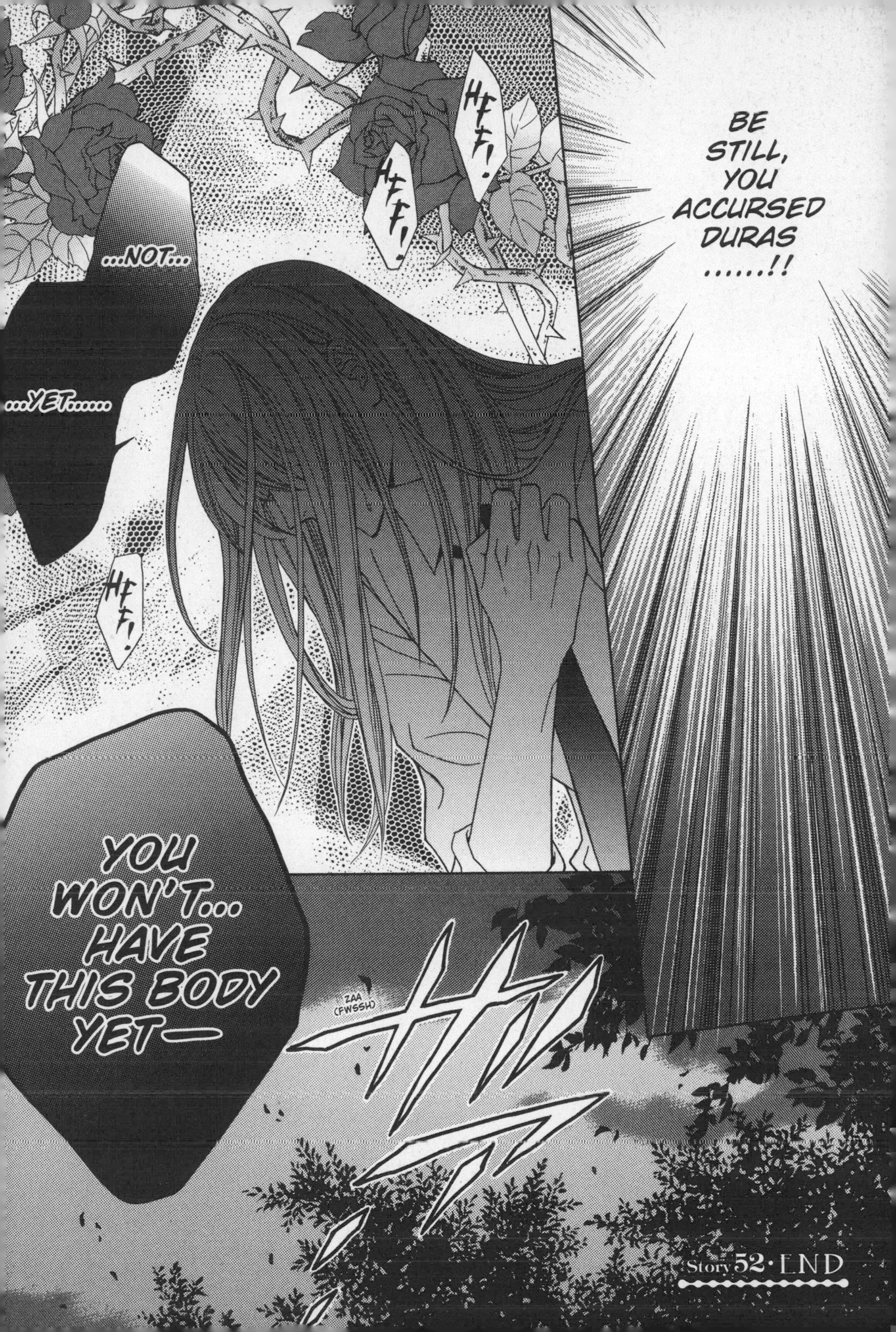
BE STILL, YOU ACCURSED DURAS ......!!
HFF!
HFF!
...NOT...
...YET......
HFF!
YOU WON'T... HAVE THIS BODY YET—
ZAA (FWSSH)
Story 52 · END

THE
BETRAYAL
KNOWS MY NAME

AFTERWORD - BEHIND THE SCENES OF URABOKU.

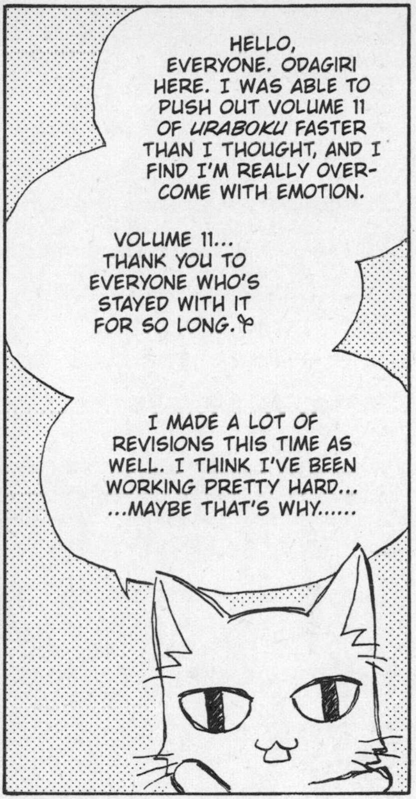
HELLO, EVERYONE. ODAGIRI HERE. I WAS ABLE TO PUSH OUT VOLUME 11 OF *URABOKU* FASTER THAN I THOUGHT, AND I FIND I'M REALLY OVER-COME WITH EMOTION.
VOLUME 11... THANK YOU TO EVERYONE WHO'S STAYED WITH IT FOR SO LONG.
I MADE A LOT OF REVISIONS THIS TIME AS WELL. I THINK I'VE BEEN WORKING PRETTY HARD... ...MAYBE THAT'S WHY......

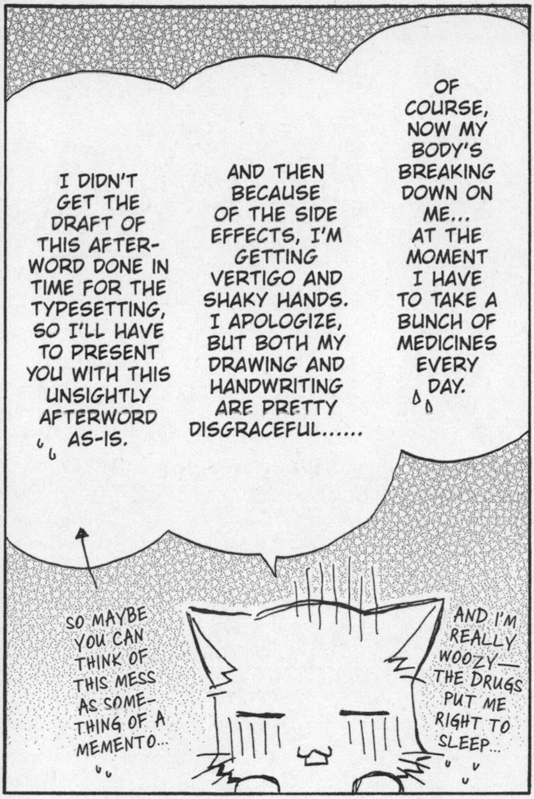
OF COURSE, NOW MY BODY'S BREAKING DOWN ON ME... AT THE MOMENT I HAVE TO TAKE A BUNCH OF MEDICINES EVERY DAY.
AND THEN BECAUSE OF THE SIDE EFFECTS, I'M GETTING VERTIGO AND SHAKY HANDS. I APOLOGIZE, BUT BOTH MY DRAWING AND HANDWRITING ARE PRETTY DISGRACEFUL......
I DIDN'T GET THE DRAFT OF THIS AFTER-WORD DONE IN TIME FOR THE TYPESETTING, SO I'LL HAVE TO PRESENT YOU WITH THIS UNSIGHTLY AFTERWORD AS-IS.
AND I'M REALLY WOOZY—THE DRUGS PUT ME RIGHT TO SLEEP...
SO MAYBE YOU CAN THINK OF THIS MESS AS SOME-THING OF A MEMENTO...

SO I WANT TO TALK SOME MORE ABOUT THE URABOKU MUSICAL—I LOVE IT SO MUCH, I MUST BE THE #1 FAN MYSELF!

THE SECOND INSTALLMENT RAN AUGUST 1ST THROUGH 5TH, AND IT WAS ENORMOUSLY POPULAR ALL THE WAY THROUGH CLOSING NIGHT. THANK YOU TO EVERYONE WHO BRAVED THE CRAZY HEAT TO GO SEE IT!

THE SECOND MUSICAL COVERED THE "KAMAKURA ARC," AND AGAIN, IT WAS REALLY A LOVELY WORK. I MEAN, I GOT TO SEE THE DRESS REHEARSAL, AND EVEN THAT MADE ME CRY (LOL). IT WAS SO AMAZING. THEY INCLUDED THE STORY OF MEIKA-CHAN, WHICH GOT COMPLETELY CUT FROM THE ANIME, AND ITS MESSAGE REALLY CAME THROUGH. TO ALL THE CAST AND CREW, THANK YOU, THANK YOU SO MUCH!!!

HERE WE ARE, TOTALLY ABSORBED IN WATCHING IT ON NICONICO'S DVR SERVICE BECAUSE THE DVD ISN'T OUT YET.

**VOLUME 2 WAS AVAILABLE FOR A LIMITED TIME ON NICONICO VIDEO. IF YOU BOUGHT A DIGITAL TICKET YOU COULD SEE IT EVEN IF YOU COULDN'T MAKE IT TO THE SHOW!☆*

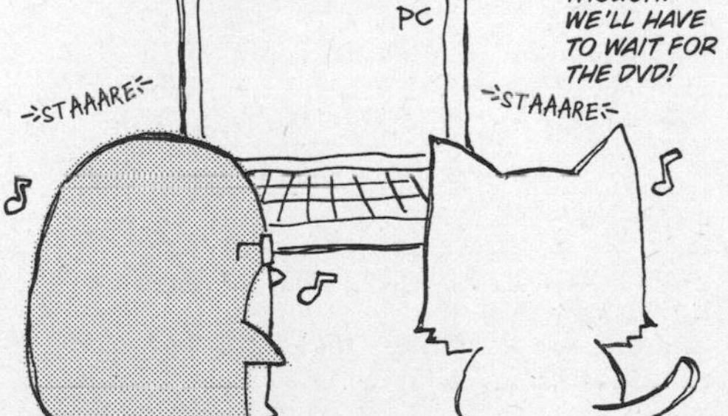
THAT'S OVER, THOUGH. WE'LL HAVE TO WAIT FOR THE DVD!
PC
STAAARE
STAAARE

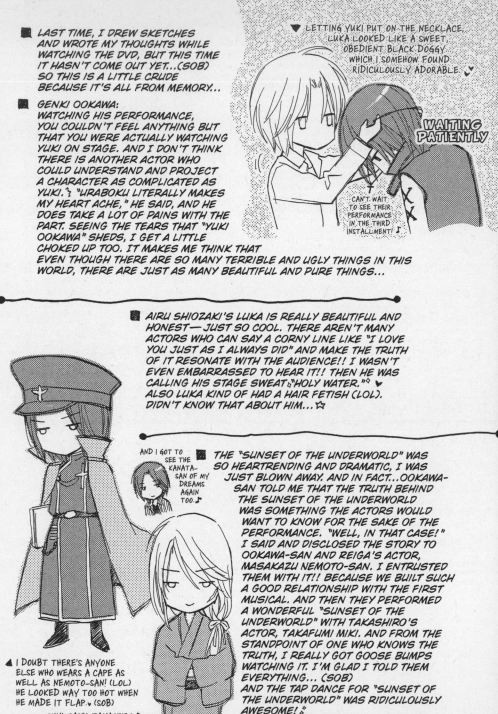

■ LAST TIME, I DREW SKETCHES AND WROTE MY THOUGHTS WHILE WATCHING THE DVD, BUT THIS TIME IT HASN'T COME OUT YET...(SOB) SO THIS IS A LITTLE CRUDE BECAUSE IT'S ALL FROM MEMORY...

■ GENKI OOKAWA:
WATCHING HIS PERFORMANCE, YOU COULDN'T FEEL ANYTHING BUT THAT YOU WERE ACTUALLY WATCHING YUKI ON STAGE. AND I DON'T THINK THERE IS ANOTHER ACTOR WHO COULD UNDERSTAND AND PROJECT A CHARACTER AS COMPLICATED AS YUKI. "URABOKU LITERALLY MAKES MY HEART ACHE," HE SAID, AND HE DOES TAKE A LOT OF PAINS WITH THE PART. SEEING THE TEARS THAT "YUKI OOKAWA" SHEDS, I GET A LITTLE CHOKED UP TOO. IT MAKES ME THINK THAT EVEN THOUGH THERE ARE SO MANY TERRIBLE AND UGLY THINGS IN THIS WORLD, THERE ARE JUST AS MANY BEAUTIFUL AND PURE THINGS...

▼ LETTING YUKI PUT ON THE NECKLACE, LUKA LOOKED LIKE A SWEET, OBEDIENT BLACK DOGGY WHICH I SOMEHOW FOUND RIDICULOUSLY ADORABLE. ♥

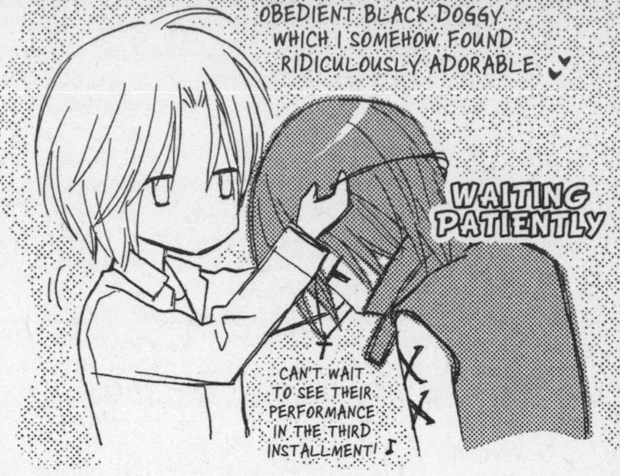
WAITING PATIENTLY
CAN'T WAIT TO SEE THEIR PERFORMANCE IN THE THIRD INSTALLMENT! ♪

■ AIRU SHIOZAKI'S LUKA IS REALLY BEAUTIFUL AND HONEST— JUST SO COOL. THERE AREN'T MANY ACTORS WHO CAN SAY A CORNY LINE LIKE "I LOVE YOU JUST AS I ALWAYS DID" AND MAKE THE TRUTH OF IT RESONATE WITH THE AUDIENCE!! I WASN'T EVEN EMBARRASSED TO HEAR IT!! THEN HE WAS CALLING HIS STAGE SWEAT "HOLY WATER." ♥
ALSO LUKA KIND OF HAD A HAIR FETISH (LOL). DIDN'T KNOW THAT ABOUT HIM...☆

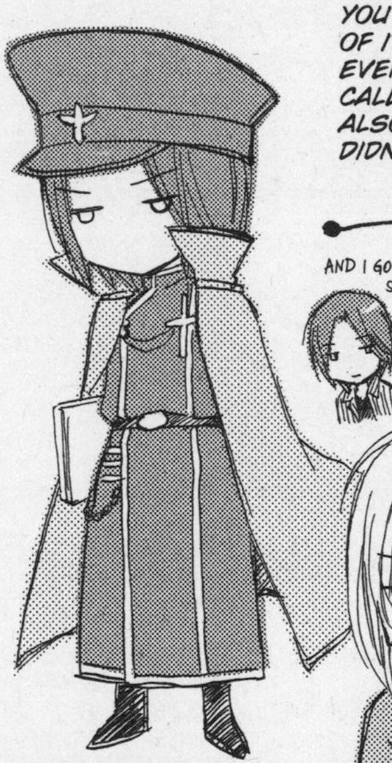

◀ I DOUBT THERE'S ANYONE ELSE WHO WEARS A CAPE AS WELL AS NEMOTO-SAN! (LOL) HE LOOKED WAY TOO HOT WHEN HE MADE IT FLAP. ♥ (SOB)

AND I GOT TO SEE THE KANATA-SAN OF MY DREAMS AGAIN TOO. ♪

■ THE "SUNSET OF THE UNDERWORLD" WAS SO HEARTRENDING AND DRAMATIC, I WAS JUST BLOWN AWAY. AND IN FACT...OOKAWA-SAN TOLD ME THAT THE TRUTH BEHIND THE SUNSET OF THE UNDERWORLD WAS SOMETHING THE ACTORS WOULD WANT TO KNOW FOR THE SAKE OF THE PERFORMANCE. "WELL, IN THAT CASE!" I SAID AND DISCLOSED THE STORY TO OOKAWA-SAN AND REIGA'S ACTOR, MASAKAZU NEMOTO-SAN. I ENTRUSTED THEM WITH IT!! BECAUSE WE BUILT SUCH A GOOD RELATIONSHIP WITH THE FIRST MUSICAL. AND THEN THEY PERFORMED A WONDERFUL "SUNSET OF THE UNDERWORLD" WITH TAKASHIRO'S ACTOR, TAKAFUMI MIKI. AND FROM THE STANDPOINT OF ONE WHO KNOWS THE TRUTH, I REALLY GOT GOOSE BUMPS WATCHING IT. I'M GLAD I TOLD THEM EVERYTHING... (SOB)
AND THE TAP DANCE FOR "SUNSET OF THE UNDERWORLD" WAS RIDICULOUSLY AWESOME!
...AAAH, MY HANDWRITING IS GETTING SO BAAAAD......

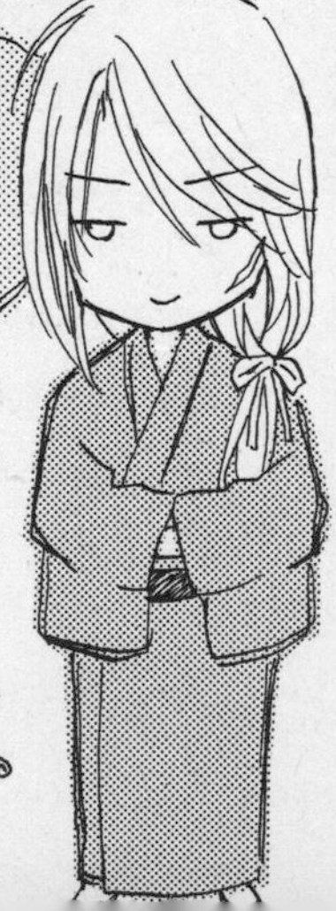

MIKI-SAN'S TAKASHIRO ▶ LOOKED REALLY GORGEOUS IN A KIMONO.

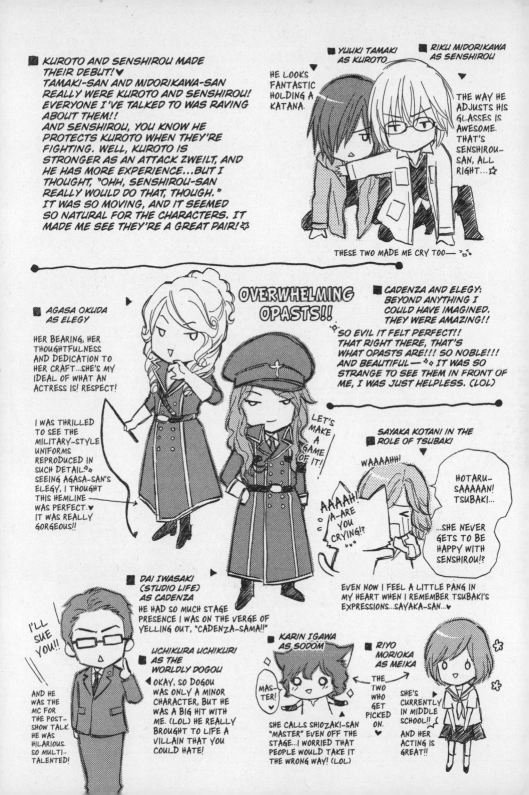

KUROTO AND SENSHIROU MADE THEIR DEBUT! ♥
TAMAKI-SAN AND MIDORIKAWA-SAN REALLY WERE KUROTO AND SENSHIROU! EVERYONE I'VE TALKED TO WAS RAVING ABOUT THEM!!
AND SENSHIROU, YOU KNOW HE PROTECTS KUROTO WHEN THEY'RE FIGHTING. WELL, KUROTO IS STRONGER AS AN ATTACK ZWEILT, AND HE HAS MORE EXPERIENCE...BUT I THOUGHT, "OHH, SENSHIROU-SAN REALLY WOULD DO THAT, THOUGH."
IT WAS SO MOVING, AND IT SEEMED SO NATURAL FOR THE CHARACTERS. IT MADE ME SEE THEY'RE A GREAT PAIR!

YUUKI TAMAKI AS KUROTO

HE LOOKS FANTASTIC HOLDING A KATANA.

RIKU MIDORIKAWA AS SENSHIROU

THE WAY HE ADJUSTS HIS GLASSES IS AWESOME. THAT'S SENSHIROU-SAN, ALL RIGHT...

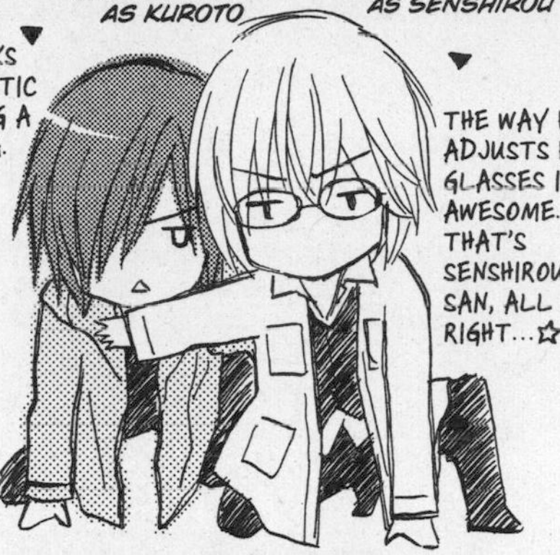

THESE TWO MADE ME CRY TOO—

OVERWHELMING OPASTS!!

CADENZA AND ELEGY: BEYOND ANYTHING I COULD HAVE IMAGINED. THEY WERE AMAZING!!
SO EVIL IT FELT PERFECT!! THAT RIGHT THERE, THAT'S WHAT OPASTS ARE!!! SO NOBLE!!! AND BEAUTIFUL— IT WAS SO STRANGE TO SEE THEM IN FRONT OF ME, I WAS JUST HELPLESS. (LOL)

AGASA OKUDA AS ELEGY

HER BEARING, HER THOUGHTFULNESS AND DEDICATION TO HER CRAFT...SHE'S MY IDEAL OF WHAT AN ACTRESS IS! RESPECT!

I WAS THRILLED TO SEE THE MILITARY-STYLE UNIFORMS REPRODUCED IN SUCH DETAIL. SEEING AGASA-SAN'S ELEGY, I THOUGHT THIS HEMLINE WAS PERFECT. ♥ IT WAS REALLY GORGEOUS!!

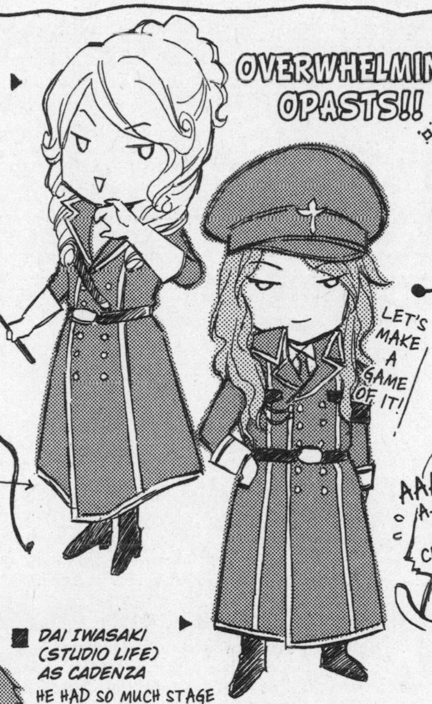
LET'S MAKE A GAME OF IT!

DAI IWASAKI (STUDIO LIFE) AS CADENZA

HE HAD SO MUCH STAGE PRESENCE I WAS ON THE VERGE OF YELLING OUT, "CADENZA-SAMA!!"

SAYAKA KOTANI IN THE ROLE OF TSUBAKI

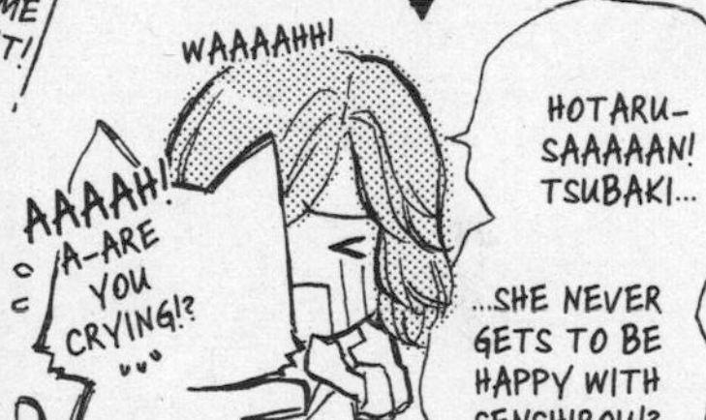
WAAAAHH!
HOTARU-SAAAAAN! TSUBAKI...
...SHE NEVER GETS TO BE HAPPY WITH SENSHIROU!?
AAAAH! A-ARE YOU CRYING!?

EVEN NOW I FEEL A LITTLE PANG IN MY HEART WHEN I REMEMBER TSUBAKI'S EXPRESSIONS...SAYAKA-SAN... ♥

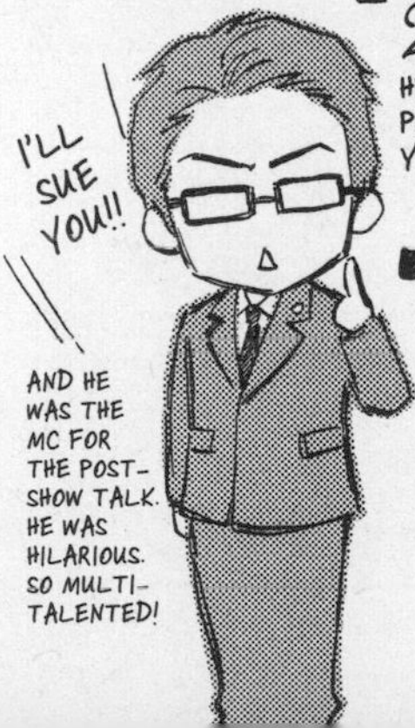
I'LL SUE YOU!!

UCHIKURA UCHIKURI AS THE WORLDLY DOGOU

OKAY, SO DOGOU WAS ONLY A MINOR CHARACTER, BUT HE WAS A BIG HIT WITH ME. (LOL) HE REALLY BROUGHT TO LIFE A VILLAIN THAT YOU COULD HATE!

AND HE WAS THE MC FOR THE POST-SHOW TALK. HE WAS HILARIOUS. SO MULTI-TALENTED!

KARIN IGAWA AS SODOM

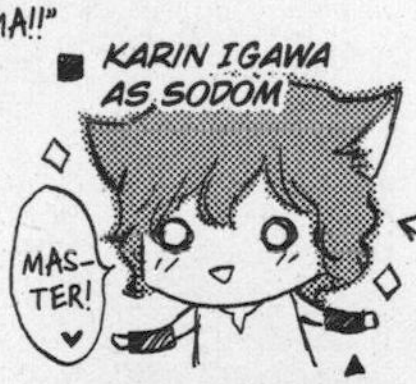
MASTER! ♥

SHE CALLS SHIOZAKI-SAN "MASTER" EVEN OFF THE STAGE...I WORRIED THAT PEOPLE WOULD TAKE IT THE WRONG WAY! (LOL)

THE TWO WHO GET PICKED ON. ♥

RIYO MORIOKA AS MEIKA

SHE'S CURRENTLY IN MIDDLE SCHOOL!! AND HER ACTING IS GREAT!!

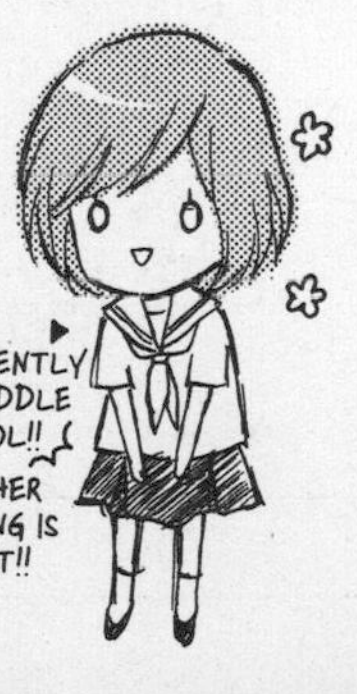

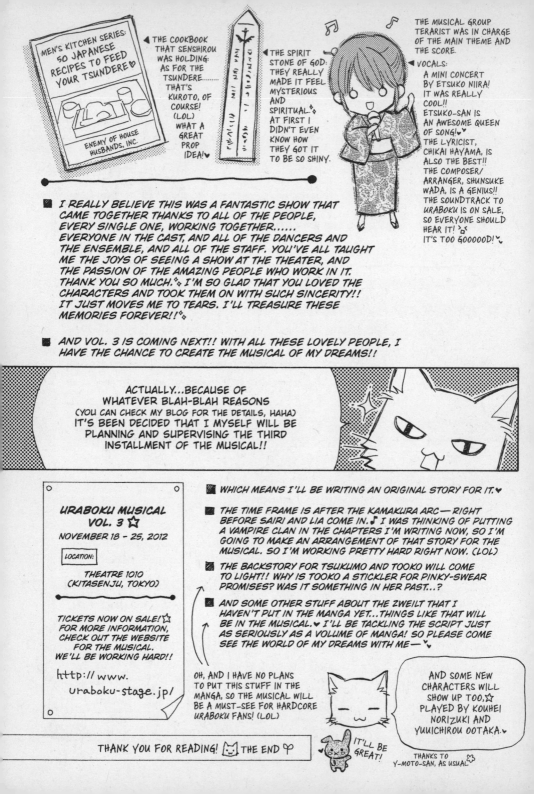

MEN'S KITCHEN SERIES: SO JAPANESE RECIPES TO FEED YOUR TSUNDERE♡

ENEMY OF HOUSE HUSBANDS, INC.

◄ THE COOKBOOK THAT SENSHIROU WAS HOLDING. AS FOR THE TSUNDERE...... THAT'S KUROTO, OF COURSE! (LOL) WHAT A GREAT PROP IDEA!

◄ THE SPIRIT STONE OF GOD: THEY REALLY MADE IT FEEL MYSTERIOUS AND SPIRITUAL.✧ AT FIRST I DIDN'T EVEN KNOW HOW THEY GOT IT TO BE SO SHINY.

THE MUSICAL GROUP TERARIST WAS IN CHARGE OF THE MAIN THEME AND THE SCORE.

◄ VOCALS: A MINI CONCERT BY ETSUKO NIIRA! IT WAS REALLY COOL!! ETSUKO-SAN IS AN AWESOME QUEEN OF SONG!♥ THE LYRICIST, CHIKAI HAYAMA, IS ALSO THE BEST!! THE COMPOSER/ ARRANGER, SHUNSUKE WADA, IS A GENIUS!! THE SOUNDTRACK TO URABOKU IS ON SALE, SO EVERYONE SHOULD HEAR IT!♪ IT'S TOO GOOOOOD!♥

■ I REALLY BELIEVE THIS WAS A FANTASTIC SHOW THAT CAME TOGETHER THANKS TO ALL OF THE PEOPLE, EVERY SINGLE ONE, WORKING TOGETHER...... EVERYONE IN THE CAST, AND ALL OF THE DANCERS AND THE ENSEMBLE, AND ALL OF THE STAFF. YOU'VE ALL TAUGHT ME THE JOYS OF SEEING A SHOW AT THE THEATER, AND THE PASSION OF THE AMAZING PEOPLE WHO WORK IN IT. THANK YOU SO MUCH.✧ I'M SO GLAD THAT YOU LOVED THE CHARACTERS AND TOOK THEM ON WITH SUCH SINCERITY!! IT JUST MOVES ME TO TEARS. I'LL TREASURE THESE MEMORIES FOREVER!!✧

■ AND VOL. 3 IS COMING NEXT!! WITH ALL THESE LOVELY PEOPLE, I HAVE THE CHANCE TO CREATE THE MUSICAL OF MY DREAMS!!

ACTUALLY...BECAUSE OF WHATEVER BLAH-BLAH REASONS (YOU CAN CHECK MY BLOG FOR THE DETAILS, HAHA) IT'S BEEN DECIDED THAT I MYSELF WILL BE PLANNING AND SUPERVISING THE THIRD INSTALLMENT OF THE MUSICAL!!

URABOKU MUSICAL VOL. 3 ☆

NOVEMBER 18 - 25, 2012

LOCATION:

THEATRE 1010 (KITASENJU, TOKYO)

TICKETS NOW ON SALE!☆ FOR MORE INFORMATION, CHECK OUT THE WEBSITE FOR THE MUSICAL. WE'LL BE WORKING HARD!!

http://www. uraboku-stage.jp/

■ WHICH MEANS I'LL BE WRITING AN ORIGINAL STORY FOR IT.♥

■ THE TIME FRAME IS AFTER THE KAMAKURA ARC— RIGHT BEFORE SAIRI AND LIA COME IN.♪ I WAS THINKING OF PUTTING A VAMPIRE CLAN IN THE CHAPTERS I'M WRITING NOW, SO I'M GOING TO MAKE AN ARRANGEMENT OF THAT STORY FOR THE MUSICAL. SO I'M WORKING PRETTY HARD RIGHT NOW. (LOL)

■ THE BACKSTORY FOR TSUKUMO AND TOOKO WILL COME TO LIGHT!! WHY IS TOOKO A STICKLER FOR PINKY-SWEAR PROMISES? WAS IT SOMETHING IN HER PAST...?

■ AND SOME OTHER STUFF ABOUT THE ZWEILT THAT I HAVEN'T PUT IN THE MANGA YET...THINGS LIKE THAT WILL BE IN THE MUSICAL.♥ I'LL BE TACKLING THE SCRIPT JUST AS SERIOUSLY AS A VOLUME OF MANGA! SO PLEASE COME SEE THE WORLD OF MY DREAMS WITH ME—♥

OH, AND I HAVE NO PLANS TO PUT THIS STUFF IN THE MANGA, SO THE MUSICAL WILL BE A MUST-SEE FOR HARDCORE URABOKU FANS! (LOL)

AND SOME NEW CHARACTERS WILL SHOW UP TOO.☆ PLAYED BY KOUHEI NORIZUKI AND YUUICHIROU OOTAKA.♥

IT'LL BE GREAT!

THANK YOU FOR READING! 🐱 THE END ♀

THANKS TO Y-MOTO-SAN, AS USUAL ☆

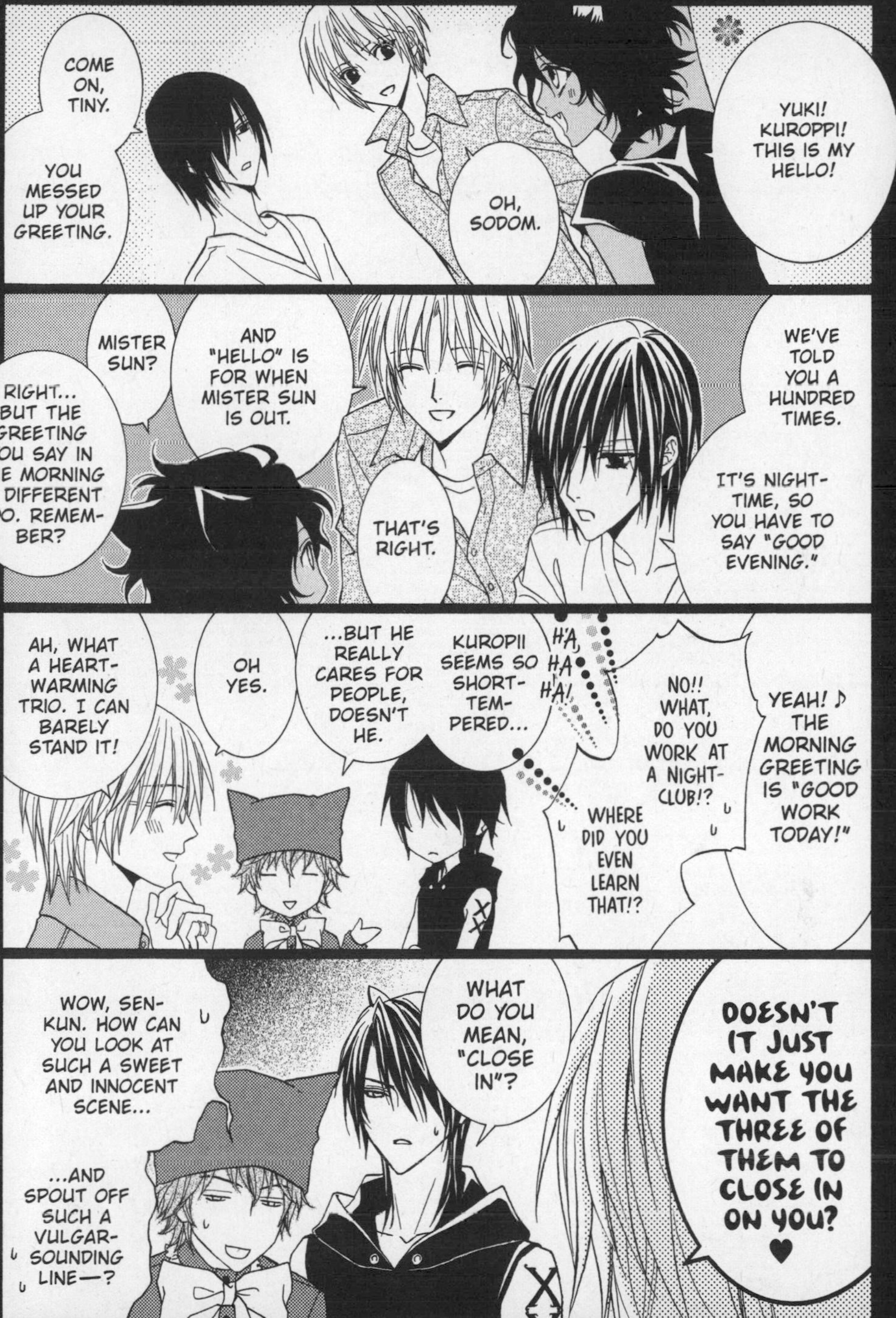
YUKI! KUROPPI! THIS IS MY HELLO!
OH, SODOM.
COME ON, TINY.
YOU MESSED UP YOUR GREETING.
WE'VE TOLD YOU A HUNDRED TIMES.
IT'S NIGHT-TIME, SO YOU HAVE TO SAY "GOOD EVENING."
THAT'S RIGHT.
AND "HELLO" IS FOR WHEN MISTER SUN IS OUT.
MISTER SUN?
RIGHT... BUT THE GREETING YOU SAY IN THE MORNING IS DIFFERENT TOO. REMEMBER?
YEAH! ♪ THE MORNING GREETING IS "GOOD WORK TODAY!"
NO!! WHAT, DO YOU WORK AT A NIGHT-CLUB!?
WHERE DID YOU EVEN LEARN THAT!?
HA, HA HA!
KUROPII SEEMS SO SHORT-TEMPERED...
...BUT HE REALLY CARES FOR PEOPLE, DOESN'T HE.
OH YES.
AH, WHAT A HEART-WARMING TRIO. I CAN BARELY STAND IT!
DOESN'T IT JUST MAKE YOU WANT THE THREE OF THEM TO CLOSE IN ON YOU? ♥
WHAT DO YOU MEAN, "CLOSE IN"?
WOW, SEN-KUN. HOW CAN YOU LOOK AT SUCH A SWEET AND INNOCENT SCENE...
...AND SPOUT OFF SUCH A VULGAR-SOUNDING LINE—?

SPECIAL THANKS

✝

K-san
H.Sanbe
H.Matsuo
R.Mozai
N.Kakeda

K.Okuda
E.Yamagishi

K.Yamamoto

...... and You

SEND COMMENTS TO: HOTARU ODAGIRI
C/O GEKKAN ASUKA EDITORIAL DEPARTMENT
KADOKAWA SHOTEN, INC.
TOKYO, JAPAN 102-8078

ODAGIRI'S BLOG: HTTP://SEKAI-KAKERA.JUGEM.JP

LATELY I'VE EVEN BEEN RECEIVING LETTERS FROM FANS OF THE ACTORS IN THE MUSICAL...
SAYING THINGS LIKE, "I'M A FAN OF XXX-SAN," AND "XXX-SAN IS SUCH A GREAT ACTOR!"
YEAH, ME TOO, THEY SURE ARE, I THINK, AND IT FEELS REALLY NICE.♥

TRANSLATION NOTES

Page 22
In Greek mythology, Leda was the wife of the king of Sparta. After she was seduced by the god Zeus when he had taken on the guise of a swan, Leda bore twins, one of whom came to be known as Helen of Troy. Here, "Leda" is written with the characters for "vertigo."

Page 102
Yuuzuki, literally "evening moon," is a more conventional reading of the characters used to write Yuki's name.